M

What Your Fourth Grader Needs to Know

FUNDAMENTALS OF A GOOD FOURTH-GRADE EDUCATION

The Core Knowledge™ Series

Resource Books for Kindergarten Through Grade Six

DOUBLEDAY
New York London Toronto Sidney Auckland

What Your Fourth Grader Needs to Know

FUNDAMENTALS OF A GOOD FOURTH-GRADE EDUCATION
(Revised Edition)

Edited by

E. D. HIRSCH, JR.

PUBLISHED BY DOUBLEDAY
a division of Random House, Inc.

DOUBLEDAY and the portrayal of an anchor with a dolphin
are registered trademarks of Random House, Inc.

Book design by Robert Bull

Library of Congress Cataloging-in-Publication Data
What your fourth grader needs to know: fundamentals of a good fourth-grade
education/edited by E. D. Hirsch, Jr.—rev. ed.
p. cm.—(The core knowledge series)
Includes index.
ISBN 0-385-49720-2
1. Fourth grade (Education)—United States—Curricula.
2. Curriculum planning—United States. I. Hirsch, E. D. (Eric Donald), 1928– II. Series.
LB1571 4th . W48 2003
372.24'2—dc21
2002041320

PRINTED IN THE UNITED STATES OF AMERICA

September 2004
First Edition

1 3 5 7 9 8 6 4 2

This book is dedicated, gratefully,
to
Linda and Gerald

Contents

II. History and Geography

III. Visual Arts

IV. Music

V. Mathematics

VI. Science

Acknowledgments

This series has depended on the help, advice, and encouragement of more than two thousand people. Some of those singled out here already know the depth of our gratitude; others may be surprised to find themselves thanked publicly for help they gave quietly and freely. To helpers named and unnamed we are deeply grateful.

Editor-in-Chief of the Core Knowledge Series: E. D. Hirsch, Jr.

Text Editors: Souzanne A. Wright, Matthew Davis, Susan Tyler Hitchcock, John Holdren

Editorial Assistance: Skyler Breeden, Peter Locke, Kathleen E. Mason, James Miller, William Rowland, Charles Shields

Art and Photo Research: Matthew Davis, Susan Tyler Hitchcock, Peter Locke, Emily E. Reddick, Jeanne Siler

Writers: This revised edition involved careful reconsideration and sometimes reuse of material in the first edition of this book, as well as others in the series. In that spirit we wish to acknowledge all of the writers and editors who contributed to either edition. Writers for the revised edition: Rebecca Beall Barnes (music), Kathryn Corrigan (language and literature), Victoria Crenson (science), Matthew Davis, Lisa Goff (art), Susan Tyler Hitchcock, Anne Isaacs (American history), Michael Marshall (language and literature), Deirdra McAfee (world history), Robert Watkins (science), Souzanne Wright (math). Writers for the original edition: Nancy Bryson (science), Marie Hawthorne (science), John Hirsch (math), John Holdren (history, language, and literature), Pamela C. Johnson (history and geography), Blair Longwood Jones (literature), Bethanne H. Kelly (literature), Elaine Moran (visual arts), A. Brooke Russell (geography, science), Peter Ryan (music, language, and literature), Lindley Shutz (language and literature), Helen Storey (language and literature)

Advisors on Subject Matter: Marilyn Jager Adams, Karima-Diane Alavi, Richard Anderson, Linda Bevilacqua, Judith Birsh, Wayne Bishop, Louis A. Bloomfield, Cheryl Cannard, Holly DeSantis, Barbara Foorman, Paul Gagnon, David Geary, Andrew Gleason, Oleg Grabar, Charles F. Gritzner, Ted Hirsch, H. Wiley Hitchcock, Henry Holt, Blair Jones, Connie Juel, Eric Karell, Morton Keller, Joseph Kett, Charles Kimball, Mary Beth Klee,

David Klein, Barbara Lachman, Karen Lang, Michael Lynch, Diane McGuinness, Sheelagh McGurn, Maurie McInnis, John F. Miller, Joseph C. Miller, Jean Osborn, Duane Osheim, Vikas Pershad, Robin Poynor, Margaret Redd, Bradly W. Reed, Donna Rehorn, Marion Roberts, Gilbert Roy, Nancy Royal, Mark Rush, Abdulaziz Sachedina, Gayle Sherwood, Janet Smith, Ralph Smith, Keith Stanovich, Paula Stanovich, Jeremy Stern, Nancy Strother, David Summers, Nancy Summers, Marlene Thompson, James Trefil, Patricia Wattenmaker, Nancy Wayne, Christiana Whittington, Lois Williams, Dorothy Wong

Advisors on Multiculturalism: Minerva Allen, Barbara Carey, Frank de Varona, Mick Fedullo, Dorothy Fields, Elizabeth Fox-Genovese, Marcia Galli, Dan Garner, Henry Louis Gates, Cheryl Kulas, Joseph C. Miller, Gerry Raining Bird, Connie Rocha, Dorothy Small, Sharon Stewart-Peregoy, Sterling Stuckey, Marlene Walking Bear, Lucille Watahomigie, Ramona Wilson

Advisors on Elementary Education: Joseph Adelson, Isobel Beck, Paul Bell, Carl Bereiter, David Bjorklund, Constance Jones, Elizabeth LaFuze, J. P. Lutz, Sandra Scarr, Nancy Stein, Phyllis Wilkin, plus all the conferees at the March 1990 conference where the first draft of the curriculum was developed

Schools: Special thanks to the schools—too many to list here—that have offered advice and suggestions for improving the *Core Knowledge Sequence*

Benefactors: The Brown Foundation, The Challenge Foundation, Mrs. E. D. Hirsch, Sr., The Olin Foundation, The Walton Family Foundation.

Our grateful acknowledgment to these persons does not imply that we have taken their (sometimes conflicting) advice in every case, or that each of them endorses all aspects of this project. Responsibility for final decisions rests with the editors alone. Suggestions for improvements are always welcome. We thank in advance those who send advice for revising and improving this series.

A Note to Parents and Teachers

Most of this book is addressed to, and intended to be read by, fourth-grade students. However, at the beginning of each chapter we have supplied a brief introduction with advice for parents and teachers. We hope these introductions will be useful for parents seeking to build on the foundation provided here, and for teachers, whether or not they teach in the growing network of Core Knowledge schools.

If you are interested in learning more about the work and ideas of teachers in Core Knowledge schools, please contact the Core Knowledge Foundation for more information: 801 East High Street, Charlottesville, VA 22902; (434) 977-7550; e-mail: coreknow@coreknowledge.org. Or visit our Web site—www.coreknowledge.org—where you will find an online bookstore, lessons created by teachers in the Core Knowledge schools, a database listing additional resources, and other supporting materials developed by the Foundation.

Introduction to the Revised Edition

This is a revision of the first edition of *What Your Fourth Grader Needs to Know*, first published in 1992. Almost nothing in that earlier book, which elicited wide praise and warm expressions of gratitude from teachers and parents, has become outdated. Why, then, revise the earlier book at all?

Because good things can be made better. In the intervening years since 1992, we at the Core Knowledge Foundation have had the benefit of a great deal of practical experience that can improve the contributions these books can make to early education. We have learned from a growing network of Core Knowledge schools. At this writing, we can build on the experiences of hundreds of schools across the nation that are following the Core Knowledge curriculum guidelines. We have also received many suggestions from parents who are using the books. And besides conducting our own research, we have continued to seek advice from subject-matter experts and multicultural advisors. All these activities have enabled us to field-test and refine the original *Core Knowledge Sequence*—the curriculum guidelines on which the Core Knowledge books are based.

What kind of knowledge and skills can your child be expected to learn at school in fourth grade? How can you help your child at home? These are questions we try to answer in this book. It presents a range of knowledge and skills—in language arts, history and geography, visual arts, music, mathematics, and science—that should be at the core of an enriching, challenging fourth-grade education.

Because children and localities differ greatly across this big, diverse country, so do fourth-grade classrooms. But all communities, including classrooms, require some common ground for communication and learning. In this book we present the specific shared knowledge that hundreds of parents and teachers across the nation have agreed upon for American fourth graders. This core is not a comprehensive prescription for everything that every fourth grader needs to know. Such a complete prescription would be rigid and undesirable. But the book does offer a solid common ground—about 50 percent of the curriculum—that will enable young students to become active, successful learners in their classroom community and later in the larger world we live in.

In this revised edition, we have retold some stories in more detail than before and placed more emphasis on the story in history. We have also included many color reproductions in the Visual Arts section. These improvements reflect contributions from many hands and minds.

Special acknowledgments are owed to the original director of the revision project, John Holdren, and to the editors of this volume, Susan Tyler Hitchcock, Matthew Davis, and Souzanne A. Wright, all four of whom have worked to make the revised edition a better book than the original. As is customary with a chief editor, however, I accept responsibility for any defects that may still be found, and I invite readers to send criticisms and suggestions to the Core Knowledge Foundation.

We hope you and your child will enjoy this book, and that it will help lay the foundations upon which to build a lifetime of learning.

E. D. Hirsch, Jr.

General Introduction
to the Core Knowledge Series

I. WHAT IS YOUR CHILD LEARNING IN SCHOOL?

A parent of identical twins sent me a letter in which she expressed concern that her children, who are in the same grade in the same school, are being taught completely different things. How can this be? Because they are in different classrooms; because the teachers in these classrooms have only the vaguest guidelines to follow; in short, because the school, like many in the United States, lacks a definite, specific curriculum.

Many parents would be surprised if they were to examine the curriculum of their child's elementary school. Ask to see your school's curriculum. Does it spell out, in clear and concrete terms, a core of specific content and skills all children at a particular grade level are expected to learn by the end of the school year?

Many curricula speak in general terms of vaguely defined skills, processes, and attitudes, often in an abstract, pseudo-technical language that calls, for example, for children to "analyze patterns and data," or "investigate the structure and dynamics of living systems," or "work cooperatively in a group." Such vagueness evades the central question: what is your child learning in school? It places unreasonable demands upon teachers, and often results in years of schooling marred by repetitions and gaps. Yet another unit on dinosaurs or "pioneer days." *Charlotte's Web* for the third time. "You've never heard of the Bill of Rights?" "You've never been taught how to add two fractions with unlike denominators?"

When identical twins in two classrooms of the same school have few academic experiences in common, that is cause for concern. When teachers in that school do not know what children in other classrooms are learning on the same grade level, much less in earlier and later grades, they cannot reliably predict that children will come prepared with a shared core of knowledge and skills. For an elementary school to be successful, teachers need a common vision of what they want their students to know and be able to do. They need to have *clear, specific learning goals,* as well as the sense of mutual accountability that comes from a shared commitment to helping all children achieve those goals. Lacking both specific goals and mutual accountability, too many schools exist in a state of curricular incoherence, one result of which is that they fall far short of developing the full potential of our children.

To address this problem, I started the nonprofit Core Knowledge Foundation in 1986. This book and its companion volumes in the Core Knowledge Series are designed to give parents, teachers, and, through them, children a guide to clearly defined learning goals in the form of a carefully sequenced body of knowledge, based upon the specific content guidelines developed by the Core Knowledge Foundation (see below, "The Consensus Behind the *Core Knowledge Sequence*").

Core Knowledge is an attempt to define, in a coherent and sequential way, a body of widely used knowledge taken for granted by competent writers and speakers in the United States. Because this knowledge is taken for granted rather than being explained when it is used, it forms a necessary foundation for the higher-order reading, writing, and thinking skills that children need for academic and vocational success. The universal attainment of such knowledge should be a central aim of curricula in our elementary schools, just as it is currently the aim in all world-class educational systems.

For reasons explained in the next section, making sure that all young children in the United States possess a core of shared knowledge is a necessary step in developing a first-rate educational system.

II. WHY CORE KNOWLEDGE IS NEEDED

Learning builds on learning: children (and adults) gain new knowledge only by building on what they already know. It is essential to begin building solid foundations of knowledge in the early grades when children are most receptive because, for the vast majority of children, academic deficiencies from the first six grades can *permanently* impair the success of later learning. Poor performance of American students in middle and high school can be traced to shortcomings inherited from elementary schools that have not imparted to children the knowledge and skills they need for further learning.

All of the highest-achieving and most egalitarian elementary school systems in the world (such as those in Sweden, France, and Japan) teach their children a specific core of knowledge in each of the first six grades, thus enabling all children to enter each new grade with a secure foundation for further learning. It is time American schools did so as well, for the following reasons.

(1) Commonly shared knowledge makes schooling more effective. We know that the one-on-one tutorial is the most effective form of schooling, in part because a parent or teacher can provide tailor-made instruction for the individual child. But in a nontutorial situation—in, for example, a typical classroom with twenty-five or more students—the instructor cannot effectively impart new knowledge to all the students unless each one shares the background knowledge that the lesson is being built upon.

Consider this scenario: in fourth grade, Ms. Franklin is about to begin a unit on early explorers: Columbus, Magellan, and others. In her class, she has some students who were in Mr. Washington's third-grade class last year and some students who were in Ms. Johnson's third-grade class. She also has a few students who have moved from other towns. As Ms. Franklin begins the unit on explorers, she asks the children to look at a globe and use their fingers to trace a route across the Atlantic Ocean from Europe to North America. The students who had Mr. Washington look blankly at her: they didn't learn that last year. The students who had Ms. Johnson, however, eagerly point to the proper places on the globe. And two of the students who came from other towns pipe up and say, "Columbus and Magellan again? We did that last year."

When all the students in a class do share the relevant background knowledge, a classroom can begin to approach the effectiveness of a tutorial. Even when some children in a class do not have elements of the knowledge they were supposed to acquire in previous grades, the existence of a specifically defined core makes it possible for the teacher or parent to identify and fill the gaps, thus giving all students a chance to fulfill their potential in later grades.

(2) Commonly shared knowledge makes schooling more fair and democratic. When all the children who enter a grade can be assumed to share some of the same building blocks of knowledge, and when the teacher knows exactly what those building blocks are, then all the students are empowered to learn. In our current system, children from disadvantaged backgrounds too often suffer from unmerited low expectations that translate into watered-down curricula. But if we specify the core of knowledge that all children should share, then we can guarantee equal access to that knowledge and compensate for the academic advantages some students are offered at home. In a Core Knowledge school, *all* children enjoy the benefits of important, challenging knowledge that will provide the foundation for successful later learning.

(3) Commonly shared knowledge helps create cooperation and solidarity in our schools and nation. Diversity is a hallmark and strength of our nation. American classrooms are often, and increasingly, made up of students from a variety of cultural backgrounds, and those different cultures should be honored by all students. At the same time, education should create a *school-based* culture that is common and welcoming to all because it includes knowledge of many cultures and gives all students, no matter what their background, a common foundation for understanding our cultural diversity.

III. THE CONSENSUS BEHIND THE CORE KNOWLEDGE SEQUENCE

The content in this and other volumes in the Core Knowledge Series is based on a document called the *Core Knowledge Sequence,* a grade-by-grade sequence of specific content guidelines in history, geography, mathematics, science, language arts, and the fine arts. The *Sequence* is not meant to outline the whole of the school curriculum; rather, it offers specific guidelines to knowledge that can reasonably be expected to make up about *half* of any school's curriculum, or perhaps a little more, thus leaving ample room for local requirements and emphases. Teaching a common core of knowledge, such as that articulated in the *Core Knowledge Sequence,* is compatible with a variety of instructional methods and additional subject matters.

The *Core Knowledge Sequence* is the result of a long process of research and consensus-building undertaken by the Core Knowledge Foundation. Here is how we achieved the consensus behind the *Core Knowledge Sequence.*

First we analyzed the many reports issued by state departments of education and by professional organizations—such as the National Council of Teachers of Mathematics and the American Association for the Advancement of Science—that recommend general outcomes for elementary and secondary education. We also tabulated the knowledge and skills through grade six specified in the successful educational systems of several other countries, including France, Japan, Sweden, and West Germany.

In addition, we formed an advisory board on multiculturalism that proposed a specific knowledge of diverse cultural traditions that American children should all share as part of their school-based common culture. We sent the resulting materials to three independent groups of teachers, scholars, and scientists around the country, asking them to create a master list of the knowledge children should have by the end of grade six. About 150 teachers (including college professors, scientists, and administrators) were involved in this initial step.

These items were amalgamated into a master plan, and further groups of teachers and specialists were asked to agree on a grade-by-grade sequence of the items. That sequence was then sent to some one hundred educators and specialists who participated in a national conference that was called to hammer out a working agreement on an appropriate core of knowledge for the first six grades.

This important meeting took place in March 1990. The conferees were elementary school teachers, curriculum specialists, scientists, science writers, officers of national organizations, representatives of ethnic groups, district superintendents, and school principals from across the country. A total of twenty-four working groups decided on revisions in the *Core Knowledge Sequence.* The resulting provisional *Sequence* was further fine-tuned during a year of implementation at a pioneering school, Three Oaks Elementary in Lee County, Florida.

In only a few years many more schools—urban and rural, rich and poor, public and private—joined in the effort to teach Core Knowledge. Based largely on suggestions from these schools, the *Core Knowledge Sequence* has been significantly revised: it was extended to seventh and eighth grades; separate guidelines were added for kindergarten; and a few topics in other grades were added, omitted, or moved from one grade to another, in order to create an even more coherent sequence for learning. A *Core Knowledge Preschool Sequence* was first published in 1997.

The Core Knowledge Foundation continues to work with schools and advisors to fine-tune the *Sequence.* The revised editions of this and other books in the Core Knowledge Series reflect the revisions in the *Sequence*. Current editions of the *Core Knowledge Sequence* and the *Core Knowledge Preschool Sequence* may be ordered from the Core Knowledge Foundation; see the end of this introduction for the address.

IV. THE NATURE OF THIS SERIES

The books in this series are designed to give a convenient and engaging introduction to the knowledge specified in the *Core Knowledge Sequence*. These are resource books, addressed primarily to parents, but which we hope will be useful tools for both parents and teachers. These books are not intended to replace the local curriculum or school textbooks, but rather to serve as aids to help children gain some of the important knowledge they will need to make progress in school and be effective in society.

Although we have made these books as accessible and useful as we can, parents and teachers should understand that they are not the only means by which the *Core Knowledge Sequence* can be imparted. The books represent a single version of the possibilities inherent in the *Sequence*. We hope that publishers will be stimulated to offer educational videos, computer software, games, alternative books, and other imaginative vehicles based on the *Core Knowledge Sequence*.

These books are not textbooks or workbooks, though when appropriate they do suggest some activities you can do with your child. In these books, we address your child directly, and occasionally ask questions to think about. The earliest books in the series are intended to be read aloud to children. Even as children become able to read the books on their own, we encourage parents to help their children read more actively by reading along with them and talking about what they are reading.

You and your child can read the sections of this book in any order, depending on your child's interests or depending on the topics your child is studying in school. You can skip from section to section and reread as much as your child likes.

We encourage you to think of this book as a guidebook that opens the way to many paths you and your child can explore. These paths may lead to the library, to many other good books, and, if possible, to plays, museums, concerts, and other opportunities for knowledge and enrichment. In short, this guidebook recommends places to visit and describes what is important in those places, but only you and your child can make the actual visit, travel the streets, and climb the steps.

V. WHAT YOU CAN DO TO HELP IMPROVE AMERICAN EDUCATION

The first step for parents and teachers who are committed to reform is to be skeptical about oversimplified slogans like "critical thinking" and "learning to learn." Such slogans are everywhere, and unfortunately for our schools, their partial insights have been elevated to the level of universal truths. For example: "What students learn is not important; rather, we must teach students to learn *how* to learn." "The child, not the academic subject, is the true focus of education." "Do not impose knowledge on children before they are developmentally ready to receive it." "Do not bog children down in mere facts, but rather, teach critical-thinking skills."

Who has not heard these sentiments, so admirable and humane, and—up to a point—so true? But these positive sentiments in favor of "thinking skills" and "higher understanding" have been turned into negative sentiments against the teaching of important knowledge. Those who have entered the teaching profession over the past forty years have been taught to scorn important knowledge as "mere facts," and to see the imparting of this knowledge as somehow injurious to children. Thus it has come about that many educators, armed with partially true slogans, have seemingly taken leave of common sense.

Many parents and teachers have come to the conclusion that elementary education must strike a better balance between the development of the whole child and the more limited but fundamental duty of the school to ensure that all children master a core of knowledge and skills essential to their competence as learners in later grades. But these parents and teachers cannot act on their convictions without an agreed-upon, concrete sequence of knowledge. Our main motivation in developing the *Core Knowledge Sequence* and this book series has been to give parents and teachers something concrete to work with.

It has been encouraging to see how many teachers, since the first volume in this series was published, have responded to the Core Knowledge reform effort. If you would like more information about the growing network of Core Knowledge schools, please call or write the Core Knowledge Foundation.

Parents and teachers are urged to join in a grass-roots effort to strengthen our elementary schools. Start in your own school and district. Insist that your school clearly state the core of *specific* knowledge and skills that each child in a grade must learn. Whether your school's core corresponds exactly to the Core Knowledge model is less important than the existence of some core—which, we hope, will be as solid, coherent, and challenging as the *Core Knowledge Sequence* has proven to be. Inform members of your community about the need for such a specific curriculum, and help make sure that your local school board members are independent-minded people who will insist that children have the benefit of a solid, specific, world-class curriculum in each grade.

Share the knowledge!

E. D. Hirsch, Jr.
Core Knowledge Foundation
801 East High Street
Charlottesville, Virginia 22902
(434) 977-7550
coreknow@coreknowledge.org
www.coreknowledge.org

What Your Fourth Grader Needs to Know

FUNDAMENTALS OF A GOOD FOURTH-GRADE EDUCATION

I.

Language
and
Literature

Introduction

This chapter presents poems, stories, brief discussions of grammar and writing, and explanations of common sayings and phrases.

The best way to bring children into the spirit of poetry is to read it aloud to them and encourage them to speak it aloud so that they can experience the music in the words. Until children take pleasure in the sound of poetry, there is little reason to analyze it technically.

Most of the stories in this book are either excerpts from longer works or abridged versions of those works. If a child enjoys a particular story, he or she should be encouraged to read a longer version. Several of the novels excerpted here are available in child-friendly versions as part of the Core Knowledge Foundation's *Core Classics* series, available on the Foundation's Web site (www.coreknowledge.org).

Parents and teachers can help draw children into stories by asking questions about them. For example, you might ask, "What do you think is going to happen next?" "Why did one of the characters act as he did?" "What might have happened if . . . ?" You might also ask the child to retell the story. Don't be bothered if children change events or characters: that is in the best tradition of storytelling and explains why there are so many versions of traditional stories.

You can also encourage children to write and illustrate their own stories. Some children may be interested in beginning to keep a journal or writing letters to friends or relatives—these are both fine ways for children to cultivate their writing skills. Another way to build vocabulary and foster language skills is by playing word games such as Scrabble, Boggle, or hangman, and doing crossword puzzles.

Experts say that our children already know more about grammar than we can ever teach them. But standard written language does have special characteristics that children need to learn. The treatment of grammar and language conventions in this book is an overview. It needs to be supplemented and rounded out by giving the child opportunities to read and write and to discuss reading and writing in connection with grammar and spelling.

In the classroom, grammar instruction is a part, but only a part, of an effective language arts program. In the fourth grade, children should be working on vocabulary and spelling. They should enjoy a rich diet of fiction, poetry, drama, biography, and nonfiction. They should be involved in the writing process, inventing topics, discovering ideas in early drafts, revising toward "publication" of polished final drafts—all with encouragement and guidance along the way. They should practice writing in many modes, including stories, poetry, journal entries, formal reports, dialogues, and descriptions.

For some children, the section on sayings and phrases may not be needed; they will have picked up these sayings by hearing them in everyday speech. But this section will be very useful for children from homes where American English is not spoken.

For additional resources to use in conjunction with this section, visit the Foundation's online bookstore and database, Resources to Build On, at the Web address above.

Poetry

Monday's Child Is Fair of Face
(author unknown)

Monday's child is fair of face,
Tuesday's child is full of grace,
Wednesday's child is full of woe,
Thursday's child has far to go,
Friday's child is loving and giving,
Saturday's child works hard for a living,
But the child that is born on the Sabbath day
Is fair and wise and good and gay.

Humanity
by Elma Stuckey

If I am blind and need someone
To keep me safe from harm,
It matters not the race to me
Of the one who takes my arm.

If I am saved from drowning
As I grasp and grope,
I will not stop to see the face
Of the one who throws the rope.

Or if out on some battlefield
I'm falling faint and weak,
The one who gently lifts me up
May any language speak.

We sip the water clear and cool,
No matter the hand that gives it.
A life that's lived worthwhile and fine,
What matters the one who lives it?

Fog
by Carl Sandburg

The fog comes
on little cat feet.

It sits looking
over harbor and city
on silent haunches
and then moves on.

Clouds
by Christina G. Rossetti

White sheep, white sheep
On a blue hill,
When the wind stops
You all stand still.
When the wind blows,
You walk away slow.
White sheep, white sheep,
Where do you go?

the drum
by Nikki Giovanni

daddy says the world is
a drum tight and hard
and i told him
i'm gonna beat
out my own rhythm

Things
by Eloise Greenfield

Went to the corner
Walked in the store
Bought me some candy
Ain't got it no more
Ain't got it no more

Went to the beach
Played on the shore
Built me a sandhouse
Ain't got it no more
Ain't got it no more

Went to the kitchen
Lay down on the floor
Made me a poem
Still got it
Still got it

Dreams
by Langston Hughes

Hold fast to dreams
For if dreams die
Life is a broken-winged bird
That cannot fly.

Hold fast to dreams
For when dreams go
Life is a barren field
Frozen with snow.

Afternoon on a Hill
by Edna St. Vincent Millay

I will be the gladdest thing
    Under the sun!
I will touch a hundred flowers
    And not pick one.

I will look at cliffs and clouds
    With quiet eyes,
Watch the wind bow down the grass,
    And the grass rise.

And when lights begin to show,
    Up from the town,
I will mark which must be mine,
    And then start down.

The Rhinoceros
by Ogden Nash

The rhino is a homely beast,
For human eyes he's not a feast.
But you and I will never know
Why Nature chose to make him so.
Farewell, farewell, you old rhinoceros,
I'll stare at something less prepoceros.

The Pobble Who Has No Toes
by Edward Lear

The Pobble who has no toes,
   Had once as many as we;
When they said, "Some day you may lose
   them all";
   He replied "Fish Fiddle de-dee!"
And his Aunt Jobiska made him drink,
Lavender water tinged with pink;
For she said, "The World in general knows
There's nothing so good for a Pobble's
   toes!"

The Pobble who has no toes,
   Swam across the Bristol Channel;
But before he set out he wrapped his nose
   In a piece of scarlet flannel.
For his Aunt Jobiska said, "No harm
Can come to his toes if his nose is warm;
And it's perfectly known that a Pobble's
   toes
Are safe—provided he minds his nose."

The Pobble swam fast and well.
   And when boats or ships came near him,
He tinkledy-binkledy-winkled a bell,
   So that all the world could hear him.
And all the Sailors and Admirals cried,
When they saw him nearing the further
   side—
"He has gone to fish, for his Aunt Jobiska's
Runcible Cat with crimson whiskers!"

But before he touched the shore—
   The shore of the Bristol Channel,
A sea-green Porpoise carried away
   His wrapper of scarlet flannel.
And when he came to observe his feet,
Formerly garnished with toes so neat,
His face at once became forlorn,
On perceiving that all his toes were gone!

And nobody knew,
   From that dark day to the present,
Whoso had taken the Pobble's toes,
   In a manner so far from pleasant.
Whether the shrimps, or crawfish gray,
Or crafty Mermaids stole them away—
Nobody knew; and nobody knows
How the Pobble was robbed of his twice
   five toes!

The Pobble who has no toes
   Was placed in a friendly Bark,
And they rowed him back, and carried
   him up
   To his Aunt Jobiska's Park.
And she made him a feast at his earnest wish
Of eggs and buttercups fried with fish,
And she said, "It's a fact the whole world
   knows,
That Pobbles are happier without their
   toes."

A Tragic Story
by William Makepeace Thackeray

There lived a sage in days of yore,
And he a handsome pigtail wore:
But wondered much, and sorrowed more,
   Because it hung behind him.

He mused upon this curious case,
And swore he'd change the pigtail's place,
And have it hanging at his face,
   Not dangling there behind him.

Says he, "The mystery I've found—
I'll turn me round,"—he turned him round;
   but still it hung behind him.

Then round, and round, and out and in,
All day the puzzled sage did spin;
In vain—it mattered not a pin—
   The pigtail hung behind him.

And right and left, and round about,
And up and down, and in and out
He turned; but still the pigtail stout
   Hung steadily behind him.

And though his efforts never slack,
And though he twist, and twirl, and tack,
Alas! Still faithful to his back,
   The pigtail hangs behind him.

Clarence
by Shel Silverstein

Clarence Lee from Tennessee
Loved the commercials he saw on TV.
He watched with wide believing eyes
And bought everything they advertised—
Cream to make his skin feel better,
Spray to make his hair look wetter,
Bleach to make his white things whiter,
Stylish jeans that fit much tighter.
Toothpaste for his cavities,
Powder for his doggie's fleas,
Purple mouthwash for his breath,
Deodorant to stop his sweat.
He bought each cereal they presented,
Bought each game that they invented.
Then one day he looked and saw
"A brand-new Maw, a better Paw!
New, improved in every way—
Hurry, order yours today!"
So, of course, our little Clarence
Sent off for two brand-new parents.
The new ones came in the morning mail,
The old ones he sold at a garage sale.
And now they all are doing fine:
His new folks treat him sweet and kind,
His old ones work in an old coal mine.
So if your Maw and Paw are mean
And make you eat your lima beans
And make you wash and make you wait
And never let you stay up late
And scream and scold and preach and pout,
That simply means they're wearing out.
So send off for two brand-new parents
And you'll be as happy as little Clarence.

Paul Revere's Ride
by Henry Wadsworth Longfellow

Listen, my children, and you shall hear
Of the midnight ride of Paul Revere,
On the eighteenth of April, in Seventy-five;
Hardly a man is now alive
Who remembers that famous day and year.

He said to his friend, "If the British march
By land or sea from the town tonight,
Hang a lantern aloft in the belfry arch
Of the North Church tower as a signal light—
One, if by land, and two, if by sea;
And I on the opposite shore will be,
Ready to ride and spread the alarm
Through every Middlesex village and farm,
For the country folk to be up and to arm."

Then he said "Good night!" and with muffled oar
Silently rowed to the Charlestown shore,
Just as the moon rose over the bay,
Where swinging wide at her moorings lay
The *Somerset*, British man-of-war;
A phantom ship, with each mast and spar
Across the moon like a prison bar,
And a huge black hulk, that was magnified
By its own reflection in the tide.

Meanwhile, his friend, through alley and street,
Wanders and watches with eager ears,
Till in the silence around him he hears
The muster of men at the barrack door,
The sound of arms, and the tramp of feet,
And the measured tread of the grenadiers,
Marching down to their boats on the shore.

Then he climbed the tower of the Old North Church,
By the wooden stairs, with stealthy tread,
To the belfry-chamber overhead,

And startled the pigeons from their perch
On the somber rafters, that round him made
Masses and moving shapes of shade—
By the trembling ladder, steep and tall
To the highest window in the wall,
Where he paused to listen and look down
A moment on the roof of the town,
And the moonlight flowing over all.

Beneath, in the churchyard, lay the dead,
In their night-encampment on the hill,
Wrapped in silence so deep and still
That he could hear, like a sentinel's tread,
The watchful night-wind, as it went
Creeping along from tent to tent,
And seeming to whisper, "All is well!"
A moment only he feels the spell
Of the place and the hour, and the secret dread
Of the lonely belfry and the dead;
For suddenly all his thoughts are bent
On a shadowy something far away,
Where the river widens to meet the bay—
A line of black that bends and floats
On the rising tide, like a bridge of boats.

Meanwhile, impatient to mount and ride,
Booted and spurred, with a heavy stride
On the opposite shore walked Paul Revere.
Now he patted his horse's side,
Now he gazed at the landscape far and near,
Then, impetuous, stamped the earth,
And turned and tightened his saddle-girth;
But mostly he watched with eager search
The belfry tower of the Old North Church,
As it rose above the graves on the hill,
Lonely and spectral and somber and still.

And lo! as he looks, on the belfry's height
A glimmer, and then a gleam of light!

He springs to the saddle, the bridle he turns,
But lingers and gazes, till full on his sight
A second lamp in the belfry burns!
A hurry of hoofs in a village street,
A shape in the moonlight, a bulk in the dark,
And beneath, from the pebbles, in passing, a spark
Struck out by a steed flying fearless and fleet;
That was all! And yet, through the gloom and the light,
The fate of a nation was riding that night;
And the spark struck out by the steed, in his flight,
Kindled the land into flame with its heat.

He has left the village and mounted the steep,
And beneath him, tranquil and broad and deep,
Is the Mystic, meeting the ocean tides;
And under the alders that skirt its edge,
Now soft on the sand, now loud on the ledge,
Is heard the tramp of his steed as he rides.

It was twelve by the village clock,
When he crossed the bridge into Medford town.
He heard the crowing of the cock,
And the barking of the farmer's dog,
And felt the damp of the river fog,
That rises after the sun goes down.

It was one by the village clock,
When he galloped into Lexington.
He saw the gilded weathercock
Swim in the moonlight as he passed,
And the meeting-house windows, blank and bare,
Gaze at him with a spectral glare,
As if they already stood aghast
At the bloody work they would look upon.

It was two by the village clock,
When he came to the bridge in Concord town.
He heard the bleating of the flock,
And the twitter of birds among the trees,

And felt the breath of the morning breeze
Blowing over the meadows brown.
And one was safe and asleep in his bed
Who at the bridge would be first to fall,
Who that day would be lying dead,
Pierced by a British musket-ball.

You know the rest. In the books you have read,
How the British Regulars fired and fled—
How the farmers gave them ball for ball,
From behind each fence and farmyard wall,
Chasing the red-coats down the lane,
Then crossing the fields to emerge again
Under the trees at the turn of the road,
And only pausing to fire and load.

So through the night rode Paul Revere;
And so through the night went his cry of alarm
To every Middlesex village and farm—
A cry of defiance and not of fear,
A voice in the darkness, a knock at the door,
And a word that shall echo for evermore!
For, borne on the night-wind of the Past,
Through all our history, to the last,
In the hour of darkness and peril and need,
The people will waken and listen to hear
The hurrying hoof-beats of that steed,
And the midnight message of Paul Revere.

Concord Hymn
by Ralph Waldo Emerson

By the rude bridge that arched the flood,
   Their flag to April's breeze unfurled,
Here once the embattled farmers stood,
   And fired the shot heard round the world.

The foe long since in silence slept;
   Alike the conqueror silent sleeps;
And Time the ruined bridge has swept
   Down the dark stream which seaward creeps.

On this green bank, by this soft stream,
   We set to-day a votive stone;
That memory may their deed redeem,
   When, like our sires, our sons are gone.

Spirit, that made those heroes dare
   To die, and leave their children free,
Bid Time and Nature gently spare
   The shaft we raise to them and thee.

Lines and Stanzas

Poetry is made up of lines. Sometimes the lines of a poem are grouped into clusters called stanzas. In Emerson's "Concord Hymn," for example, there are four stanzas, each of which contains four lines. The first and third lines of each stanza rhyme, and so do the second and fourth.

George Washington

by Rosemary Benét and Stephen Vincent Benét

Sing hey! for bold George Washington,
That jolly British tar,
King George's famous admiral
From Hull to Zanzibar!
No – wait a minute – something's wrong –
George *wished* to sail the foam.
But, when his mother thought, aghast,
Of Georgie shinning up a mast,
Her tears and protests flowed so fast
That George remained at home.

Sing ho! for grave Washington,
The staid Virginia squire,
Who farms his fields and hunts his hounds
And aims at nothing higher!
Stop, stop, it's going wrong again!
George *liked* to live on farms,
But, when the Colonies agreed
They could and should and would be freed,
They called on George to do the deed
And George cried, "Shoulder arms!"

Sing ha! for Emperor Washington,
That hero of renown,
Who freed his land from Britain's rule
To win a golden crown!
No, no, that's what George *might* have won
But didn't, for he said,
"There's not much point about a king,
They're pretty but they're apt to sting,
And, as for crowns—the heavy thing
Would only hurt my head."

Sing ho! for our George Washington!
(At last I've got it straight.)
The first in war, the first in peace,
The goodly and the great.
But, when you think about him now,
From here to Valley Forge,
Remember this—he might have been
A highly different specimen,
And, where on earth would we be, then?
I'm glad that George was George.

Stories and Myths

The Fire on the Mountain

This story takes place in Ethiopia.

People say that in the old days in the city of Addis Ababa there was a young man by the name of Arha. He had come as a boy from the country of Guragé, and in the city he became the servant of a rich merchant, Haptom Hasei.

Haptom Hasei was so rich that he owned everything that money could buy, and often he was very bored because he had tired of everything he knew, and there was nothing new for him to do.

One cold night, when the damp wind was blowing across the plateau, Haptom called to Arha to bring wood for the fire. When Arha was finished, Haptom began to talk.

"How much cold can a man stand?" he said, speaking at first to himself. "I wonder if it would be possible for a man to stand on the highest peak, Mount Sululta, where the coldest winds blow, through an entire night without blankets or clothing and yet not die?"

"I don't know," Arha said. "But wouldn't it be a foolish thing?"

"Perhaps, if he had nothing to gain by it, it would be a foolish thing to spend the night that way," Haptom said. "But I would be willing to bet that a man couldn't do it."

"I am sure a courageous man could stand naked on Mount Sululta throughout an entire night and not die of it," Arha said. "But as for me, it isn't my affair since I've nothing to bet."

"Well, I'll tell you what," Haptom said. "Since you are so sure it can be done, I'll make a bet with you anyway. If you can stand among the rocks on Mount Sululta for an entire night without food or water, or clothing or blankets or fire, and not die of it, then I will give you ten acres of good farmland for your own, with a house and cattle."

Arha could hardly believe what he had heard.

"Do you really mean this?" he asked.

"I am a man of my word," Haptom replied.

*"Since you are so sure it can be done,"
Haptom said, "I'll make a bet with you."*

"Then tomorrow night I will do it," Arha said, "and afterward, for all the years to come, I shall till my own soil."

But he was very worried, because the wind swept bitterly across that peak. So in the morning Arha went to a wise old man from the Guragé tribe and told him of the bet he had made. The old man listened quietly and thoughtfully, and when Arha had finished he said:

"I will help you. Across the valley from Sululta is a high rock which can be seen in the daytime. Tomorrow night, as the sun goes down, I shall build a fire there, so that it can be seen from where you stand on the peak. All night long you must watch the light of my fire. Do not close your eyes or let the darkness creep upon you. As you watch my fire, think of its warmth, and think of me, your friend, sitting there tending it for you. If you do this you will survive, no matter how bitter the night wind."

Arha thanked the old man warmly and went back to Haptom's house with a light heart. He told Haptom he was ready, and in the afternoon Haptom sent him, under the watchful eyes of other servants, to the top of Mount Sululta. There, as night fell, Arha removed his clothes and stood in the damp, cold wind that swept across the plateau with the setting sun. Across the valley, several miles away, Arha saw the light of his friend's fire, which shone like a star in the blackness.

The wind turned colder and seemed to pass through his flesh and chill the marrow in his bones. The rock on which he stood felt like ice. Each hour the cold numbed him more, until he thought he would never be warm again, but he kept his eyes upon the twinkling light across the valley, and remembered that his old friend sat there tending a fire for him. Sometimes wisps of fog blotted out the light, and then he strained to see until the fog passed. He sneezed and coughed and shivered, and began to feel ill. Yet all night through he stood there, and only when the dawn came did he put on his clothes and go down the mountain back to Addis Ababa.

Haptom was very surprised to see Arha, and he questioned his servants thoroughly.

"Did he stay all night without food or drink or blankets or clothing?"

"Yes," his servants said. "He did all of these things."

"Well, you are a strong fellow," Haptom said to Arha. "How did you manage to do it?"

"I simply watched the light of a fire on a distant hill," Arha said.

"What! You watched a fire? Then you lose the bet, and you are still my servant, and you own no land!"

"But this fire was not close enough to warm me, it was far across the valley!"

"I won't give you the land," Haptom said. "You didn't fulfill the conditions. It was only the fire that saved you."

"He thought he would never be warm again, but he kept his eyes upon the twinkling light across the valley."

Arha was very sad. He went again to his old friend of the Guragé tribe and told him what had happened.

"Take the matter to the judge," the old man advised him.

Arha went to the judge and complained, and the judge sent for Haptom. When Haptom told his story, and the servants said once more that Arha had watched a distant fire across the valley, the judge said:

"No, you have lost, for Haptom Hasei's condition was that you must be without fire."

Once more Arha went to his old friend with the sad news that he was doomed to the life of a servant, as though he had not gone through the ordeal on the mountaintop.

"Don't give up hope," the old man said. "More wisdom grows wild in the hills than in any city judge."

He got up from where he sat and went to find a man named Hailu, in whose house he had been a servant when he was young. He explained to the good man about the bet between Haptom and Arha, and asked if something couldn't be done.

"Don't worry about it," Hailu said after thinking for a while. "I will take care of it for you."

Some days later Hailu sent invitations to many people in the city to come to a feast at his house. Haptom was among them, and so was the judge who had ruled Arha had lost the bet.

When the day of the feast arrived, the guests came riding on mules with fine trappings, their servants strung out behind them on foot. Haptom came with twenty servants, one of whom held a silk umbrella over his head to shade him from the sun, and four drummers played music that signified the great Haptom was here.

The guests sat on soft rugs laid out for them and talked. From the kitchen came the odors of wonderful things to eat: roast goat, roast corn and durra, pancakes called *injera* and many tantalizing sauces. The smell of the food only accentuated the hunger of the guests. Time passed. The food should have been served, but they did not see it, only smelled vapors that drifted from the kitchen. The evening came, and still no food was served. The guests began to whisper among themselves. It was very curious that the honorable Hailu had not had the food brought out. Still the smells came from the kitchen. At last one of the guests spoke out for all the others:

"Hailu, why do you do this to us? Why do you invite us to a feast and then serve us nothing?"

"Why, can't you smell the food?" Hailu asked with surprise.

"Indeed we can, but smelling is not eating; there is no nourishment in it!"

"And is there warmth in a fire so distant it can hardly be seen?" Hailu asked. "If Arha was warmed by the fire he watched while standing on Mount Sululta, then you have been fed by the smells coming from my kitchen."

The people agreed with him; the judge now saw his mistake, and Haptom was shamed.

He thanked Hailu for his advice and announced that Arha was then and there the owner of the land, the house, and the cattle.

Then Hailu ordered the food brought in, and the feast began.

The Wonderful Chuang Brocade

This folktale is from a region in southern China called Chuang.

For thousands of years the people of China have been famous for their rich art in silken brocades. The Chuang people of Kwangsi Province are especially well known for their beautiful designs and pictures. Some of them tell stories such as this one.

In this province, at the foot of high peaks, in a thatched cottage, lived an old widow with her three sons: Lemo, Letui, and Leju. The old mother was a most wonderful weaver of brocades, which merchants and folks bought from her to make vests, bedcovers, and blankets. Her sons were woodcutters.

One day the old mother went to sell a fine brocade she had made. In the merchant's shop hung a painting of wondrous beauty. It showed a village with a rich, tall palace with colorful gardens around it. Beautiful flowers and ripe vegetables were everywhere; ducks, chickens, and cows were all over. Never had she seen a more beautiful scene. Quickly she sold her brocade and bought the painting, forgetting the rice and other foods she needed.

At home she proudly showed the painting. "How happy I would be to live in that palace with its gardens," she said to her sons.

"That is a dream, *Ah-mee*," spoke Lemo, the oldest son.

"Maybe we will live in such a place in our next life," said Letui, her second son.

Then Leju, the youngest, said, "*Ah-mee*, you must weave a brocade just like the painting, and when you look at your work you will think you are living in the palace with those gardens."

"You are right, son," said the old mother, and she set to work at once.

Day in, day out, and nights as well, she worked at the wooden loom with silk threads, and the scenes of the painting grew in beauty on the brocade.

Day in, day out, and nights as well, she worked at the wooden loom with silk threads, and the scenes of the painting grew in beauty on the brocade.

She never stopped working. Her old eyes hurt from the smoke of the pine-oil lamps, but she did not stop. After one year, tears filled her eyes, but instead of stopping, she put her tears into the brocade and made of them a singing river and a shining pond full of fishes. After two years, drops of blood fell from her eyes onto the brocade. Out of these she wove bright red flowers and a glowing sun.

So the old near-blind mother worked for three years until she finished putting the painting into the brocade. The sons were so proud of her work, they took it out of their dark hut and put it in front of the door where there was enough daylight to see and admire it. Everyone who saw it exclaimed, "What a wonderful Chuang brocade!"

All of a sudden a weird whirring wind came along and . . . *whisht!* it picked up the brocade and carried it high, high up into the sky and . . . The brocade disappeared.

The old mother fainted, everyone shouted . . . but the brocade was gone. The mother became very ill and no doctor could help her. She was forever crying for her brocade!

Seeing this, Lemo said, "Mother, stop grieving! I will find your beautiful brocade and bring it back to you."

"Go, son, and may good fortune go with you."

Lemo set out over mountains and across rivers. One day he came to a mountain pass, on one side of which stood a stone house. To the right was a stone horse, its mouth wide open, bent over an arbutus bush full of red berries.

At the door sat an old white-headed woman.

"Who are you and where are you going, young man?" she asked Lemo.

He told her the tale of his mother's beautiful brocade—how hard and long she had worked at it and how the wind had carried it away, and how very ill she had become.

"Young Lemo, I know all this. The winds of the mountains tell me many things. Your brocade is now in the Sun Mountain of the East with the beautiful fairies who live there. They saw the brocade and sent the wind for it. They are now copying your mother's beautiful work, and you can get it back only with the help of the stone horse. But the horse will help you only if you give him two of your teeth for the ones he is missing in his mouth so that he can eat the berries from the arbutus bush. Then he will take you far and wide to the Sun Mountain in the East.

"On the way you will come to a mountain of leaping flames through which you must pass. You must do it in silence and without fear. If you cry out even once, you will turn into charcoal.

"Then you will come to a sea full of jagged ice with knife-cutting cold winds tearing at you, but you must not cry out or even shiver with cold. If you do, you will be crushed by the wild tossing ice and buried in the icy water.

"If you go through these trials, you will get your mother's brocade."

Lemo was silent. His face turned blue with fear and he hung his head and thought—for a long time. To lose his teeth and endure such terrible trials!

The old woman watched him. Then she said, "Son, your face tells your thoughts. It says: it is too much! But you tried, so there is a little iron box full of gold nuggets. Go back home and live well."

Lemo took the box and thanked her and left. But he was thinking hard. "If I go home I must share the gold with all my family! There will be little for me . . . No! I will go to the city and live on my wealth!" So he turned his steps toward the big city.

The old mother waited and waited, pining for her beautiful brocade. "If only I could see it before I die," she cried continually.

Letui, her second son, said, "Mother, I will bring you your brocade," and he set off at once.

He, too, came to the stone house with the old lady and her stone horse, and she told him just what she had told Lemo.

Letui also thought and thought, and the old woman knew what was in his mind. "Son," she said, "I can tell you think the trials are too much for you, but you started bravely, so here is a little iron box with gold nuggets. Go back and live happily." But Letui thought as did Lemo, so instead of going home, he too turned toward the city.

At home the old mother waited, crying for her handiwork until her eyes gave out and she became completely blind!

Leju, the youngest son, said, "Mother, I will go on the road to find your beautiful brocade and bring it back to you. You will be with kind neighbors who will take care of you while I am away."

Horse and rider went through the burning mountain and the icy sea. But Leju sat firm on the horse, thinking only of helping his mother.

He bade her good cheer and went off. Like his brothers, he came to the stone house with the stone horse and the old woman. She told him how he could get the brocade only with the help of the horse, and of the dangers he must face.

Instead of thinking long as his brothers had, Leju gave two of his teeth to the horse and mounted it. The horse ate the berries and then went off swift as the wind. Horse and rider went through the burning mountain and the icy sea. But Leju sat firm on the horse, thinking only of helping his mother, and so he reached the Sun Mountain and the palace where the lovely fairies were busy copying *Ah-mee*'s masterpiece.

Leju spoke to them, telling them of his mother's sickness and blindness, and of how she continued to cry for her lost brocade.

"We will finish copying your mother's wonderful work by tomorrow morning," said one of the maidens. "Then you can take it back to your *Ah-mee*."

They gave him delicious fruits to eat, and he fell asleep. But during the night the fairies hung a big glowing pearl on the rafter and wove by its light.

A maiden in a red dress finished first. She looked at her own work, and then at *Ah-mee*'s. She sighed, "I am afraid mine is not nearly as fine. I wish I could live in the beautiful place that is on her brocade." So she began weaving her own image right near the fish pond that *Ah-mee* had woven.

Leju slept in the palace of the fairies, but the next morning, before the maidens arose, he took his mother's brocade, mounted the stone horse, and in the wink of time they were back at the stone house where the white-haired woman sat waiting for him.

"Leju, your mother is very ill," she said. "Hurry back. The sight of her brocade will bring her health." Then she took the two teeth from the horse's mouth and put them back into Leju's. Next she put a pair of magic deerskin shoes on his feet and bade him good luck.

The shoes were like wings and took him swiftly to his home, where his mother was lying in bed, thin as a stick and barely alive.

"*Ah-mee*," he shouted, "I have brought you your brocade. Here!"

No sooner did she touch it than she began to feel well again. Her eyes opened wide and once again she could see! She got up and took her beloved work out into the open sunshine and then . . . a miracle happened! The embroidery of her brocade became a real place. Trees! Flowers! All were there before the rich palace, and by the fish pond stood the lovely maiden in her red dress.

Leju married the maiden, and the two lived happily all their lives.

One day two beggars came to their village. They were Lemo and Letui. They had spent all their gold, drinking, eating, and making merry in the city, and now they were dressed in rags and begging for food. When they saw the beautiful garden where *Ah-mee*, Leju, and his wife were walking and singing, they quietly slipped away, too ashamed to face their mother and brother.

King Arthur and the Knights of the Round Table

Old legends tell of an ancient British king named Arthur and of his queen, Guinevere. The legends tell how they held court at Camelot, where they were attended by the famous Knights of the Round Table. These knights upheld the code of chivalry, defending the defenseless and fighting for justice.

Arthur himself was the son of King Uther Pendragon. To protect his son, King Pendragon put Arthur in the care of Merlin, a sorcerer. Merlin could cast magic spells and change his appearance to look like an animal or another person. He was also called a seer because he could see the future—for everyone except himself. Merlin allowed Arthur to be raised by a knight, Sir Ector. Sir Ector did not know that Arthur was the king's son, and Arthur did not know this either.

When Arthur was still a very young man, King Pendragon died, leaving no other heir to the throne. The British lords began to feud with each other over who should be king. The feuding went on until one Christmas day something amazing happened. As the lords came out of church, they found a square marble stone in the churchyard. In the middle of it was an anvil and into the anvil was thrust a sword. The stone gripped the naked sword by the point, and on the blade was written in gold letters: Whosoever pulls out this sword from this stone and anvil is the true-born King of Britain.

All of the great lords tried to pull out the sword, but all failed. When all of the great men had tried, Arthur grasped the sword by the hilt and gave it a light, quick pull—and out it came. The great men of the kingdom were astonished and they knelt before Arthur and acknowledged him as the rightful King of Britain.

A few weeks later, Arthur and Merlin were out riding when they came to a lake in the middle of which Arthur saw a sight as strange as the stone and anvil in the churchyard. Rising out of the water was an arm clothed in soft white silk holding a sword. Farther off, Arthur saw a boat move across the water with a damsel in it.

Arthur pulls out the magic sword as Sir Ector and Kay look on.

"That is the Lady of the Lake," said Merlin. "Speak well to her and she will give you her sword."

The boat approached the land, and the lady greeted Arthur.

"Damsel," he replied, "what sword is that, that yonder arm holds above the water? I wish it were mine, for at the moment I have none."

"Sir Arthur, King," she answered, "that sword is mine, and if you will give me a gift when I ask, you shall have it."

Arthur replied, "I will give you whatever gift you shall ask for."

"Very well," she said, "get into the boat and row to the sword. Take it with you."

So Arthur and Merlin tied up their horses and rowed across the lake to the mysterious arm. As soon as Arthur grasped the hilt of the sword, the hand let go and the arm sank back into the water. As they rowed back to the shore, the king examined the sword and saw that it was truly magnificent. Its name was carved into the blade—Excalibur. It would be Arthur's sword in many battles to come.

Arthur chose the Lady Guinevere as his wife and queen and received his famous round table as a gift from Guinevere's father. Arthur's knights met at the round table to discuss important affairs.

Of all the Knights of the Round Table, Sir Lancelot was the bravest and strongest. No knight had ever defeated Lancelot in combat. On horse or on foot, he was the champion. He was the king's dear friend. He would help any woman in need, but he had sworn a special, lifelong vow of service to Guinevere.

One night Lancelot was staying in a castle where an elderly couple had given him shelter. After dinner, Lancelot put his armor and sword beside him and soon fell asleep in his upstairs room.

During the night a violent knocking on the gate below woke him. He ran to the window and, by the light of the moon, saw a knight being chased by other knights. Lancelot donned his armor, tied his bedsheet to the window, and slid down. He strode right into the middle of the fighting knights. To his surprise, he noticed the single knight's shield to be that of Sir Kay, the King's steward. Lancelot leaped at the three knights and in seven strokes he beat them all to the ground.

Sir Lancelot.

"Sir knight," they said, "we yield to you as to a champion of unmatched strength."

He answered, "I will not accept your yielding to me. You must yield to this knight or else I will kill you."

"Fair knight, we cannot do that, because we would have beaten that knight if you had not come," the three knights said.

"Well, you can choose whether you will die or live," said Sir Lancelot. "If you yield, it must be to Sir Kay."

So the three yielded to Sir Kay, and Sir Lancelot ordered them to go to the court at Camelot and beg the queen for mercy, saying that Sir Kay sent them there as her prisoners.

Over the years Lancelot sent many a defeated knight to Camelot, commanding each to bow down before Guinevere. Eventually, however, the love between Lancelot and Guinevere helped tear Camelot apart. Lancelot and Arthur, who had once been best friends, fought many battles against one another and the kingdom again descended into turmoil. During one battle, Arthur was mortally wounded.

Although Camelot ended unhappily, people still remember it as a time of peace and nobility, when chivalry shone as brightly as a polished suit of armor and adventure was always waiting around the next turn in the road.

Saint George and the Dragon

Saint George, the patron saint of England, traveled around the world doing chivalrous deeds. Once, in Africa, he spent a night at an old hermit's house.

"Sir knight," said the hermit, "I am sorry that it is your destiny to arrive in our country at a time when we are in great distress. We are cursed with a terrible dragon. Every day we must present this monster with a young girl, whom  the beast devours. If we fail to do this, the dragon blows such a horrible stench from its nostrils that disease sweeps through the land. This dragon has devoured almost all of the young girls in our country, and tomorrow the king's own daughter is to be sacrificed to the monster. Therefore the king has proclaimed that, if any knight is so adventurous as to combat with this dragon and preserve his daughter's life, that man shall have great rewards."

Hearing this, Saint George made a solemn vow that he would either save the king's daughter or lose his life in that honorable enterprise. In the morning he buckled on his armor, mounted his horse, and had the old hermit guide him to the place where the sacrifices were made. As they approached the spot, the knight saw a beautiful damsel, dressed like a bride in pure Arabian silk being led to the sacrifice. He told the princess to return to her father's palace. He would fight the dragon and save her from her cruel fate.

Then the noble knight rode into the valley where the dragon had his lair. When the dragon saw him, it made a hideous roaring noise, loud as thunder. The dragon was fearful to behold. It was fifty feet long with scales of glittering silver. The beast swung its powerful tail and smote the knight so hard that both horse and rider were thrown to the ground. Two of Saint George's ribs were broken in the fall, but the brave knight did not give up. He prayed to God to give him the strength and agility to slay the monster. Then with a bold, courageous heart, he charged the beast and drove his spear into a soft spot under the dragon's wing, where there were no scales. The spear found its way to the dragon's heart, and the dying beast sent forth a gushing stream of purple gore.

When the king heard what the knight had done, he offered him a large reward. But Saint George refused to take the money. He encouraged the king to give the money to the poor. Then he mounted his horse and rode away, in search of further noble adventures.

Robin Hood
(Excerpt from the novel by J. Walker McSpadden)

English legends tell of a great outlaw hero named Robin Hood, who is said to have lived in England in the Middle Ages. Robin Hood lived in Sherwood Forest with his band of merry men, hunting for deer with his bow and arrow, stealing from the rich and giving to the poor, and doing battle with the wicked Sheriff of Nottingham.

One day Robin Hood was walking along a path in Sherwood Forest when he saw a little footbridge that led across a stream. As he drew near the bridge, he saw a tall stranger coming from the other side. Robin quickened his pace, and the stranger did likewise, each thinking to cross first. They met at the middle of the log, and neither would yield an inch.

"Give way, fellow!" roared Robin.

The stranger smiled. He was almost a head taller than Robin. "Nay!" he retorted. "I give way only to a better man than myself."

"Give way, I say," repeated Robin, "or I shall have to show you a better man."

His opponent budged not an inch, but laughed

loudly. "Now," he said good-naturedly, "I'll not move after hearing that speech, even if I might have before. I have sought this better man my whole life long. Therefore show him to me."

"That I will right soon," said Robin. "Stay here while I cut a cudgel like that you have been twiddling in your fingers." So saying, he leapt to his own bank again and cut a stout staff of oak, a good six feet in length. Then back he came boldly, whirling the staff above his head and calling, "Make ready for the tune I am about to play upon your ribs! One! Two!"

"Three!" roared the giant, striking at Robin mightily.

The fight was fast and furious. It was strength pitted against skill. The mighty blows of the stranger went whistling around Robin's ducking head, while his own swift undercuts gave the stranger an attack of indigestion. Yet each stood firmly in his place, not moving backward or forward a foot for a good half hour. The giant's face was getting red, and his breath came snorting forth like a bull's. Robin dodged his blows lightly, then sprang in swiftly and unexpectedly and gave the stranger a wicked blow upon the ribs.

The stranger reeled and nearly fell, but regained his footing.

"By my life, you can hit hard!" he gasped, giving back a blow as he staggered.

That blow was a lucky one. It caught Robin off his guard, striking him on the head and dropping him neatly into the stream.

The cool, rushing current quickly brought him to his senses. But he was still so dazed that he groped blindly for the swaying reeds to pull himself up on the bank. His opponent could not help laughing heartily, but he also thrust down his long staff to Robin, crying, "Lay hold of that!"

Robin took hold and was hauled to dry land like a fish. He lay on the warm bank awhile to regain his senses; then he sat up and rubbed his head.

"By all the saints," said he, "my head hums like a beehive on a summer morning."

Then he picked up his horn, which lay nearby, and blew three shrill notes that echoed among the trees. A moment of silence followed, then the rustling of leaves and crackling of twigs could be heard, and from the glade two dozen yeomen burst, all clad in Lincoln green like Robin.

"Good master," cried the man named Will Stutely, "how is this? There is not a dry thread on you."

"This fellow would not let me pass the footbridge," replied Robin, "and when I tickled him on the ribs, he answered with a pat on my head that sent me into the stream."

"Then shall he taste some of his own porridge," said Will. "Seize him, lads!"

"Nay, let him go free," said Robin. "The fight was a fair one. Are you ready to quit?" he continued, turning to the stranger with a twinkling eye.

"I am content," said the other, "for I like you well and wish to know your name."

"My men, and even the Sheriff of Nottingham, know me as Robin Hood the outlaw."

"Then am I right sorry that I beat you," exclaimed the man, "for I was on my way to join your company. But now that I have used my staff on you I fear you will not have me."

"Nay, never say it," cried Robin. "I am glad you fell in with me, though I did all the falling!"

As the others laughed, the two men clasped hands, and the strong friendship of a lifetime began.

Robinson Crusoe
(Retold from the novel by Daniel Defoe)

The English writer Daniel Defoe wrote Robinson Crusoe (1719) *after hearing the story of a Scottish man who lived alone on a deserted island for almost five years. Defoe began with the factual story, imagined how such a character must have felt, and added elements of danger and adventure to make a fictional story that readers would enjoy.*

I, Robinson Crusoe, was born in the year 1632 in England. As a young lad I took to the sea, against the wishes of my father. In times to come I would often recall his warnings that I would live to regret my decision, for in September of 1659, I was shipwrecked off the coast of South America during a dreadful storm and washed up on the shore of a deserted island, all the rest of the ship's company being drowned, and myself almost dead.

My initial joy at finding myself alive soon gave way to wild despair as I looked about me and realized that I was alone, with no means of sustaining myself. I soon discovered, however, that the bulk of the ship remained intact some distance from shore, and by fashioning a raft from pieces of the wreckage, I was able to carry away some provisions and tools.

Among these were a tin of biscuits, some dried meat, a bit of rum and tobacco, a spyglass, several axes and other implements, and several guns with a quantity of gunpowder and shot that had luckily not been dampened by the sea. With these last I managed to shoot enough birds and wild goats to provide myself with food when my supplies began to give out. And when my clothes fell to pieces, I made myself a short jacket and breeches of goatskin, as well as a cap to protect my head from sun and rain. With my hairy attire, my sunburned skin, and my growing beard, I would have caused fright or else raised a great deal of laughter had any Englishman been there to see me.

Crusoe and his parrot.

I protected myself from wild beasts and any savages who might roam the island by building a small fort. This was of great comfort to me, for I feared being discovered by the fierce cannibals known to inhabit that part of the world.

With continual labor, I was in time able to fashion almost everything needed to make my dwelling comfortable, including a table and shelves for storing my possessions and some clay pots. I managed to trap and tame a she-goat and her kid, and in time I acquired an entire flock. For companionship I had a dog and two cats, the only other survivors of the wreck. To these I added two parrots, which I tamed and taught to speak a few words. With these my subjects about me, I thought myself quite the master of my little kingdom.

One day I discovered corn growing near the entrance to my cave. I carefully watered the plants until they ripened, then I saved all the grain for planting season. After the next harvest, I again saved all for planting, continuing in this manner until I had an ample crop to eat.

I explored the island and found wild grapes in abundance, which I gathered and dried as raisins. I also built a small canoe out of a tree trunk, and this I used to explore the coast.

For fifteen years, I busied myself with caring for my crops and flocks, maintaining my fort, and exploring the island. Then one day as I went to my boat, I was surprised to see the print of a man's naked foot very plain in the sand. Thunderstruck, I looked and listened, but neither saw nor heard anyone; nor were there any other footprints. I fled in terror to my fort, wondering whether I should fear savage cannibals or the devil himself.

For the next few years, I kept fearful watch and made sure my guns were always loaded, but I saw no other signs of a visitor to the island. Then, early one morning in my twenty-third year of residence, I spied a campfire on the shore. I approached cautiously and, peeping from the trees, perceived with horror that some savage cannibals had come to my island, bringing their captured enemies and evidently intending to kill and eat them here on the shore. There were at least twenty of them. As I watched, they dragged two miserable wretches from their boats, one of whom they immediately struck down with a club. Suddenly the other captive broke and ran, heading straight toward me. Two of his enemies pursued him, but he easily outstripped them and, as I saw him approach, it occurred to me that he might become the companion and servant I had long wished for. So I came to the rescue, knocking down one pursuer with the butt of my gun and shooting the other as he raised his bow and arrow to shoot me.

When the savages left, the rescued man threw himself down before me and made gestures of thanks. I named my new companion Friday, for I calculated it was on that day that I rescued him.

Friday was strong and well-formed, handsome of feature, and quick to learn. I soon taught him to assist me in my work and to speak some English. I taught him to say master and let him know that was to be my name. I also taught him to say yes and no, and to know the meaning of them. I likewise taught him to shoot, though not without some difficulties, for he could not at first under-stand how the gun worked and was aston-ished and not a little frightened by the noise it made. His astonishment did not wear off for a long time, and I believe, if I had let him, he would have worshipped me and my gun. For some time he would not touch the weapon, and once I found him speaking softly to it, imploring it not to kill him. With my guidance, however, he soon learned to use it skillfully.

Friday's lessons in shooting proved valu-able, for one day, after we had lived together pleasantly for several years, our island was once again visited by cannibals bringing bound captives upon whom they planned to feast. I saw with horror that one of their prisoners was wearing Euro-pean clothes — perhaps one of my own countrymen. "Friday," I said, "we must re-solve to fight them; can you fight?"

Crusoe and Friday.

Friday said he could fight, but added, in his broken English, "There come many great number."

"No matter for that," I said, "our guns will frighten those we do not kill."

We rushed from the woods and fired upon the cannibals, killing or wounding many of them. The survivors fled to their canoes and paddled away, leaving the European alive. We untied him and gave him food and drink, for which he thanked us in Spanish. Then, hearing a groaning noise, we looked and found an old man who lay bound in the bottom of one of the canoes. When Friday heard him speak and looked in his face, his reaction was wonderful. He kissed the man, hugged him, cried, laughed, jumped about, danced, sang, and then cried again. When at last he came to his senses, he told me that it was his father, who had also been taken by the savages.

The Spaniard and Friday and I began to think about how we might escape, but only a few days later we were surprised by the arrival of an English ship. And so I left the island, the nineteenth of December, as I found by the ship's account, in the year 1686, after I had been upon it twenty-eight years, two months, and nineteen days. I returned with Friday to England to find that the investments I had made many years before had fared well in the hands of honest friends and that I was a prosperous man.

Gulliver's Travels
(Adapted from the novel by Jonathan Swift)

After the appearance of Robinson Crusoe *in 1719, stories about voyages, shipwrecks, and distant islands became popular. Jonathan Swift's* Gulliver's Travels *(1726) benefited from this popularity, but Swift's book was unlike any other travel book ever written. In the book Gulliver describes his fantastic experiences in Lilliput, where the people stand only six inches tall, and in Brobdingnag, where the people are thirty-six feet tall and the cats are as large as oxen. As the excerpt below begins, Gulliver has been shipwrecked and washed up on an unknown shore, where he has taken a nap to recover his strength.*

When I awoke, it was just daylight. I attempted to rise, but was not able to stir for I found my arms and legs were strongly fastened to the ground and my hair tied down in the same manner. I likewise felt several slender cords across my body, from my armpits to my thighs. I could only look upward. The sun began to grow hot, and the light bothered my eyes.

In a little time I felt something moving on my left leg, advancing over my breast, and coming almost to my chin. Bending my eyes downward as much as I could, I perceived it

to be a human creature not six inches high, with a bow and arrow in his hands. In the meantime, I felt at least forty more of the same kind following the first. I was in the utmost astonishment and roared so loudly that they all ran back in fright, but they soon returned, crying out in shrill voices, "Hekinah Degul!"

Struggling to get free, I managed to break the strings and wrench out the pegs that held my left arm to the ground, but the creatures ran off again before I could seize them. I heard one of them cry, "Togol phonac!" and instantly felt a hundred arrows discharged upon my left hand, which pricked me like so many needles. I now thought it prudent to lie still, and when the people observed I was quiet, they discharged no more arrows.

About four yards from me, near my right ear, I heard a knocking noise, like people at work. Turning my head that way, as far as the pegs and strings would permit me, I saw a stage erected about a foot and a half above the ground. It was capable of holding four of the inhabitants, with two or three ladders to mount it. From there, one of them, who seemed to be an important person, made a long speech, of which I understood not one syllable.

Before he began, he cried out, "Langro Dehul san!" Immediately fifty of the inhabitants came and cut the strings that fastened the left side of my head, which gave me the liberty of turning it to the right and seeing the person speaking and his gestures. He made a great speech in which I could observe many gestures of threats and others of promises, pity, and kindness.

I answered in few words, but in the most humble manner. I was almost famished with hunger, having not eaten a morsel for several hours. I put my finger on my mouth several times to show that I wanted food. The important person understood me very well and commanded that several ladders should be placed against my sides, on which more than a hundred of the inhabitants mounted and walked towards my mouth, carrying baskets full of meat. I observed the flesh of several animals, but could not distinguish them by the taste. There were shoulders, legs, and loins shaped like those of mutton, but smaller than the wings of a lark. I ate them two or three at a mouthful and took three loaves of bread at a time, each about the size of a musket ball. They supplied me as fast as they could, showing a thousand marks of wonder and astonishment at my bulk and appetite.

I then made another sign that I wanted drink. They flung up one of their largest barrels, rolled it towards my free hand, and knocked out the lid. I drank it off in a single gulp, which was easy enough, for it hardly held half a pint. They brought me a second barrel, which I drank in the same manner, and made signs for more, but they had no more to give me. When I had performed these wonders, they shouted for joy and danced upon my breast, crying "Hekinah Degul!"

They daubed an ointment upon my hands and face, which, along with a sleeping potion they had placed in my wine, soothed me into a deep slumber. When I awoke, I found myself on a large cart, being carried toward Lilliput, the capital city of my captors, who I later learned were called Lilliputians. Fifteen hundred of their largest horses, each about four and a half inches high, were employed to draw me toward the metropolis. When we arrived, the Emperor of Lilliput and his court rode forth to greet me, and I was taken to an empty temple outside the city where I was to lodge.

The great gate to the temple was about four feet high and almost two feet wide. The Emperor's blacksmith brought ninety chains, like those that hang from a lady's watch in Europe, and almost as large, which were locked to my left leg with thirty-six padlocks. When the workmen found it was impossible for me to break loose, they cut all the strings that bound me and allowed me to stand up.

The noise and astonishment of the people at seeing me stand up are not to be expressed. When I got to my feet, I looked about me, and must confess I never beheld a more entertaining prospect. The country round appeared like a continued garden, and the enclosed fields, which were generally forty feet square, resembled so many beds of flowers. These fields were intermingled with woods, in which the tallest trees appeared to be seven feet

high. I viewed the town on my left hand, which looked like the painted scene of a city in a theater.

That night I got into my house, with some difficulty. At first I slept on the ground. Later the Emperor ordered a bed to be made. Six hundred beds of their ordinary size were brought in and sewn together.

The Emperor held frequent councils to debate what course should be taken with me. They feared my breaking loose or causing a famine due to my huge diet. Some suggested starving me or shooting me with poison arrows, but were unsure how to dispose of me safely once I was dead. When the Emperor saw how gently I treated his people, however, he decided to provide me with sufficient food and to grant me certain liberties, provided I would swear a peace with him and his empire. When I agreed, I was granted my freedom.

Treasure Island

(Retold with excerpts from the novel by Robert Louis Stevenson)

Robert Louis Stevenson published Treasure Island *in 1883, but the story takes place in the 1700s, not long after the events of* Robinson Crusoe *and* Gulliver's Travels. *The story is told by a boy named Jim Hawkins. One day Jim meets an old sea captain who tells him to keep an eye out for a "seafaring man with one leg." After the captain dies suddenly, Jim discovers a treasure map among the dead man's belongings. Jim shares his discovery with three adults — Captain Smollett, Squire Trelawney, and Doctor Livesay. They hire a one-legged ship's cook by the name of Long John Silver and set sail for Treasure Island, with Jim as cabin boy.*

Several weeks later our ship, the *Hispaniola*, was ready. The squire had hired as the ship's cook a one-legged pub owner named Long John Silver, who carried a parrot on his shoulder. From time to time the parrot would call out, "Pieces of eight! Pieces of eight!" Silver explained that he had lost his other leg while serving in the Royal Navy. At first I feared that Long John might be the one-legged sailor of whom the captain had spoken, but I soon changed my mind. Long John seemed to me the best possible ship-mate, for as we walked along the docks together, he explained what the sailors were about, told me stories of ships and seamen, and repeated nautical terms until I had learned them perfectly, telling me I was "smart as paint."

Our captain was Mr. Smollett and at first all went well. Then one night I chanced to overhear Long John whispering with another crew member, telling him that if he would "join up," he could "end the cruise a wealthy man." As I listened, I realized, to my horror, that Silver and several of the other crew members were pirates who had sailed with the old captain who had stayed at our inn. They were planning to mutiny and take the treasure for themselves. After some discussion, the other man agreed to join Silver and the other pirates, saying "there's my hand on it."

Jim tells the Squire, the Doctor, and the Captain of Silver's plot.

"You're a brave lad, and smart as paint," replied Silver. When I heard him address this man in the same words of flattery he had used on me, I wanted to kill him. But I kept hidden and listened as Silver continued: "Just speak soft and keep sober till I give the word. We'll wait, but when the time is right, let 'er rip! I claim Trelawney. I'll wring his neck with these hands!"

I told the squire, the doctor, and the captain what I had heard. They were shocked to learn about Silver, but vowed to be on guard and to strike first.

The next day we reached the island, and I went on shore with some others. I hid among the trees and spied on Silver as he tried to recruit more men for his plot. When one man refused to join him, Silver knocked him down with his crutch and buried his knife up to the hilt in the sailor's back. Afraid he might kill me too, I turned and ran into the forest. I had not gone far when I came upon a sunburned man with long hair, ragged clothing, and a scruffy beard. He ran toward me, calling out in a voice that sounded like a rusty lock. He said his name was Ben Gunn. He had been marooned on the island by some angry shipmates after leading them on an unsuccessful quest for pirates' gold. He was rich, he confided (which made me doubt his sanity), but he had lived off wild goats' flesh and coconuts all this time. I decided to tell him our story, and he promised to help us if we would help him escape the island. He told me where I might find his little homemade boat, hidden in a cove.

Suddenly I heard the sound of cannons and realized that

Silver's pirates attack the stockade.

the fight between my friends and the pirates had already begun. I took leave of Ben Gunn and ran back toward the boat, till I saw the English flag flying above the trees. I ran toward it and found a stockade I had seen marked on the map, which was being stoutly defended by my friends. They had fled there with arms and provisions, and now the pirates were approaching. I scaled the wall to welcoming cries and went to work keeping the guns loaded, while my friends fired continually, killing a number of the rogues who rushed upon the fortress. At last the pirates retreated, leaving many of their own dead, and several of ours.

I told my friends about my meeting with Ben Gunn. The squire, the doctor, and the captain had a conference, after which the doctor took a musket and set off briskly through the trees. I guessed he was going to see Ben Gunn. It was stiflingly hot in the stockade, and blood and dead bodies lay all around. I envied the doctor walking in the cool shadow of the woods with the birds about him, and a mischievous idea entered my head: suppose I went looking for Ben Gunn's boat? But I was only a boy, and I knew they would never let me go alone, so I filled both pockets of my coat with biscuits, grabbed two pistols, and snuck away.

Once I found the little boat, I had another mischievous idea. When night fell, I rowed quietly out to the *Hispaniola*. There were only two pirates on board, and they were engaged in a drunken argument, unaware of me. When the argument ended, one pirate lay dead, and the other, the coxswain Israel Hands, nursed a knife wound in the leg. At this point I made my appearance, waving my pistols and announcing that I was taking command of the ship. Hands seemed to give in, apparently too badly injured to resist. I lowered the hateful Jolly Roger, hurled it overboard, and raised the British flag. Then I did my best to steer the boat to a cove on the other side of the island. Just as we reached the cove, Hands came lurching toward me with a dagger. I drew my pistols and pointed them squarely at him. Hands made as if he would surrender, but then, in an instant, back went his right hand over his shoulder. He hurled a knife, which sang through the air like an arrow, pinning my sleeve to the mast. Without knowing what I was doing, I fired both pistols, and, with a choked cry, the pirate plummeted into the water.

I assumed that my friends still held the stockade, and, as I made my way back in the darkness, there was no way to tell otherwise. But when I entered, I was greeted by Silver's parrot screeching, "Pieces of eight! Pieces of eight!" I was taken prisoner by the pirates, who told me that my friends had abandoned the stockade and the map in exchange for their freedom, and had now retreated to another part of the island. My heart sank when I heard this, and I was not a little astonished, for I could not imagine why my friends would give Silver the map. But I had problems of a more pressing nature, for the buccaneers wanted to kill me on the spot. But Silver cried out "Avast there!" He had decided to keep me alive, just in case he should need a hostage.

The next morning Silver led us off to seek the treasure. He was armed to the teeth, with his parrot perched upon his shoulder gabbling. He tied one end of a line about his waist and the other around mine, and, as he hobbled along, I followed obediently behind him, led like a dancing bear. Even with the map, we had trouble finding the spot. As we approached the tall tree near which it was supposed to lie, we came upon a human skeleton, its bony hand seeming to point the way to the treasure. In another moment we came to the spot. There on the ground was a deep ditch and the remains of a huge chest, split open and emptied of its contents. The treasure had been taken!

The pirates turned upon Silver for leading them on a fool's errand. They drew their pistols, vowing to kill both him and me, but just then shots rang out from the other direction. I turned and saw my friends coming, led by Ben Gunn. Some of the buccaneers fell, and the rest quickly surrendered.

Dr. Livesay and the others led me and the captive pirates to Ben's cave, where the treasure lay safely stowed, as it had been ever since Gunn had found it. They chided me for sneaking away from the stockade but allowed me to rejoin their party. We loaded the treasure aboard the *Hispaniola* and headed for home, leaving all the pirates save Long John Silver to survive as Ben had done, with the help of some arms and provisions. It was our intent to see Silver brought to justice, but one evening when we stopped in a port, he jumped ship with a sack of gold coins and got away. All of us had an ample share of the treasure and used it wisely or foolishly, according to our natures. It is said there is more treasure buried on the island, but nothing would bring me back there again. The worst dreams I ever have are when I hear the surf booming about its coasts or when I start upright in bed, with the voice of Silver's parrot ringing in my ears: "Pieces of eight! Pieces of eight!"

Rip Van Winkle

(Condensed from the story by Washington Irving)

In a village in the Catskill Mountains, there lived a simple, goodnatured fellow by the name of Rip Van Winkle. He was a kind neighbor, and the children would shout with joy whenever he approached. Rip Van Winkle was a lovable soul who was ready to attend to anybody's business but his own. But as to keeping his own farm in order, he found it impossible, and his children were as ragged as if they belonged to nobody.

Rip was one of those happy fools who take the world easy, eat white bread or brown, whichever can be got with least thought or trouble, and would rather starve on a penny than work for a pound. If left to himself, he would have whistled his life away in perfect contentment, but his wife was continually dinning in his ears about his idleness, his carelessness, and the ruin he was bringing on his family. Rip would shrug his shoulders, shake his head, cast up his eyes, but say nothing. This always provoked a fresh volley from his wife, so that he left the house to go outside—the only side that belongs to a henpecked husband.

Rip used to console himself, when driven from home, with the company of a group of sages and fellow idlers who convened on a bench in front of an inn. Sitting beneath a portrait of His Majesty King George the Third (New York in those days was still a province of England), they talked over village gossip and told stories. If by chance an old newspaper should fall into their hands from some passing traveler, they would listen as Van Bummel, the schoolmaster, read them its contents, and it would have been worth any statesman's money to hear the discussions that followed. Nicholas Vedder, a patriarch of the village, made his opinions known by the manner in which he smoked his pipe. Short puffs indicated anger; when he was pleased, he would inhale the smoke slowly and emit it in light and delicate clouds.

One day, seeking to escape the labor of the farm and the clamor of his wife, Rip shouldered his gun and walked high into the Catskills to hunt for squirrels. All day the mountains echoed and re-echoed with the reports of his gun. Finally he threw himself on a green knoll that looked down into a deep glen, wild and lonely. Rip lay musing on the scene as evening gradually advanced, and sighed as he thought of going home.

As he was about to descend, he heard a voice calling, "Rip Van Winkle! Rip Van Winkle!" He perceived a strange figure toiling up the rocks and bending under the weight of something on his back. He was surprised to see any human being in this lonely place, but supposing it to be one of his neighbors in need of assistance, he hastened down to help. The stranger was a short old fellow with a grizzled beard. His dress was of the antique Dutch fashion and he bore a stout keg that Rip supposed was full of liquor. He made signs for Rip to assist him, and together they clambered up a narrow gully. Every now and then long rolling peals like thunder seemed to issue out of a deep ravine. Passing through this ravine, they came to a hollow that looked like a small amphitheater.

In the center was a company of odd-looking persons playing at ninepins. The thunderous noise Rip had heard from afar was the sound of the ball rolling toward the pins. Like Rip's guide, they were dressed in an outlandish fashion, with enormous breeches. What seemed particularly odd to Rip was that these folks maintained the gravest faces, the most mysterious silence, and were, in fact, the most melancholy party he had ever witnessed. They stared at Rip in such a way that his heart turned within him and his knees banged together for fear.

Rip's guide emptied the keg into large flagons. The company quaffed the liquor in profound silence and then returned to their game. As Rip's apprehension subsided, he ventured to taste the beverage. One taste provoked another, and at length his senses were overpowered and he fell into a deep sleep.

Upon waking, he found himself on the green knoll whence he had first seen the old man. It was a bright sunny morning. "Surely," thought Rip, "I have not slept here all night." He recalled the strange men. "Oh! That wicked flagon! What excuse shall I make to Dame Van Winkle?" He looked around for his gun, but found only an old firelock encrusted with rust. Suspecting he had been robbed, he determined to revisit the scene of the previous evening to demand his gun. As he rose to walk, he found himself stiff in the joints. With some difficulty, he found the gully up which he and his companion had ascended, but could find no traces of the ravine that had led to the amphitheater. He shouldered the rusty firelock and with a heart full of trouble turned his steps homeward.

As he approached the village he met a number of people, but none whom he knew, which somewhat surprised him for he had thought himself acquainted with everyone in the country round. Their dress, too, was of a different fashion. They all stared at him with surprise and stroked their chins. When Rip did the same, he found to his astonishment that his beard had grown a foot long! A troop of children ran at his heels, hooting after him and pointing at his gray beard. There were houses in the village that he had never seen before, with unfamiliar names inscribed over the doors. He began to wonder whether both he and the world around him were bewitched.

With some difficulty he found his own house. The roof had fallen in and the door was off its hinges. He entered and called for his wife and children, but all

"My own dog has forgotten me," sighed poor Rip.

was silent. He spotted a dog that looked like his own and called out to him, but the dog snarled and showed his teeth. "My own dog has forgotten me," sighed poor Rip.

He hastened to the village inn. Before it there now hung a flag adorned with stars and stripes. He recognized the face of King George on the sign, but now his red coat was blue, his head wore a cocked hat, and underneath the figure was printed GENERAL WASHINGTON. There was a crowd of people around the door, but none that Rip knew. He inquired, "Where's Nicholas Vedder?"

There was silence, then an old man replied, "Nicholas Vedder! Why he is dead and gone these eighteen years!"

"Where's Van Bummel, the schoolmaster?"

"He went off to wars and is now in Congress."

Rip's heart sank at hearing of these sad changes. He said in despair, "I'm not myself. I was myself last night, but I fell asleep on the mountain, and everything's changed, and I can't tell who I am!"

The bystanders looked at each other in puzzlement. Then a comely woman pressed through the throng. She had a child in her arms, which, frightened by the gray-bearded man's looks, began to cry. "Hush, Rip," cried she, "the old man won't hurt you." The name of the child and the air of the mother awakened a train of recollections in his mind. He caught the mother and child in his arms and said to the woman, "I am your father—young Rip Van Winkle once—old Rip Van Winkle now! Does nobody know poor Rip Van Winkle?"

All stood amazed, until an old woman, peering into his face for a moment, exclaimed, "Sure enough! It is Rip Van Winkle! Welcome home again, old neighbor. Why, where have you been these twenty years?"

Rip's story was soon told, for the whole twenty years had been to him but as one night. Many were skeptical, but an old man who was well-versed in the local traditions corroborated his story in the most satisfactory manner. He assured the company that the Catskill Mountains had always been haunted by strange beings; that the great discoverer Hendrick Hudson kept a vigil there with his crew of the *Half Moon*; that his father had once seen them in their old Dutch clothing playing at ninepins in the hollow of the mountain.

Rip's daughter took him home to live with her, her mother having died some years before after breaking a blood vessel in a fit of passion. Having arrived at that happy age when a man can be idle with impunity, Rip took his place once more on the bench at the inn door and was reverenced as one of the patriarchs of the village. He used to tell his story to every stranger that arrived. Some doubted the truth of it, but the old Dutch villagers almost universally gave Rip full credit. Even to this day, whenever a thunderstorm comes up on a summer afternoon, they say that Hendrik Hudson and his crew are at their game of ninepins; and it is a common wish of all henpecked husbands in the neighborhood, when life hangs heavy on their hands, that they might have a quieting draft out of Rip Van Winkle's flagon.

The Legend of Sleepy Hollow
(Condensed from the story by Washington Irving)

Not far from the eastern shore of the Hudson River is a little valley known as Sleepy Hollow. A drowsy, dreamy atmosphere seems to hang over the land, as if it were under the sway of some witching power. The whole neighborhood abounds with local tales, haunted spots, and twilight superstitions, but the dominant spirit that haunts this region is the apparition of a figure on horseback without a head. It is said to be the ghost of a Hessian trooper, whose head was carried away by a cannonball during the Revolutionary War. The ghost rides forth nightly to the scene of battle in search of his head, and he travels with great speed to get back to the churchyard before daybreak.

In this out-of-the-way place there lived a worthy fellow by the name of Ichabod Crane, who instructed the children of the vicinity. The name Crane was well suited to him. He was tall and exceedingly lank, with narrow shoulders, long arms and legs, and hands that dangled a mile out of his sleeves. He had huge ears, large green eyes, and a long nose. To see him striding along on a windy day, with his clothes fluttering about him, one might have mistaken him for a scarecrow escaped from a cornfield.

From his schoolhouse could usually be heard the voices of his pupils, reciting their lessons, interrupted now and then by the voice of the master or by the sound of his birch switch as he urged some unfortunate along the path of knowledge.

According to custom, Ichabod Crane was boarded and lodged at the houses of the farmers whose children he instructed. With these he lived a week at a time, thus making the rounds of the neighborhood. His appearance at a home was apt to occasion a stir, for the ladies thought his taste and accomplishments vastly superior to those of the rough country farmers. He had read several books quite through and was a perfect master of Cotton Mather's *History of New England Witchcraft*, in which he most firmly believed. It was often his delight, after school was dismissed, to study old Mather's direful tales until dusk. Then, as he wended his way home, every sound of nature fluttered his overexcited imagination: the moan of the whippoorwill, the cry of the tree toad, or the dreary hooting of the screech owl.

He loved to pass long winter evenings with the old Dutch wives as they sat spinning by the fire and listened with interest to their tales of ghosts and goblins—in particular, the legend of the headless horseman. But the pleasure in all this was dearly purchased by the terrors of his subsequent walk homeward. What fearful shapes and shadows beset his path! How often did he dread to look over his shoulder, lest he should behold some uncouth being close behind him!

In addition to his other vocation, Ichabod Crane was the singing master of the neighborhood. Among his musical disciples was Katrina Van Tassel, the only child of a substantial Dutch farmer. She was a blooming lass of eighteen, ripe and rosy-cheeked as one of her father's peaches. She soon found favor in Ichabod's eyes, not merely for her beauty but for her vast inheritance. Old Van Tassel was a thriving, liberal-hearted farmer and a doting father. Every window and crevice of his vast barn was full to bursting with the treasures of the farm. Sleek porkers grunted in their pens and regiments of turkeys went gobbling through the farmyard. The pedagogue's mouth watered as he pictured every pig roasted with an apple in its mouth and every turkey daintily trussed up with a necklace of savory sausages. As he rolled his eyes over the fat meadowlands and the orchards burdened with ruddy fruit, his heart yearned after the damsel who was to inherit them, and he determined to gain her affections.

He was to encounter, however, a host of fearful adversaries: Katrina's numerous rustic admirers.

The most formidable of these was burly Brom Van Brunt, a local hero of some renown. His Herculean frame had earned him the nickname of Brom Bones. Brom Bones was famous for his horsemanship and always ready for either a fight or a frolic, though he had more mischief than ill will in him. With all his roughness, there was a strong dash of good humor at bottom. Whenever a madcap prank occurred in the neighborhood, people whispered that Brom Bones must be at the bottom of it.

When Brom Bones began wooing Katrina, most other suitors gave up the chase, not wanting to cross the lion in his affections. But Ichabod Crane persevered in his quest. He was therefore delighted when, one fine autumn morning, a farmhand came to the school door with an invitation for Ichabod to attend a merrymaking at Van Tassel's. He turned his students loose an hour before the usual time, yelping in joy, brushed his only suit of rusty black, and fussed over his appearance before a broken looking glass. He borrowed a horse so that he could arrive gallantly mounted. The horse was gaunt and swaybacked; his rusty mane and tail were knotted with burrs; one eye had lost its pupil and was glaring and spectral and the other had the gleam of the devil in it. He must have had fire and mettle in his day, for he bore the name of Gunpowder. Ichabod was a suitable figure for such a steed; his elbows stuck out like a grasshopper's, and as he rode the motion of his arms was not unlike the flapping of a pair of wings.

The castle of Van Tassel was thronged with the flowering beauties of the adjacent country. It was not the charms of the buxom lasses that caught our hero's gaze as he entered the parlor, however, but those of a Dutch country table piled high with autumn food. There was the doughty doughnut, the crisp cruller, and a whole family of cakes. And then there were l apple and peach and pumpkin pies, besides ham and smoked beef, dishes of preserved plums, peaches, pears, and quinces; not to mention roasted chickens, and bowls of milk and cream. As Ichabod sampled every dainty, he chuckled to think that he might one day be lord of all this splendor.

Ichabod danced proudly with the lady of his heart, his

Ichabod dances with Katrina, while Brom Bones looks on.

loosely hung frame clattering about the room, while Brom Bones sat brooding by himself in the corner. When the revel began to break up, Ichabod lingered behind to have a little talk with the heiress Katrina, fully convinced that he was now on the high road to success. Something, however, must have gone wrong at the interview, for he soon sallied forth from the mansion with an air quite desolate. He went straight to the stable and with several hearty kicks roused his steed.

It was the witching time of night when Ichabod traveled homeward. All the ghost stories that he had heard over the years now came crowding upon his recollection. The night grew darker; the stars seemed to sink deeper in the sky. He had never felt so lonely. A splash by the side of a bridge caught his ear. In the dark shadow, he beheld something huge, misshapen, black, and towering. The hair rose upon his head. He stammered, "Who are you?" He received no reply. The shadowy object put itself in motion and bounded into the middle of the road. It appeared to be a horseman of large dimensions, mounted on a black horse of powerful frame. Ichabod quickened his steed, in hopes of leaving the mysterious horseman behind. The stranger, however, quickened to an equal pace. The odd silence of Ichabod's companion was soon fearfully accounted for. For upon seeing his fellow traveler in relief against the sky, gigantic in height, and muffled in a cloak, Ichabod was horror struck to perceive that he was headless and that he carried his head before him on his saddle. In desperation Ichabod rained kicks upon Gunpowder. The specter followed close behind. Away they dashed, stones flying.

An opening in the trees now cheered him with the hope that the church bridge was at hand, the place where, legend said, the horseman should stop. Ichabod cast a look behind to see if his pursuer would vanish. Instead, he saw the goblin rising up in his stirrups, in the very act of hurling his head at him. Ichabod tried to dodge the horrible missile, but too late. It encountered his cranium with a tremendous crash. He tumbled into the dust, and Gunpowder and the goblin rider passed by like a whirlwind.

The next morning the old horse was found quietly cropping grass at his master's gate. The students were assembled at the schoolhouse, but no schoolmaster arrived. The tracks of horses' hoofs were traced to the bridge. On the bank was found the hat of the unfortunate Ichabod and close beside it a shattered pumpkin.

There was much gossip and speculation about the disappearance of Ichabod Crane. Some said he had been carried off by the headless horsemen; others reported that he had simply left town in humiliation at having been dismissed by Katrina. Shortly after his rival's disappearance, Brom Bones conducted Katrina in triumph to the altar. Whenever the story of Ichabod was related, Bones looked exceedingly knowing and always burst into hearty laughter at the mention of the pumpkin. The old country wives, however, maintain to this day that Ichabod was spirited away, and it is said that one may still hear his voice, chanting a melancholy psalm tune among the solitudes of Sleepy Hollow.

Learning about Language

Parts of Speech

In English, there are eight parts of speech, which means there are eight possible jobs a word can have in a sentence. Here are seven of these parts of speech and examples of how each one can be used in sentences:

Parts of Speech	Examples of Use
Noun: a word that names a person, place, animal, thing, or idea	I love **pizza** and **lemonade**. **Measles** is a terrible **disease**.
Adjective: a word that modifies, intensifies, or tells about a noun	It was a **dark** and **stormy** night. She is one **smart** girl.
Pronoun: a word that takes the place of a noun	**She** loved to play hide and seek, but **they** did not.
Verb: a word that describes an action or a state of being	We **caught** and **released** 17 fish. I **am** an insomniac.
Adverb: a word that adds to the meaning of a verb by telling how, or in what manner, the action occurred	She reads **well**. We ran **quickly** and **joyfully** to the porch.
Conjunction: a word that joins words, ideas, or phrases in a sentence	I bought bread **and** olives. Since they pulled my teeth, I can **neither** eat **nor** sleep.
Interjection: a word thrown into a sentence for emphasis	I like it, but, **good grief**, it sure is expensive! **Wow**! Your hair is green.

Words have jobs, just like people. And, they can change jobs just as we do. For example, you might think that the word **run** is always a verb because it describes an action. But look at the way it is used in each of the following sentences.

I **run** two miles a day.

Here, **run** is a **verb**; it describes an action.

My **run** lasts about 20 minutes.

Here, **run** is a **noun**; it names a thing.

In order to really understand a sentence you have to recognize the words and also understand what job each word is doing in the sentence.

Complete Sentences

A complete sentence includes a subject and a predicate. The subject tells what or whom the sentence is about. The predicate tells what the subject is or does. In the sentences below the subjects are in bold and the predicates are underlined.

I like soccer.
Robert Louis Stevenson wrote a famous book.
Pollyanna was a girl who always looked on the bright side of life.

The subject is usually a noun or a pronoun, and it usually comes at the beginning of the sentence.

The predicate must always include a verb, and may also include adverbs and other parts of speech. It usually comes after the subject, as it does in both of the sentences printed above.

If you leave out either the subject or the predicate, you won't have a complete sentence. You'll have a fragment. Here are two fragments:

Visited the land of Lilliput.

Robinson Crusoe.

To fix the first fragment, you need to add a subject. Ask yourself who visited the land of Lilliput, then complete the sentence:

Gulliver <u>visited the land of Lilliput</u>.

To fix the second fragment, you need to add a verb, so your sentence will have a predicate. Ask yourself what Robinson Crusoe did, then rewrite:

Robinson Crusoe <u>survived on a deserted island</u>.

Subject-Verb Agreement

Whenever you write sentences, make sure that your subject and your verb agree. We don't say "he run" or "they runs." We say "he runs" and "they run." A singular subject takes a singular verb, and a plural subject takes a plural verb. See if you can pick the right verb form for each of the following sentences:

Pizzas **is/are** delicious.
My friends **live/lives** down the street.
A flock of seagulls **was flying/were flying** overhead.

The last sentence is a little tricky. It might seem like there are many seagulls, so the subject must be plural. But really the subject of the sentence is "flock," and there's only one flock. That's why we say "A flock of seagulls was flying overhead."

Run-on Sentences

Another problem you can run into in writing is when you try to put too much in one sentence, like this:

We read *Treasure Island* it is an exciting story.

This is called a run-on sentence. One way to fix a run-on sentence is by dividing it into two separate sentences:

We read *Treasure Island*. It is an exciting story.

Kinds of Sentences

There are different kinds of sentences. A declarative sentence makes a statement and usually ends with a period.

It's hot today.

The man began to sweat in the bright sunlight.

An interrogative sentence asks a question and ends with a question mark.

Did you ask Mom?

An imperative sentence is an order or a command. Imperative sentences are sometimes written with a period and sometimes, when they are said with great emotion, with an exclamation point.

Read chapter two.

Go to your room!

Exclamatory sentences are sentences that are exclaimed, or shouted out, like "Go to your room!" or "That's gross!" Both of these are complete sentences, but sometimes when we are very excited, we don't speak in complete sentences. Then we might make exclamatory *statements* like these:

Gross!

Yippee! The big jackpot!

Commas

Commas tell readers when to pause within a sentence and which groups of words to read together. Here are some situations in which we use commas:

between the day and the year in dates	October 18, 2000
between the city and the state in an address	Charlottesville, VA
between items in a series	That man is mad, bad, and dangerous to know.
after the words *yes* and *no*	No, you may not stay up all night.
before conjunctions that combine parts of sentences	Sticks and stones may break my bones, but names can never harm me.
inside quotation marks, when writing dialogue	"I'm so glad to see you," said Pollyanna.

Apostrophes

Apostrophes are used to show possession. Singular nouns with a few exceptions show possession by adding 's.

My **uncle's** putt stopped just short of the hole.

Many plural nouns already have an "s" at the end; these words show possession by just adding an apostrophe.

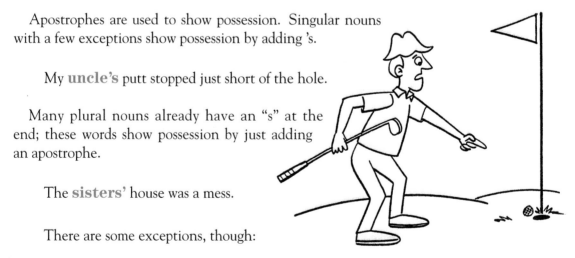

The **sisters'** house was a mess.

There are some exceptions, though:

The **men's** room is bigger than the **women's** room.

Apostrophes are also used in contractions to show that some letters have been omitted. The contraction *that's* is short for "that is." The apostrophe tells you the letter "i" has been left out. Similarly, the contraction *we're* is short for "we are."

Quotation Marks

Use quotation marks when you want to distinguish somebody else's words from your own words. For instance, if you were writing a story about a fortune-teller, you might use quotation marks like this.

"I see good things in your future," said the mysterious woman, staring into her crystal ball.

Quotation marks are also used for titles of poems, songs, short stories, and magazine articles.

We read "Dreams," a poem by Langston Hughes.

Synonyms and Antonyms

A synonym is a word that means the same thing, or almost the same thing, as another word. Quick and fast are synonyms, and so are costly and expensive. See if you can match the italicized words on the left with the synonyms on the right.

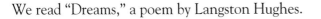

bad	buccaneer
friend	evil
pirate	buddy
try	spotless
clean	attempt

Antonyms are words that are opposites. Soft and hard are antonyms. So are good and evil. See if you can match the italicized words on the left with their antonyms on the right.

advance	expensive
true	fail
succeed	shy
cheap	retreat
bold	false

Homophones

Homophones are words that sound the same but have different meanings. It's important to choose the right word when you're writing.

There are twenty rocks in my collection.
The fans cheered for **their** team.
They're from Florida.

I've got **your** book.
You're my best friend.

It's cold!
The bird built **its** nest in our yard.

Did you **hear** that?
Come over **here**.

Let's go **to** the mall.
I have **two** pairs of shoes.
You come, **too**.

Prefixes

Prefixes are groups of letters that are added to the front of words to make new words, with different meanings.

im- and *in-* mean not. So something that's impossible is not possible, and someone who's inconsistent is not consistent.

non- also means not. A nonfiction book is not fictional—that is, it's a true story. A nonviolent protest is not violent.

mis- means wrong, wrongly, bad, or badly. If you misspell a word, you spell it wrong. And if you misbehave, you behave badly.

en- means in or into. To endanger someone is to put that person in danger. And to entrap someone is to draw the person into a trap.

pre- means before, or earlier. A pregame show takes place before the game, and a prehistoric event took place long ago, before people began recording history.

Suffixes

Suffixes are a lot like prefixes, but they are added to the *end* of a word.

-y is a suffix that can be used to make adjectives. Does anyone you know display greed? Then that person is greedy. Are you ready to go to sleep? Then you must be sleepy.

-ly and *-ily* are suffixes that are often used to make adverbs. Take the adjective quick, add *-ly*, and you get the adverb quickly. In the same way, easy becomes easily.

-ful is a suffix meaning full of. A thoughtful person is full of thoughts, and a playful baby is full of play.

-able or *-ible* is a suffix that means capable of or worthy of a specific action. If a shirt is capable of being washed, we say it is washable. If you can bend and flex your arms and legs well, we say you are flexible.

-ment is a suffix used to make verbs into nouns. If everybody in the room agrees (verb), you have achieved agreement (noun). If you are amazed (verb), you are in a state of amazement (noun).

It's useful to know commonly used prefixes and suffixes because sometimes you can figure out what a difficult word means by breaking it down into prefixes, roots, and suffixes. For example, you may never have read or heard the word misrule. But if you break it into two parts—mis-rule—you can guess that it means to rule badly.

Writing and Research

Once you've learned how to write sentences, you can practice putting sentences together into paragraphs and longer works. Here are some things you might try writing:

1. A letter to a friend or family member
2. A short story
3. A summary of what you did today
4. A description of an object or of a person
5. A poem
6. A report

To write a report, first choose a topic you'd like to learn more about. Then go to your school library or public library and ask the librarian to help you find information on your topic. (You can also find information by searching the Internet.) As you learn interesting facts or read quotations that you think you might want to use in your report, write down what you found and also where you found these things. Whenever you find something in a book, write down the title of the book, the author, where the book was published, by whom, and when. Most of this information can be found in the first few pages of a book.

When you write your report, think of it as a set of paragraphs, each of which should have its own purpose. Before you start writing, you should have a good idea what each paragraph in your essay is intended to accomplish. For instance, if you were writing a report on Babe Ruth, you might have a paragraph telling when Ruth lived and who he played for, another on his achievements as a hitter, and a third on his record as a pitcher. Your last paragraph should be your conclusion, in which you restate your point and finish up your report.

At the end of your report, you'll want to include a bibliography. A bibliography is a list of books and articles you used to write your report. Here's what some entries from a bibliography on Babe Ruth might look like:

Creamer, Robert. *The Babe Comes to Life.* New York: Fireside, 1992.

Smelser, Marshall. *The House That Ruth Built: A Biography.* Lincoln, Nebraska: University of Nebraska Press, 1993.

Thomson, Charles. "Why the Babe Was the Greatest." *Sports Illustrated*, January 17, 1976, pages 23–32.

Notice that the entries in a bibliography are listed alphabetically, by the author's last name.

Writing a report isn't easy, but, like other things in life, you can get good at it by practicing.

Sayings and Phrases

Every culture has some sayings and phrases that can be difficult for outsiders to understand. In this section we introduce a handful of common English sayings and phrases and give examples of how they are used.

As the crow flies

When a bird flies from place to place, it flies through the air and takes the most direct route. But when people drive, they have to follow roads and often have to go farther. When people give a distance "as the crow flies," they mean the shortest distance between the two points, not the distance you would have to travel if you followed roads.

As Dan and his mom drove along the river, they could see the beach on the opposite side. Dan asked, "How far is it to the beach?"

"It's only about a quarter of a mile as the crow flies," his mother said. "But we have to drive three miles north to the bridge and then three miles south once we cross the bridge."

Beauty is only skin deep.

People use this saying to mean that you can't judge a person's character by how good he or she looks.

"That new girl sure is pretty," Kim said.

"Yeah, but I wonder if she's nice, too," Carol said. "After all, beauty is only skin deep."

The bigger they are, the harder they fall.

When a huge oak falls in the forest, it makes a tremendous crash. When a small sapling falls, you can barely hear it. When people use this saying, they mean that the larger or more powerful something is (it could be a person, a team, a country, or something else), the bigger the shock will be when a setback occurs.

"But, Coach," Sam said, "we'll never be able to beat Central. They're the defending state champions and haven't lost a game yet this season!"

"Never mind that," said the coach. "If we play our best game, we can beat them—and the bigger they are, the harder they fall!"

Birds of a feather flock together.

We use this saying to mean that similar people, or people who have similar interests, like to be with each other.

"Those guys always eat lunch together," Jenny said, nodding toward a group of boys in the cafeteria.

"Yeah," said June. "They're on the same baseball team and they love to talk about mitts and bats and home runs."

Jenny nodded. "Birds of a feather flock together!"

Blow hot and cold

This phrase comes from one of Aesop's Fables, in which a man blows on his fingers to warm them up and then blows on his soup to cool it down. In both cases, the man is opening his mouth, but what comes out is very different. If a person says one thing and later says the opposite, we say that the person is blowing hot and cold.

"Is Felicia going to try out for the soccer team this year?" Stacy asked.

"I don't know," Tricia replied. "Last week she was saying yes, but this week she's saying no. She's really blowing hot and cold."

Break the ice

Before ice-breaking ships were invented, sailors who wanted to sail during the winter had to walk out onto frozen water and break up the ice before the boat could move forward. Nowadays people use the saying break the ice to refer to ending an awkward silence by beginning a conversation.

It was the first day of summer camp. The four girls began to unpack their clothes and make their beds in silence. None of the girls knew each other, and no one knew what to say. Finally, one of them broke the ice by saying, "Hey, where's everybody from?"

Bull in a china shop

If a person is clumsy in a place where things can be upset or broken, or handles a delicate situation badly, we say the person is acting like a bull in a china shop.

Leroy slammed the door behind him. A painting fell off the wall and his mother's crystal vase wobbled on the dining room table. "I'm home!" he yelled, then tripped on the doormat and fell onto the floor.

"Honestly, Leroy," his mother said as she helped him up, "sometimes you're just like a bull in a china shop!"

Bury the hatchet

This phrase comes from Native American culture. When two nations declared war on each other, they were said to take up the hatchet. When they agreed to end their war, they were said to bury the hatchet. To bury the hatchet is to stop holding a grudge and make peace with someone else, to let bygones be bygones and forgive and forget.

Colin could not forgive his sister for breaking his tennis racquet. He kept up a sulky silence when he was around her. Finally, his sister said, "Oh, Colin, can't we bury the hatchet? I hate it when you are mad at me!"

Can't hold a candle to

Before electricity, servants had to hold candles for their masters so the masters could see. When we say one person or thing can't hold a candle to another person or thing, we mean that the first is not nearly as good as the second.

"How's the frozen pizza?" the girls' mother asked.
"It's okay," said Isabel. "But it can't hold a candle to your homemade pizza!"

Don't count your chickens before they hatch.

Because not every egg in a nest hatches into a baby chicken, people use this saying to mean that you may be disappointed if you count on having something before it is really yours.

"I can't wait to listen to these CDs I just bought on the boom box I'm getting for my birthday!" Nathan said.
"But how do you know you're going to get a boom box for your birthday?" Annie asked. "Don't count your chickens before they hatch!"

Don't put all your eggs in one basket.

Once upon a time a girl went to her family's henhouse to gather eggs for breakfast. Instead of taking only a few eggs, she packed all the eggs into her basket. On the way back to the house, she tripped and broke the eggs so there was nothing left for her family to eat. She then wished she had not put all her eggs in one basket. If someone tells you not to put all your eggs in one basket, the person is reminding you what can happen when you rely too heavily on one plan and don't think about what could go wrong.

"Dan's older brother wants to go to Harvard. He says he won't even apply to any other colleges."

"But what will he do if he doesn't get into Harvard? Maybe he shouldn't put all his eggs in one basket."

Etc.

Etc. is an abbreviation of et cetera [et SET-er-uh], a Latin phrase meaning and the rest. It can also mean and so forth, and so on, or "and other things like the ones I've just mentioned."

I like large dogs: St. Bernards, Irish Wolfhounds, Great Danes, etc.

Go to pot

This phrase was originally used in the kitchen. All of the leftover scraps that weren't good for anything else went to pot. That is, they were thrown into a big pot to make a stew. Eventually, the meaning changed. Now when we say something has gone to pot, we mean it has not been taken care of and has gone bad or been ruined.

"Have you checked the garden recently?" Dan asked.

"No," Pete replied, "not for a week or so."

"You'd better get out there, or the weeds will take over and the whole thing will go to pot."

Half a loaf is better than none.

This means that having something is better than having nothing, even if it's not exactly what you want.

When Theo's father gave him five dollars, he complained that he wasn't given ten. "Theo," his mother said, "there are many people who don't have a penny. You need to learn that half a loaf is better than none."

Haste makes waste.

This saying means that when you rush you don't do as good a job as when you are careful and take your time.

It was Sammy's night to do the dishes. He quickly rinsed all of the dinner plates, then ran the silverware under the faucet.

"What's your hurry?" his father asked.

"I told Karl I'd meet him at the park!"

"If you aren't more careful cleaning these dishes," his father said, picking up a plate with a spot of spaghetti sauce on the rim, "you'll have to do them over again. Then you'll really be late. Haste makes waste!"

Laugh, and the world laughs with you; weep, and you weep alone.

This saying means that when you are happy, people want to share your happiness, but when you are sad, people don't want to be with you.

"Come on, Tom, cheer up!" Kimiko shook Tom's shoulder. "Why are you in such a bad mood?"

"Oh, I don't know," Tom said. "Nobody likes me."

"Well, what do you expect, with that big frown across your face." Kimiko smiled. "Laugh, and the world laughs with you; weep, and you weep alone!"

Lightning never strikes twice in the same place.

We use this expression to mean that if something unfortunate has happened, the chances are that it probably won't happen again in exactly the same way.

"Hey, Kareem, don't stand there! Remember last month when a lightbulb fell and hit Mr. Vasquez right on the head?"

"Yeah, I remember. But what are the chances of that happening again? Lightning never strikes twice in the same place."

Live and let live.

This saying means mind your own business and let other people live as they wish to live.

"You need a haircut, Daryl." Kenya put her hands on her hips. "And look at those ugly shoes! You need to buy some new ones."

"Listen, Kenya. I like the way my hair looks, and I think these are cool shoes," Daryl said. "I'm going to keep dressing the way I want to dress. As for you, you'd better learn to live and let live."

Make ends meet

When someone is having trouble making enough money to pay the bills, we say the person is struggling to make ends meet.

"Where's your dad?" Sarah asked.

Elizabeth explained, "He's at work. He has to work overtime every night to pay the bills, and on weekends, too. He says it's what he has to do to make ends meet."

Make hay while the sun shines.

Farmers need dry weather to make hay, so they take advantage of sunny weather when it comes. This saying means that you should take advantage of good times when you have them, because they may not last forever.

Jason and Frank were watching TV. They watched a commercial in which a famous player flew through the air and made an amazing dunk.

"Why does he even bother making commercials?" asked Jason. "He makes millions just playing basketball."

"Go easy on the man," said Frank. "He's just trying to make hay while the sun shines. You think he'll be able to dunk like that in ten years?"

Money burning a hole in your pocket

Sometimes money gets spent so quickly that it almost seems like it's burning a hole in your pocket.

"A lot of people on my paper route gave me tips for Christmas," Luke said. "I'm rich!"

"So why don't you open a savings account and start putting your money in the bank?" Luke's big sister asked. "Otherwise, that money's just going to burn a hole in your pocket!"

On the warpath

When a group of Native Americans declared war, they were said to be on the warpath. Nowadays we use the phrase to describe anyone who is angry, in a bad mood, or eager to get into a fight.

"Just because Paul lost his camera doesn't mean he can go around yelling at everybody," Roger said.

"I know," Celia replied, "but he thinks someone stole it, and he's going to be on the warpath until that camera shows up!"

Once in a blue moon

A blue moon is the second full moon in a calendar month. Blue moons are rare. So something that happens only once in a blue moon, happens very rarely.

"Sarah," Rebecca said excitedly, "remember that skirt I liked? I just found it at the mall. It was on sale for 75 percent off!"

"Wow! How often does that happen?" Sarah replied.

"Once in a blue moon!" cried Rebecca.

One picture is worth a thousand words.

Often a picture can explain something better than words.

"Here's a picture of Rick after he won his diving medal." Sonia showed Mrs. Smith the photograph.

"Goodness!" Mrs. Smith said. "Doesn't he look proud!"

"Yes, he does," Sonia said. "Just look at his face. A picture is worth a thousand words!"

An ounce of prevention is worth a pound of cure.

People use this saying to mean that it's better to anticipate a problem and try to prevent it than to wait until it gets really bad later on.

"If you don't brush your teeth more often, you'll get cavities," Al's sister said, "and then you'll have to get fillings when you go to the dentist."

"Yikes, I don't want that to happen!" Al said. "I suppose you're right: an ounce of prevention is worth a pound of cure."

RSVP

When RSVP is written on an invitation, it means that the people who are inviting you would like you to tell them whether or not you will be able to come. RSVP is an abbreviation of the French phrase **R**épondez **S**'il **V**ous **P**lait, *which means Please Reply.*

Helen was excited about receiving an invitation to Laura's birthday party. When she saw RSVP written on the invitation, she rushed to the phone. "Hello, Laura? It's Helen. I just called to RSVP. I would never miss your birthday party!"

Run-of-the-mill

We use this saying to describe anything that is very ordinary.

"How was your day, Carmen?" Mrs. Morello asked.

"It was pretty run-of-the-mill," Carmen replied. "But I'm really looking forward to our field trip to the museum tomorrow."

Seeing is believing.

This saying means that you can't necessarily believe that something exists or is true unless you see the evidence for yourself.

"You should have seen the fish I caught," Eddie said. "It was this big!" He spread his arms as wide apart as he could.

"Yeah, right," said Daniel, shaking his head. He knew Eddie liked to exaggerate.

"I'm not kidding!" exclaimed Eddie. He ran into the house, then staggered out holding a gigantic fish.

"Wow!" said Daniel. "Seeing is believing."

Shipshape

When a ship is ready to sail, with all its decks cleaned and equipment in good order, it is shipshape. We use this saying to describe anything that is in perfect order.

Mrs. Walters waved her hand around the messy classroom. The desks were littered with sheets of colored paper, pots of paint, pans of water, and paintbrushes. "Listen up!" she called out. "Nobody goes to lunch until this room is shipshape."

Through thick and thin

If you're riding a horse in the forest, it's harder to ride through thick woods than it is to ride through thin woods. But a determined rider will ride through thick and thin to get to his destination. We use this expression to describe someone who persists through good times and bad.

"Maleek and I are best friends," Dwayne explained. "He's stuck with me through thick and thin."

Timbuktu

Timbuktu is a famous town in Africa. When people use this term, however, they usually mean a place that seems exotic or very far away.

When the factory closed, Susan asked her mother, "Does this mean that Dad is going to be transferred to a new location?"

Susan's mother replied, "It looks that way. Let's just hope they don't send him to Timbuktu."

Two wrongs don't make a right.

We use this saying to remind each other that you can't correct a wrong action by doing something else that's wrong.

"Carl hit me, so I hit him back!" Bill said.

"What's the point of that?" Bill's big brother asked. "It didn't make anything better, did it? Two wrongs don't make a right, you know."

When it rains it pours.

When people say this they mean that something that starts out bad can turn into a disaster.

Keith limped into the kitchen and collapsed on a chair.

"What happened to you?" his brother asked.

Keith grimaced. "What a rotten day! First I missed the bus and had to walk to school. When I got there, I got in trouble for being late. Then I messed up on my math test, left my lunch at home this morning, turned my ankle in gym class, and now I think I'm getting a cold. I'll tell you, when it rains, it pours!"

You can lead a horse to water, but you can't make it drink.

This saying means that you can show people what you want them to do, but you cannot force them to do it.

Vera disliked bowling. All of her friends insisted that she come with them to the bowling alley, though, because they needed an extra person on their team.

"Who cares whether or not you hit a bunch of pins with a stupid ball," Vera thought to herself. When it was her turn to play, she crossed her arms over her chest and refused. She explained, "Just because you got me to come with you doesn't mean I'm going to play. You can lead a horse to water, but you can't make it drink!"

II.

History and Geography

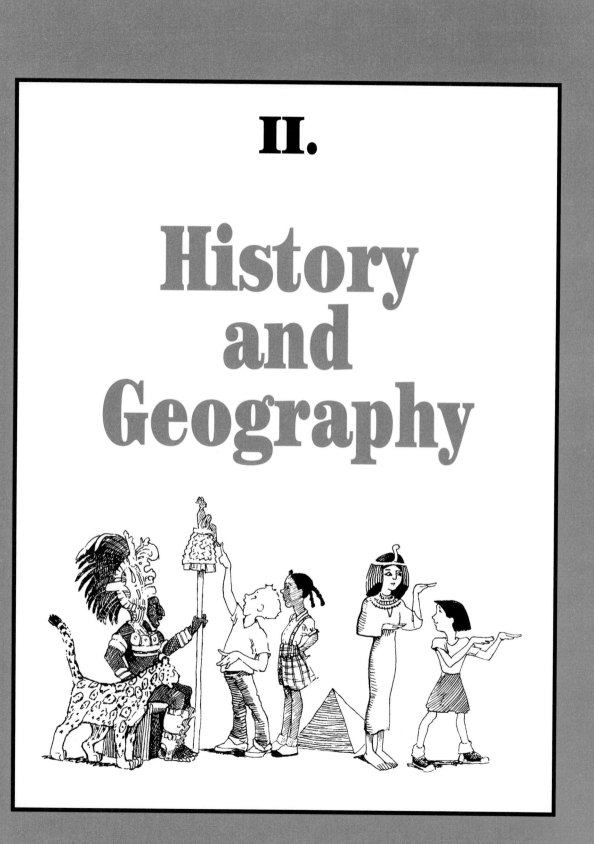

Introduction

This chapter treats geography, world history, and American history. Geography has been described as the study of what's where, why it's there, and why we should care. It looks at how humans are challenged by, adapt to, utilize, and change the natural environments in which they live. By fourth grade, students should know the rudiments of world and American geography. They should be able to read and color maps—and make simple maps of their own. They can be shown maps of their own town and state, invited to study maps during field trips and family vacations, and, as their skills develop, allowed to navigate. Children can learn more about geography from atlases, books on foreign lands, subscriptions to geography magazines like *National Geographic for Kids*, and by collecting stamps.

In both world and American history we have tried to emphasize the *story* in history, without an undue emphasis on dates. Some crucial dates—like 1066, 1492, and 1776—should be memorized. Most others serve a useful purpose without being committed to memory, for they help to reinforce the child's sense of chronology and establish a foundation for more sophisticated historical understanding in years to come.

The world history topics for fourth grade build on the topics introduced in third grade. In third grade students studied ancient Rome. In fourth grade they learn about the culture that developed in Europe when the western Roman Empire collapsed. They also learn about other civilizations that flourished in this era, including China, several African kingdoms, and an Islamic civilization.

In American history children build on their knowledge of the colonial period from third grade as they learn about the Revolutionary War, the Constitution, the first presidents, and some early American reformers. The ideas and events discussed are central to our national identity and to our understanding of what it means to be a citizen of the United States.

Several of the readings in the Language and Literature section can be connected with topics in this chapter: Robin Hood and King Arthur with the Middle Ages, and the poems by Longfellow, Emerson, and the Benéts with the American Revolution.

Parents and teachers are encouraged to build on the foundation provided here by discussing history with children and seeking out additional books on topics of interest. We especially recommend the Pearson Learning/Core Knowledge history series, described on our Web site.

World Geography

Maps

If you read *Treasure Island* earlier in this book, you already know how useful maps can be. In the story, the map tells Jim Hawkins and his friends where Treasure Island is and also

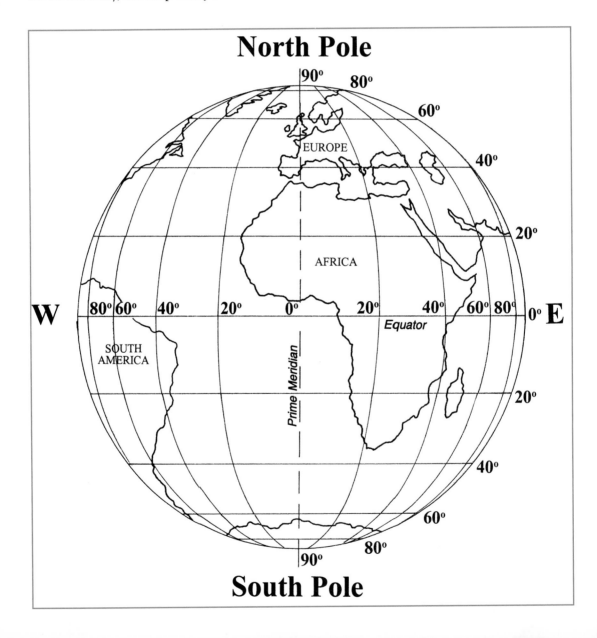

where the treasure is buried. Maps can be useful in real life, too. But you have to know how to use them.

Look at the map on page 70. This map shows half the earth, as it might look from a spaceship in orbit. You may already know that the imaginary line that divides the globe around the middle is called the equator. But what about all those other lines parallel to the equator? And what about the lines that run north and south on the map? What are they for?

Mapmakers draw imaginary lines and divide the world into sections in order to locate places accurately. The lines running parallel to the equator are called parallels; they measure degrees of latitude north and south of the equator. The lines that run from pole to pole are called meridians; they measure degrees of longitude east and west of the prime meridian. You can remember the difference between meridians and parallels by remembering that parallels are *parallel* and **m**eridians **m**eet at the poles.

Can you see how the parallels and meridians intersect? Each point of intersection is a coordinate. Looking at the map, you can also see that each parallel and each meridian has its own number. We'll learn more about these numbers, and about coordinates, in a minute.

How does the map below differ from the first map you looked at? The first map looks almost like a picture of a globe. But this one looks more like a globe cut open along a north-to-south seam through the Pacific Ocean and stretched flat. Mapmakers do this to show the whole world on one map.

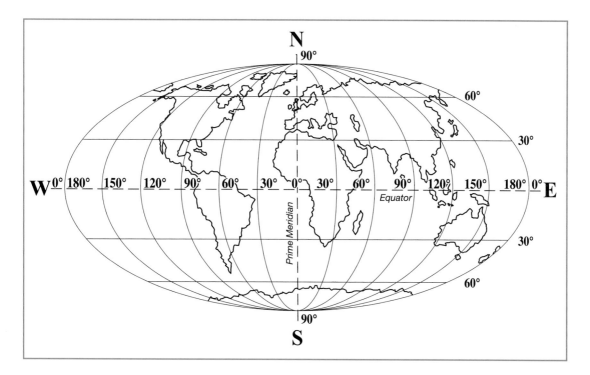

Hemispheres

Mapmakers and people who use maps sometimes divide our earth into large sections shaped like half a grapefruit. These sections are called hemispheres. *Hemisphere* is a Greek word meaning half a sphere. On the stretched-out map on page 71, you can see that the equator divides the globe into two hemispheres. Everything north of the equator is in the Northern Hemisphere; everything south of the equator is in the Southern Hemisphere.

The earth can also be divided into Eastern and Western Hemispheres. The meridian that divides these two hemispheres runs through Greenwich [GREN-itch], England. Many years ago, when the system of longitude and latitude we use today was set up, Greenwich was the home of a famous observatory, where astronomers gazed at the stars. Mapmakers agreed to use this location for an imaginary line just as important as the equator, but running from the North Pole to the South Pole. It is called the prime meridian.

Can you find the prime meridian on the map? Look for the meridian that runs north and south through England and is marked 0° . The small, raised circle after the zero is a symbol that stands for degree. Degrees are the units we use to measure longitude and latitude. Everything to the west of the prime meridian on the stretched-out map is in the Western Hemisphere, and everything to the east is in the Eastern Hemisphere. Find the Eastern and Western Hemispheres on the map on p. 71 and then, if possible, on a globe.

Coordinates

Now that you know about the prime meridian and the equator, you can find the coordinates for any place in the world. Let's find the coordinates for Greece to see how it is done.

Follow Your Finger

To look at the hemispheres in more detail you'll need a globe. First find the prime meridian. With your finger trace this line to the equator. Do you see that the prime meridian is marked 0°?

Next trace your finger along the equator moving west from the prime meridian. See how the degree numbers on the meridians go up as you go west? When you reach the 180th meridian (180°), you've gone exactly halfway around the world. The 180th meridian (also called the international date line) is the continuation of the prime meridian on the other side of the globe. The 180° line and the prime meridian (0°) divide the globe into the Eastern and Western hemispheres.

Continue tracing your finger along the equator to the west. What hemisphere are you crossing now? What happens to the longitude degree marks as you move back toward the prime meridian? Do the numbers keep getting larger or do they get smaller?

To begin with, you'll need to find Greece on the map on page 70 by looking for the Mediterranean Sea. Can you find Italy's boot? Greece is the peninsula sticking into the Mediterranean just east of Italy. You can see that a parallel and a meridian intersect over Greece. The parallel is marked 40° and the meridian is marked 20°.

So the coordinates of Greece are 40° and 20°. But when we write these coordinates we write 40°N, 20°E because Greece is 40° north of the equator and 20° east of the prime meridian. 40°N tells you the latitude of Greece, and 20°E tells you its longitude. Put the two together, and you've got a location.

Can you find 20°S, 20°E on the same map? What continent is this spot in? How about 20°S, 40°W?

Map Scale

Take a look at the three maps that follow. Notice how each map focuses on a smaller area and shows more detail. The map of the United States shows forty-eight states, while the state map shows just one state, and the city map shows only one city within that state. The map of the United States shows much more of the earth's surface than the state map, and the state map shows much more than the town map.

Each of these three maps is drawn to a different scale. Scale is the proportion between the distance on the map and the actual distance on the earth's surface. For instance, on

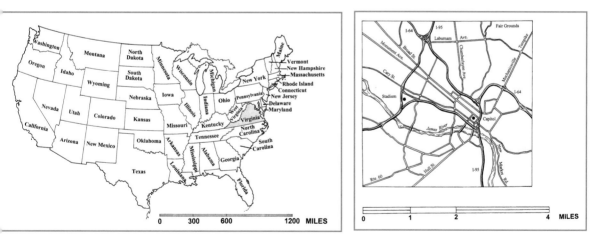

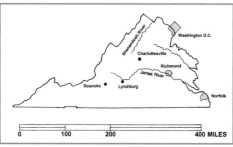

one map a distance of one inch might represent one real mile; on another an inch might represent one hundred miles.

To figure out how much real distance is represented on a map, you'll need to find the map scale. The map scale looks like a ruler and is often located at the bottom of the map or in a corner. On the national map, the scale is in the lower right corner. It tells you that the distance to the first mark represents three hundred miles in real life. On the state map the same distance represents one hundred miles, but on the city map it represents only one mile.

You can use the scale to measure distances from place to place. Get a ruler or a piece of string and use it to measure the distance from the stadium to the capitol on the city map. It should be about one inch. Then place your ruler or string next to the scale for the city map to find out how much real distance one inch represents: a little more than a mile and a half. So the distance between the stadium and the capitol—as the crow flies—is about a mile and half. You could probably walk between the two places if you wanted to.

Now look back at the state map and measure the distance from Lynchburg to Norfolk. You should find that this is also about one inch. Does that mean it would be as easy to walk from Lynchburg to Norfolk as it was to walk from the stadium to the capitol? Not so fast! You need to figure out what that one inch stands for on *this* map. If you place your inch next to the scale, you'll see that one inch on this map represents more than one hundred miles, but less than 200—perhaps about 175 miles. If you tried to walk that far, you'd have very tired feet!

What a Relief!

The map of the United States on p. 73. is a political map. It shows political boundaries, like the boundaries between the states. But it does not tell you what the land itself looks like. You can't tell from this map whether Kansas is full of mountains or flat as a board. If you want to learn how flat or hilly a particular piece of land is, you need to consult a special kind of map, called a relief map.

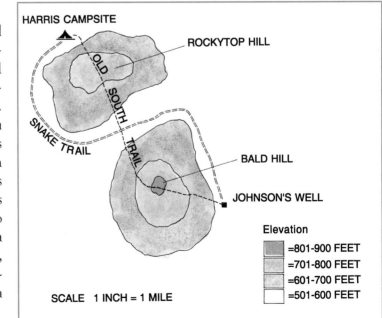

Take a look at the relief map opposite. It shows two hills, Rockytop Hill and Bald Hill. Can you use the key in the lower right to figure out which hill is higher? The top of Bald Hill is shaded orange. That means it's between 801 and 900 feet above sea level. The highest part of Rockytop Hill is shaded grey, which means it's between 701 and 800 feet above sea level. So Bald Hill is higher.

What if you wanted to hike from Harris Campsite to Johnson's Well? There are two paths you could take: Snake Trail or Old South Trail. Which path is more direct? Which path is hillier? About how far would you walk if you followed Old South Trail? How about Snake Trail? (Hint: you may want to use a piece of string to measure the twisty paths.)

Mountains of the World

One of the things a relief map can show you is where the tallest mountains are located. Look at the map below. It shows some of the major mountain ranges of the world and some of the tallest peaks. Let's learn a little about these ranges and peaks.

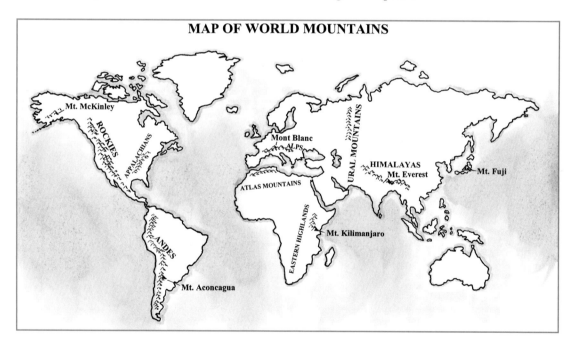

MAP OF WORLD MOUNTAINS

American Mountains

The Andes [AN-deez] in South America stretch nearly 4,500 miles from the southern tip of the continent to the Caribbean coast. The highest mountain in the Andes, Mount Aconcagua, rises 22,831 feet above sea level.

The Andes Mountains and the surrounding territory were the home of the ancient Inca

The worn peaks of the Appalachians.

people. The Incas built a famous city, Machu Piccu, on top of one of the mountains in the Andes.

The Appalachian Mountains extend nearly 1,800 miles, from Alabama to the Gulf of Saint Lawrence. They include the White Mountains of New Hampshire, the Allegheny Mountains of Pennsylvania and West Virginia, the Blue Ridge Mountains of Virginia, and the Great Smoky Mountains of North Carolina and Tennessee.

The Appalachians have played an important role in our country's history. During the early years of American history,

most settlers stayed east of the Appalachians, along the coast. Eventually, however, Daniel Boone and others found passes that led through the Appalachians. This opened the way for settlement in the Midwest and the Great Plains.

West of the Appalachians lie the Rocky Mountains. The Rockies stretch more than 3,000 miles, from New Mexico through the United States and Canada, and north to Alaska. Mount McKinley, in Alaska, is the highest mountain in North America at 20,320 feet.

The Rockies are much higher than the Appalachians—so much higher that the Appalachians look like hills in comparison. Because they are so tall, the Rockies were an even bigger barrier to settlers. But

The jagged peaks of
the Rocky Mountains, in Colorado.

eventually paths like the Oregon Trail were blazed, and thousands of settlers followed these trails across the Rockies to Washington, Oregon, and California.

Why a Tall Mountain Is a Young Mountain

A rule geographers have discovered about mountains is that young mountains tend to be high mountains, while old mountains tend to be lower. The Rockies and the Appalachians are good examples. Scientists tell us the Rockies are about 130 million years old and the Appalachians about 280 million years old.

Because the Appalachians are so old, their peaks have been worn down over millions of years by weathering and erosion. That explains why the Appalachians have a rounded look and seldom rise above 6,000 feet. The Rockies, on the other hand, have not been worn down as much. Many peaks are rugged and jagged, and dozens rise more than 14,000 feet above sea level.

The High Peaks of the Himalayas

Although the Rockies are tall, they're not nearly as tall as the Himalayas, in Asia, where many peaks reach over 25,000 feet. This range includes the world's tallest mountain, Mount Everest, which rises 29,028 feet above sea level.

Until 1953 no person had ever climbed to the top of Mount Everest. Freezing temperatures, ferocious winds, snow avalanches, and blizzards stopped all who tried. Another obstacle was thin air. Human beings need oxygen to survive, but not all of the air in our atmosphere contains the same amount of oxygen. As you climb farther above sea level, the amount of oxygen in the air decreases—the air gets thinner. On top of Mount Everest the air is so thin that even the slightest movements can leave you gasping for breath.

The first people to overcome all these obstacles and reach the peak were New Zealand beekeeper Edmund Hillary and his Tibetan guide Tenzig Norgay in May 1953.

Edmund Hillary and Tenzig Norgay are all smiles after becoming the first to climb to the peak of Mount Everest.

African Mountains

The Atlas Mountains stretch for 1,500 miles along the northwest coast of Africa. These mountains are named for the Greek god Atlas who had to support the sky on his shoulders through eternity. With an average height of 11,000 feet, the Atlas Mountains are tall enough to keep coastal rains from moving inland and watering the Sahara Desert.

Mount Kilimanjaro.

The tallest mountain in Africa, at 19,340 feet, is Mount Kilimanjaro. This beautiful, towering peak is actually the remains of an ancient volcano. Even though it is close to the equator, where temperatures are usually warm, Kilimanjaro is so high that it wears a cap of ice throughout the year.

The Alps

The Alps cover much of Switzerland and Austria, as well as parts of France and Italy. The highest peak in the Alps is 15,771-foot Mont Blanc.

If you've studied Roman history, you may know about the Carthaginian general Hannibal, who bravely marched his army of soldiers and attack elephants across the Alps to invade Italy.

In 1991 two hikers in the Alps came across a human body frozen in the snow. Tests revealed that the body was roughly 5,000 years old. Freezing temperatures had preserved the man's body so well that it was like an ice mummy. Scientists were able to determine how old the man was when

This is a sketch of what Ötzi, the Ice Man of the Alps might have looked like when he was alive, about 5,000 years ago.

he died, what he was wearing, and even what he had eaten for his last meal. The ice man—nicknamed Ötzi—was about forty when he died. He stood about five feet tall, wore a fur cap and leather shoes, and carried an ax as well as a bow and arrows. The iceman of the Alps has given scientists valuable new information about how people lived in prehistoric times.

Europe in the Middle Ages

Think of kings and queens, of knights and castles, of King Arthur and his Knights of the Round Table, of Robin Hood and Joan of Arc. Welcome to the Middle Ages!

"Middle of what?" you ask. The phrase *Middle Ages*, and the adjective *medieval*, refer to the period of European history between ancient and modern times. Some historians say that the Middle Ages ran from A.D. 476 to 1453. Others don't use exact dates, but they agree generally within this time span.

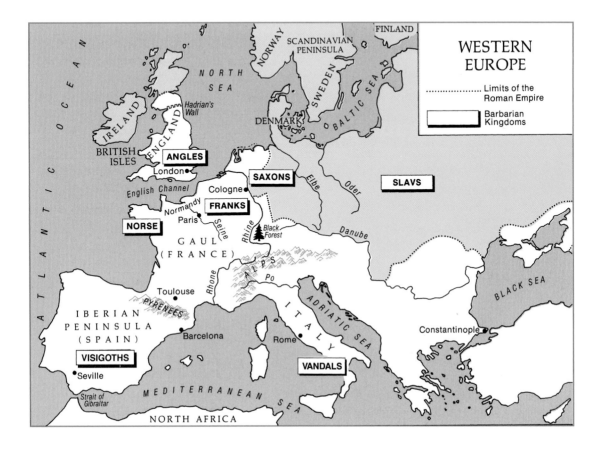

After Rome

The Middle Ages began when the vast Roman Empire collapsed. The Romans had controlled all the lands along the coast of the Mediterranean Sea, including Greece, Turkey, Egypt, and northern Africa. Julius Caesar had conquered what is now France, and other Roman generals had crossed the Pyrenees and gained control of the Iberian Peninsula, including modern-day Spain and Portugal. The Romans had even crossed the English Channel and colonized England, Wales, and part of Scotland. The only parts of Europe that remained free from Roman control were Ireland, northern Scotland, Scandinavia, and the lands east of the Danube and Rhine rivers.

By the 300s and 400s, the Roman Empire had grown too big and had too many problems for one man to rule. So it was split in two. The western emperor, based in Rome, ruled Italy, France, Spain, England, and other western lands. The eastern emperor had his capital in Constantinople (now called Istanbul) and ruled Greece, Turkey, the Balkan Peninsula, and the Middle East.

As early as the year 200, new people started entering Roman territory. They were tough, and eventually they learned to outfight the Roman armies. By A.D. 476, these people had overthrown the western Roman emperors and set up barbarian kingdoms. Some of these kingdoms eventually became modern countries like France and England. But in the east the other Roman emperors kept on ruling. The Eastern Roman Empire (also known as the Byzantine Empire) lasted until 1453.

> The ancient Greeks and Romans called foreigners barbarians because they couldn't understand their languages. When the foreigners spoke, the Greeks heard only "bar . . . bar . . . bar."

The Barbarians

The fiercest barbarians, the Huns, originally lived north of China. The Huns tried to break through the Great Wall of China. Then, in the mid-400s, they turned and swept westward all the way to Europe, under the leadership of their king, Attila [ah-TILL-ah]. One historian wrote that the Huns were men "of a very ugly pattern," so uncivilized that "they make no use of fire [and] feed upon the roots which they find in the fields, and the half-raw flesh of any sort of animal." Everywhere the Huns went they caused terrible destruction. They became famous for their wild and savage ways.

Other tribes succeeded in taking over other Roman territories. The Visigoths sacked the city of Rome in A.D. 410 and eventually settled in Spain. The Vandals looted Italy so badly

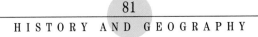
that the word *vandalism* is still used to describe destruction of other people's property. The Franks were Germans who settled in modern France, which is named for them. The Angles took over Britain and gave their name to England ("Angle-land"). At the same time, the Saxons also invaded Britain. The languages of the Angles and Saxons eventually grew together to form Anglo-Saxon, or Old English, the earliest form of the English language, spoken a thousand years ago. Many of our most common words can be traced back to Anglo-Saxon—words like *man, house,* and *dog.*

Were the Dark Ages Really So Dark?

You may have heard the term the Dark Ages. This name is sometimes applied to the first 300 years or so after the fall of Rome, and sometimes to the whole medieval period. The phrase was coined by the Italian poet Petrarch, who lived much later, in the 1300s. Petrarch loved the culture of the ancient Greeks and Romans and felt that nothing good had happened after the fall of Rome. He saw the Middle Ages as a time of violence, poverty, and ignorance. That's why he labeled the period the Dark Ages.

Today we know that Petrarch was unfair to the Middle Ages. The Middle Ages had their fair share of poverty and warfare, and only a few people could read and write. But all of these problems were common both before and after the Middle Ages, and we now understand that it is unfair to describe the whole period as an age of darkness. As you will see, medieval civilization produced great achievements in government, religion, and art.

The Rise of the Christian Church

For the Christian Church, the early Middle Ages were a time of growth. Christianity had become the official religion of the Roman Empire under Emperor Constantine in the 300s, and the religion continued to prosper even after the western Roman Empire collapsed.

The early Christians called barbarians and other non-Christians "heathens" [HEE-thens], and they felt that it was their duty to convert them to Christianity. Most of the invading tribes eventually did accept Christianity.

The leader of the western Christian church, the Bishop of Rome, was called the pope. The pope claimed to be Jesus Christ's representative on earth. During the Middle Ages, popes became more and more powerful figures, forming partnerships with kings and nobles throughout western Europe.

Pope Gregory VII, head of the Roman Catholic Church from 1073–1085.

As time went on, conflicts developed between the eastern followers of the church, who spoke Greek, and the western followers, who spoke Latin. In 1054, the two sides split in a quarrel about beliefs. The eastern church became known as Orthodox, because it claimed its beliefs were orthodox (correct). The western church called itself Catholic, because it claimed to be worldwide (which is what the word *catholic* means). Today we still have the two religions that were formed by that split in the Middle Ages—Orthodoxy and Roman Catholicism.

The western church grew wealthy and powerful. Kings and nobles donated gifts of land and gold and the Roman Catholic Church eventually became richer than any king in Europe.

Monks—men who chose to devote their lives to the Church—were usually the best-educated people in Europe in those days. Monks spent their lives in monasteries, working and praying. Women who devoted their lives to the church and lived together were called nuns. During the Middle Ages, monks and nuns studied the writings of ancient Greeks and Romans. They took special care and copied the writings by hand. Thanks to them, we know more about ancient history and philosophy.

Beginning around the year 800, church leaders and monasteries started schools for children. About 300 years later, the Church established the first universities.

A monk copying a manuscript.

Charlemagne

Do you remember learning about the Franks? In 771 a ruler took control of the Frankish land. His name was Charlemagne [SHAR-luh-main], which means Charles the Great. Charlemagne reigned more than forty-five years. He increased the size of his empire by conquest. Ultimately, Charlemagne unified most of the western lands of the old Roman Empire. The pope recognized Charlemagne's considerable power and crowned him emperor in the West. In return, Charlemagne protected the pope.

Charlemagne had a great interest in education and culture. He invited learned men from all over Europe to his court. He encouraged new ideas and rewarded men who were loyal to him. Those who worked for him in the military or the government received land as their payment.

When Charlemagne died in 814, his empire disintegrated. More barbarians (like the Vikings) overran Europe. But Charlemagne had a lasting influence on European history. His practice of rewarding men with land spread throughout western Europe and became the basis for a way of life that is sometimes called feudalism, or the feudal system.

Feudalism

The phrase feudal system is almost as controversial today as the phrase Dark Ages. It was never used in the Middle Ages. The phrase was invented later, and many historians don't think it's a good term. Still, the word has stuck in many peoples' minds, to the point where it's difficult to talk about the Middle Ages without using the term.

When we talk about feudalism we mean a way of living in which land was exchanged for service. The person who received the land was called the vassal; he promised to serve the person who gave him the land, who was called the lord. The name for the land grant made by the lord was a fief [feef].

Some vassals served a king. Others served a rich and powerful man in their region. Vassals were supposed to keep the fief only as long as they served their king or lord faithfully. Vassals, lords, and kings swore oaths to observe these rules, and the church taught that breaking these oaths was a terrible sin.

The more vassals who swore loyalty to a particular lord, the more powerful the lord became. A woman might become a lord if her husband died and she had no son or other male relative, but in general men dominated medieval government and society.

Lords were responsible to their king. A king expected that his lords would supply fighters when he needed them. These fighters were called knights. In battle they wore metal armor designed to protect their bodies from heavy swords and other weapons. They often fought on horseback. Knights swore loyalty to their lord and their king. They received their pay in land or in money from those they conquered.

Although kings and lords were the most powerful people in the Middle Ages, most of the work was done by the peasants, or serfs, who worked on the manors, or farms, owned by the lords. Serfs could not move away from the village without the lord's permission. They grew food, tended animals, and wove cloth. Serfdom was a

A knight.

hard life, but serfs were not slaves: the lord could not sell them or members of their families, and he was supposed to protect them and respect their rights.

In general, medieval society was like a pyramid, with the kings and lords on top, knights below, and serfs on the bottom.

Lords and Castles

Many times a medieval lord controlled a whole village and the surrounding land. The lord could interpret and enforce laws. He made money by collecting taxes and dues from his serfs and by making them share their crops or livestock. Sometimes he ran a mill or brewery for them, making them pay to grind their flour or turn their grain into beer.

At the same time, the serfs knew that in case of war or a raid from attackers, the lord would offer them protection in his castle. Protection was important because medieval life could be violent. Peasants often got into fights. Nobles feuded among themselves and often raided each other's lands. Kings fought wars and faced rebellions from lords. To defend themselves, nobles built castles, in which they lived and stored weapons. Early medieval castles were simple wooden forts. Later, kings built stronger castles out of stone. Castle walls sometimes enclosed a series of small buildings, like a little town. The castle needed a water supply within the walls, and food was stored so that people could withstand a siege [seej].

Life in a Castle

Castles were designed for defense—not comfort. Life in a castle was not very pleasant. Most castles had only a few rooms: a great hall, a kitchen, and possibly a private chamber for the lord and his wife. Usually the great hall was where everyone came together. People slept, ate, played, and worked in the great hall. Heat came from smoky buckets of coals or from fireplaces. Windows were small and candles threw little light. Stone walls and floors were cold and uncomfortable. The bathrooms were outhouses in the castle walls, with straw instead of toilet paper!

Neither the noble father nor mother spent much time with their children. Nursemaids tended the young children. Books were extremely rare, but children of the Middle Ages had a chance to play with toys and hear stories. Traveling storytellers and musicians (called minstrels), clowns (called jesters), and troops of actors often visited a castle. Sometimes they even lived in the castle, ready to entertain whenever requested. Children and adults all enjoyed dancing. They played outdoor sports as well. Our games of tennis, croquet, and bowling all began as lawn games in the Middle Ages.

Young noble boys were sometimes taught by tutors. At seven, many were sent away to be educated, typically at the castle of a relative. There they would generally serve as pages. Pages were boys who worked for knights and noblemen, performing simple tasks such as waiting on table. After seven years of service, a page could rise to the next level and become a squire. Squires were still servants, but they began to train for military service and could accompany their lords to battle.

The lines below are from a famous poem called *The Canterbury Tales,* written during the Middle Ages by an English poet named Geoffrey Chaucer. In this poem, a group of English men and women ride together on a pilgrimage to the cathedral at Canterbury. The lines describe one of the pilgrims, a squire. First notice the old-fashioned kind of English it uses—maybe you can guess some of the words. Then read what it says in modern English.

Short was his gowne, with sleves longe and wyde.
Wel koude he sitte on hors and faire ryde.
He koude songes make and wel endite,
Juste and eek daunce, and weel purtreye and write.
So hoote he lovede that by nyghtertale
He sleep namoore than dooth a nyghtyngale.
Curteis he was, lowely, and servysable,
And carf biforn his fader at the table.

His gown was short, with sleeves long and wide.
He could sit well on a horse and ride well.
He could make songs and compose well,
Joust and also dance, and draw and write well.
He loved so hotly that at night
He slept no more than a nightingale does.
He was courteous, humble, and willing to serve,
And carved in front of his father at the table.

Chaucer's squire.

Squires who succeeded in their years of training became knights. Not all boys who became knights were of noble birth, but a knight's equipment—horse, armor, and weapons—was very expensive, so most knights came from wealthy families. Only boys could look forward to this honor, though. Noble girls were brought up to be ladies—they were taught sewing, embroidery, weaving, singing, dancing, and how to use herbs for healing. A few girls learned to ride (sidesaddle, with their long skirts draped over one side).

The Life of a Knight

Young men eager to become knights could prove their strength and abilities by taking part in tournaments. Tournaments, or jousting matches, were mock battles staged for practice, fun, and fame. Here is an announcement of a jousting match from around the year 1400:

Six gentlemen this 3rd day of May next, shall come before the high and mighty redoubted ladies and gentlemen to appear at just before noon, to joust with all comers on said day until six that afternoon.

And the said ladies and gentle women shall give unto the best jouster of all a costly diamond. Unto the next best a ruby worth half as much. And to the third a sapphire worth half of that. And on the said day there should be officers of arms to measure that the spears are of the same length.

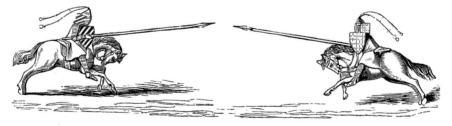

Chivalry

During the Middle Ages, noblemen and noblewomen developed their own ideals, customs, and rules for behavior. We call this set of rules the code of chivalry [SHIV-al-ree], after the French word *chevalier* [she-val-YAY], which means horseman or knight. According to the code of chivalry, knights were supposed to guard women, help the poor, serve the church, and treat all fellow knights as brothers. Knights were expected to be brave in war and to rescue damsels in distress. They were expected to treat knights captured in war as honored guests until a ransom, or reward money, was received and the captured knight was free to go home.

Medieval Towns

By the 1200s and 1300s, many people were moving from country villages into bigger towns and cities, where they found jobs. Lords tried to keep serfs at home by treating them better. They gave them more freedom and offered lower taxes and rents. But still many serfs left for the towns and cities. By 1300, there were few serfs left in western Europe, although serfdom lingered on in eastern Europe.

In the 1300s, even the largest cities like Florence and Paris had fewer than 100,000 people. But they were crowded and noisy, busy with street vendors and shopkeepers, and with traders bringing things from distant towns to sell. Most towns held markets two or three times a week, where local farmers sold produce and craftsmen and traders sold everything from candles to clothes. In a typical town, up to half the adult males were craftsmen who made tools, furniture, and other important items by hand.

Learning Your Trade

Medieval craftsmen and merchants formed associations called guilds. A town might have a carpenters' guild, a butchers' guild, a shoemakers' guild, and a cloth merchants' guild, among others. The vast majority of guild members were men, but sometimes women were allowed to join. Guilds made strict rules about how, when, and where people could trade. Only guild members could do business in towns, and prices were fixed by the guild. If a member made something that didn't meet guild standards for workmanship, he might have to pay a fine or might be kicked out of the guild.

Medieval children began training for a trade or business between the ages of seven and nine. A father paid a master craftsman or merchant to train his son as an apprentice. Apprentices lived in the home of the master who taught them. They had to work for that master for seven years. Eventually an apprentice became a journeyman, traveling from town to town to learn more from different masters. If he was smart and lucky, a journeyman might finally become a master, join a guild, set up a shop, get married, and start a family—and then teach his trade to a new apprentice.

Charters and Churches

As medieval towns grew, kings and nobles granted townspeople the right to govern themselves through a mayor and town council. They spelled out these rights in town charters. Towns were still not very democratic, for the richest merchants and craftsmen held almost all the power. Still, it was in the Middle Ages that the idea was born that people had rights and liberties and could govern themselves.

Medieval people took their religion very seriously. They built hospitals and other institutions to help people in need, and they believed that by helping those in need, they were expressing their own love for God. They also built large and beautiful churchs and cathedrals that expressed their love of God and their pride in their city. Sometimes it would take more than one hundred years to complete a great medieval church, so that the people who started building it would be dead long before it was done. Today these churches are considered some of the world's most wonderful works of architecture.

There was a less happy side to the deep religious feelings of medieval life, however. Some people expressed ideas that did not agree with what the pope and other church leaders said. Church leaders called these contradictory opinions heresy and the people who held them heretics, and often they were treated cruelly. Some Christians also mistreated the Jews who lived in medieval cities. At times, conflicts over what was the true religion added to the violence of medieval life.

England: The Rise of a Medieval Kingdom

Remember how England was conquered by the barbarian Angles and Saxons? After many years of fighting, the Anglo-Saxon people came together under a single king and converted to Christianity.

One of the most important Anglo-Saxon kings was called Edward the Confessor. Edward the Confessor got his name because he was a very religious man, always eager to confess his sins to God and try to follow the rules of the church. He died in 1066, leaving no children. An important nobleman, Harold Godwinson, was chosen as the next king. But over in Normandy—a part of France just across the English Channel—a duke named William had other ideas.

William the Conqueror

Normandy got its name from the Norsemen (or Vikings) who had settled in northern France 150 years earlier. The Normans became so powerful that their duke was more wealthy and powerful than the king of France. Norman armies were the best in Europe. But Duke William of Normandy wanted more.

Claiming to be the true king of England, in September 1066 he sailed across the English Channel with 700 ships carrying 7,000 knights.

The armies of King Harold and Duke William met in October of 1066 at the Battle of Hastings. After a bloody battle in which Harold was killed, the Normans defeated the Anglo-Saxon army. Duke William was crowned King William I. He was also called William the Conqueror.

The Anglo-Saxons hated William. They didn't want to be ruled by a foreigner. William turned all his Norman knights into English noblemen and gave them titles and property in England.

Despite the hatred that he aroused, William the Conqueror made his mark on English history. He organized a government and sent sheriffs throughout the land to collect taxes from all the people. He built castles all over England, stationing soldiers to put down rebellions. He also hired people to make a list of all the property and landowners in the land. These people put together a book called the Domesday Book. It was the first time records were kept about who had a right to what land—and it made it easier for William and the kings who came after him to collect taxes.

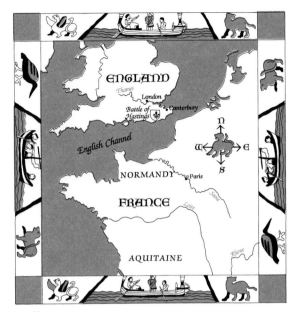

Henry II

Henry II.

After William the Conqueror died in 1087, England had other kings—some strong and some weak. One of the most notable was Henry II, who became king of England in 1154.

Henry demanded all kinds of taxes from the nobles and sent soldiers, sheriffs, and judges throughout his kingdom to collect these taxes. He also set up a new system of law that is still the basis of today's courts in England and America. For the first time a jury (a group of citizens) listened to a case to determine if someone was guilty of a crime. People could also appeal a verdict. If a person didn't like the decision made in his local lord's court, he could ask the king for another trial in the royal court.

Murder in the Cathedral

For the first few years of Henry's reign, his main assistant was Thomas Becket. Becket helped Henry create a powerful government. The king trusted Becket, and Becket was almost as wealthy and powerful as the king himself.

Then Henry made a mistake. In an attempt to gain control over the Church in England, he appointed Becket as Archbishop of Canterbury, the most powerful church leader in all of England. Henry figured that his best friend would run the Church in a way that suited the king, but things didn't work out that way. As soon as Becket became Archbishop of Canterbury, something amazing happened. Becket became more religious than he had ever been before and started taking his new job very seriously. When Henry and the Church disagreed, Becket sided with the Church.

Furious, Henry ordered Becket arrested. Becket escaped to France. The pope threatened to kick Henry out of the Church (which would mean that his subjects wouldn't have to obey him) unless Henry allowed Becket to return as archbishop. Finally Henry gave in and Becket returned to England, where he immediately began opposing Henry again.

Henry was annoyed. During a royal dinner, with many nobles in attendance, he is said to have complained about Becket: "Will no one rid me of this troublesome priest?" Was Henry just sulking, or was he encouraging his knights to assassinate Becket? We'll never know for sure. But four knights who heard King Henry's words took them seriously. They murdered the archbishop while he was kneeling in prayer in Canterbury Cathedral.

All Europe was struck with horror. The pope declared Becket a saint. Thousands of people came to Canterbury to pray at his tomb, and many said that miracles occurred there. For instance, it was said that blind people who visited Becket's tomb suddenly were able to see.

Henry ruled for nearly twenty years after Becket's death, but he was overcome by guilt. He begged the pope for forgiveness and gave back everything he had ever taken from the Church. Still, he could not forgive himself. To punish himself even more for Becket's death, he walked barefoot for three miles along the rocky road to

The murder of Becket in Canterbury Cathedral.

Canterbury, till his feet bled. Then he prayed for forgiveness and allowed priests to whip him—though how hard, we don't know.

Meanwhile, Henry II's ambitious wife, Eleanor of Aquitaine [AH-qui-tain], plotted with their three sons to overthrow him. Henry banished Eleanor as a traitor. He had her locked up in a castle in France. His sons fled to France as well. Henry died, thinking himself a failure. But actually he had done something historic—he had made the king the supreme ruler over all the feudal lords of England.

From the Magna Carta to Parliament

John, the youngest of Henry's sons, became king in 1199. He fought many wars and wasted lots of money. He also lost most of England's land in France. The English lords grew more and more disgusted by his recklessness. In 1215, following a major English defeat, they forced King John to sign a charter limiting his rights. The proud lords called this charter Magna Carta, which is Latin for great charter.

The Magna Carta is one of the most important documents in English history. It sets forth the idea that there is a common law that all people must follow—not just peasants but also knights, nobles, and kings. The Magna Carta also states that the king must respect the rights of the other nobles and consult with them if he wants to make new laws.

Edward I, King John's grandson, wanted to strengthen the royal government. In 1295 he formed a Model Parliament [PAR-lah-ment]. It was a group of knights and nobles and churchmen who approved laws proposed by the king. Although England was still a long way from being a modern democracy, this was the origin of England's modern parliament.

King John signing the Magna Carta.

The Black Death

A terrible disease swept through Europe late in the 1340s. Called the Black Death, it got its name from the black lumps that it caused on a sick person's skin. The modern name for it is bubonic [byoo-BON-ick] plague. The bacteria that cause bubonic plague are spread to humans by fleas that have bitten infected rodents. With all the rats in the crowded towns and cities of medieval Europe, the disease spread fast.

People who caught the Black Death developed painful bumps on their bodies and sometimes began to spit blood. Two-thirds of those who caught the disease died. So many died that they had to be stacked in mass graves. The Italian writer Boccaccio [bo-COTCH-chee-oh] said that the plague spread "like a fire through dry grass."

No one knew how to stop this horrible new disease. Most people were afraid even to visit the sick. They tried different treatments—wrapping a patient with cold towels or encouraging him to sniff perfume, since many people believed the plague was caused by hot, stinky air. Many people, especially church leaders, thought that God had sent the plague to punish people for their sins. Some people walked from town to town, whipping themselves and each other. They believed that if they punished themselves for their own sins and those of their neighbors, God might stop the Black Death.

In just three years, one out of every three people in Europe died. Then, suddenly, around 1351, the plague seemed to disappear. But it returned—in 1363, again in 1369, and on many more occasions for the next 300 years.

The Hundred Years' War

From 1337 to 1453, the armies of the kings of France and England fought each other in what is known as the Hundred Years' War. The battles took place in France. Both armies raided French villages for food and money, causing widespread hunger and terrible hardship. During long breaks in the fighting, soldiers without jobs or pay wandered around Europe, demanding money in return for protecting people—and robbing them if they didn't pay.

Because of plague and the Hundred Years' War, western Europe suffered horribly. Many people died and many villages simply disappeared. Trade slowed down and even stopped in some areas. Desperate peasants rebelled, and soldiers crushed these rebellions.

Joan of Arc

One of the most remarkable figures to emerge during the Hundred Years' War was a French teenager known as Joan of Arc. Joan was born around 1412, when the war had already been raging for seventy-five years. As a young girl, she had mystical experiences and claimed that God wanted her to lead the French people and drive out the invading English. Amazingly, France's young uncrowned king (called the dauphin [doe-FAN]) allowed this peasant girl to head an army. Wearing knight's armor and riding at the head of a large body of soldiers, Joan met the English army and forced it out of the town of Orléans [or-lay-AWN] in 1429. Then she had the *dauphin* crowned King Charles VII.

But the French leaders believed they had gotten all they needed from Joan. In 1430, she was captured in a battle, and Charles made no effort to pay a ransom and save her. The English accused her of heresy, witchcraft, and wearing men's clothes. (A girl wearing pants was considered unnatural and improper—and, thought the English, any girl who could beat their soldiers in battle surely must be a witch!) An English-controlled court found her guilty. Joan of Arc was burned at the stake.

Joan was only nineteen years old when she died, but she achieved what the French kings and armies had not. Her victory at Orléans was a turning point. After that, the English began to lose the Hundred Years' War. The inspired courage of a young French peasant girl had changed history.

Joan of Arc leading the French troops.

The End of the Middle Ages

Things were so miserable during the Hundred Years' War that some people thought it was the end of the world. Today we know it wasn't the end of the world, but 1453, the end of the Hundred Years' War, is the date some historians consider the end of the Middle Ages. It was an important year in history elsewhere, too. In 1453 Turkish invaders captured Constantinople, marking the end of the Byzantine, or eastern Roman, Empire.

The Rise of Islam

The word *Islam* [IHS-lahm] means submission in the Arabic language, and for those who believe in the religion of Islam, it means submission to one God. Islam is a religion practiced by more than a billion people around the world today and by more than 5 million people in the United States. We call these people Muslims [MUZ-lims].

Muslims follow the teachings of Muhammad [moo-HAH-mahd], who lived on the Arabian Peninsula during the medieval period, from 570 to 633. Muslims believe that about 1,400 years ago, in the city of Mecca [MEK-kah], Muhammad received the word of God, whom they name *Allah* [ah-LAH], the Arabic word for God.

The Prophet Muhammad

Muhammad was born in Mecca. Mecca was home to a holy building called the *Ka'ba* [KAH-bah]. In Muhammad's time, travelers who came to Mecca filled the *Ka'ba* with idols, or statues of the many gods they worshiped. Local merchants wanted this practice to continue, because every traveler bringing an idol to the *Ka'ba* also spent money while visiting Mecca.

Muhammad was a trader himself. He loved his neighbors and his city, but he was uncomfortable with the way people were worshiping many gods and filling the *Ka'ba* with idols. To think over his concerns, he went alone into the desert and the mountains to meditate.

According to Islamic tradition, as Muhammad was meditating in a cave, the Angel Jibrail [JIB-rill] appeared to him.

"Read!" Jibrail ordered.

The *Ka'ba* in Mecca is a holy site for Muslims.

"I cannot read," Muhammad answered. Few people in those days knew how to read.

Jibrail squeezed Muhammad tightly. "Read!" he said again. "Read in the name of your Lord, who created you from a drop of blood."

Muhammad told his wife he had received a message from God. For a long time, she was the only one who believed him.

Several years later, Muhammad is said to have undergone another miraculous experience. Muslims believe that Muhammad was taken up into the sky by angels. He traveled from Mecca to Jerusalem, where he prayed with earlier prophets, including Abraham and Jesus. As he stood on a rock in the city of Jerusalem, he ascended (or went up) into heaven and received God's instruction to tell people to pray five times a day. Muslims built the Dome of the Rock in Jerusalem to commemorate this great event. (see pp. 157).

Trouble in Mecca

Muhammad began telling people in Mecca about his experiences and the ideas that were coming to him. At the time, the people of Mecca followed various religions. There were some Jews and Christians who believed in a single God, but there were many others who worshipped many gods. Muhammad's insistence that there was only one God upset some of these people, and they tried to stop him from spreading his message. But Muhammad continued sharing his ideas. Gradually, more people came to believe that he was a true prophet.

Muhammad taught that every action or thought should be guided by the will of God. He urged Muslims to see themselves as God's creatures, placed on earth to serve God and humanity. He told his followers that God judges people's actions when they die. If they have done good, they will be rewarded; if they have done evil, they will be punished.

At first, Islam was just a local religion with a few followers, but as Islamic ideas spread, Muhammad and his followers came into conflict with the powerful traders in Mecca. These traders made a living by welcoming visitors to Mecca and trading with them. They thought these traders might not come to Mecca anymore if they heard that Muhammad was stirring up trouble. Finally, they forced Muhammad to leave the city. In 622, he and his followers moved north to a city that is now called Medina.

Muhammad's journey to Medina is called the *Hijra* [HEEZH-rah]. It is a very important event in the history of Islam—so important that it is the starting point for the Muslim calendar. Muslims will refer to an event that happened 1050 years after the *Hijra*, in the same way that Christians will refer to events that happened after the birth of Jesus.

The *Hijra* also led to the construction of the first mosque [MOSK], or Muslim place of worship. The night he arrived in Medina, Muhammad began to build a rough structure, now considered the first mosque of Islam.

There are mosques all over the world. Every mosque has minarets [min-ah-RETS], or towers from which a holy man calls the faithful to prayer five times a day. Before entering a mosque, Muslims must remove their shoes and wash at a special fountain. They sit on rugs laid down on the mosque floor in a room designed to face toward Mecca. When the prayer leader arrives, the faithful stand, raise their hands together above their heads, and follow a series of prayer movements. They end by kneeling and lowering their heads to the ground.

The moon rising between the two minarets of the Grand Mosque in Mecca.

Muhammad's Return

In Medina, Muhammad continued to hear messages from Allah. Muhammad expected all people in Medina, no matter what their religions, to live in peace and harmony. The Jews in Medina refused to accept Muhammad as the leader of the city. Mecca was trying to attack Medina and take it over, and the Jews in Medina had been helping the armies from Mecca. That made it even harder for Muhammad and the Jews to agree. Finally, in 630, Muhammad himself led an army in a raid on Mecca. He was leading what Muslims call a *jihad* [gee-HAHD], which is a war fought for religious beliefs. His goal was to rid the city of polytheistic worshippers.

Muhammad and his men took Mecca without much fighting. Muhammad removed all the idols from the *Ka'ba* and dedicated the temple to the worship of the one God of Islam.

Two years after restoring the *Ka'ba* to the worship of one God, Muhammad delivered his last sermon. He asked his followers to obey God and treat each other with justice and kindness. After giving this sermon, Muhammad felt that his life was complete. He returned to Medina and died at the age of 63.

The Qur'an

While Muhammad was alive, many of his followers committed his teachings to memory. After Muhammad died, his followers wrote down the things he had taught them. Muhammad's ideas are still read as holy words today, written down in a book called the *Qur'an* [kohr-AN].

The *Qur'an* is the holy book of the Islamic religion. Its title means "reading," and it recalls the instruction to read, given to Muhammad by the angel Jibrail. The *Qur'an* is written in Arabic. Muslims always study it in its original language, even if they do not speak

Girls studying the *Qur'an*.

Arabic. Muslims believe that the *Qur'an* contains the actual words of God, so learning to read and recite those words is an act of worship.

Some of the important words of Islam can be spelled in different ways. *Qur'an* is sometimes spelled *Koran*, Mecca is also spelled *Makkah*, and Ka'ba is sometimes written as Kaaba.

The Five Pillars of Islam

Devoted Muslims compare their religion to a building that is supported by five pillars. The Five Pillars of Islam are five rules that form the central philosophy of the Islamic faith.

The First Pillar: *Shahada* [sha-HA-dah] in Arabic

As a statement of their faith, Muslims say, "There is no God but Allah and Muhammad is his prophet." This simple statement is the basis of all Muslim be-

A child looks on as adult Muslims pray in the streets of Mecca.

lief. It is the first thing whispered into a child's ear when he is born and the last thing a Muslim hopes to utter at the moment of death.

The Second Pillar: *Salat* [sah-LAHT] in Arabic

Salat means prayer. Muslims recite prayers from the *Qur'an* at dawn, midday, afternoon, evening, and night. At each of these five times of day, they stop what they are doing to bow down in worship in the direction of Mecca.

The Third Pillar: *Sawm* in Arabic

Sawm means fasting, or going without food and drink. Muslims fast during daylight hours throughout the holy month that they call *Ramadan* [rah-mah-DAHN]. Muslims believe fasting brings spiritual rewards. When the fast is over, at the end of *Ramadan*, Muslims celebrate with a festival.

The Fourth Pillar: *Zakat* [ZACK-at] in Arabic

Through *zakat*, or giving to others, Muslims share and show kindness in a practical way to those less fortunate.

The Fifth Pillar: *Hajj* [hahzh] in Arabic

The *Hajj* is a word for the pilgrimage, or religious journey, to Mecca. All healthy Muslims are expected to make a pilgrimage to Mecca at least once in their lives. Today, more than two million Muslims go to Mecca every year.

Spreading the Word of Islam

After Muhammad's death, Muslims began conquering other lands, taking over territories so they could govern them according to the rules of their religion. One by one, the great cities of the ancient Middle East—Damascus in Syria, Antioch in Turkey, Tyre in Lebanon, and finally Jerusalem in today's Israel—were taken over by Muslims. Islamic armies and settlers pushed east to India and China and west across North Africa. In 711, Muslims crossed the Mediterranean and moved into nearby Spain. They began marching over the Pyrenees Mountains to France, but French soldiers met and stopped them.

Muslims lived in Spain for the next seven centuries. They built strong forts, beautiful mosques, and graceful palaces, like the *Alhambra* (see p. 156). They developed irrigation systems to grow their crops better and brought plants to Spain from all over the world: cherries, apples, pears, almonds, sugar cane, and bananas.

It's hard to imagine a world without 1, 2, or 3. But do you remember that the Romans used other numerals? They wrote I for 1, V for 5, and X for 10. In our daily life, we use Arabic numerals, used by Muslim scholars from the Arab world, who may have learned them from scholars in India. Muslims introduced these symbols to Europeans. Nowadays, the whole world uses Arabic numerals.

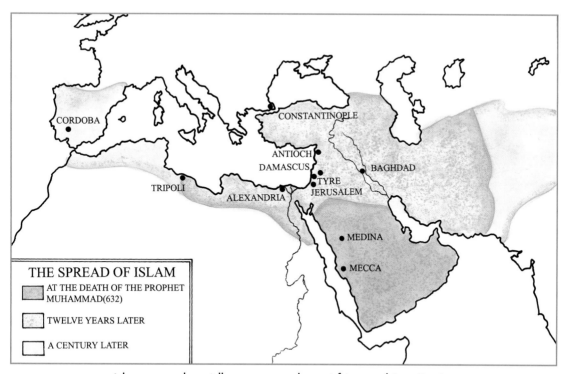

THE SPREAD OF ISLAM

AT THE DEATH OF THE PROPHET MUHAMMAD(632)

TWELVE YEARS LATER

A CENTURY LATER

Islam spread rapidly across northern Africa and into Spain.

The angel Jibrail urged Muhammad to read, and reading and learning have been important in the Islamic religion ever since. Spain's city of Córdoba [KOHR-do-vah] became a great center of Muslim learning and culture. Muslim scholars studied the *Qur'an* along with other works of science and philosophy from many cultures, including ancient Greece. The Muslim philosopher Avicenna (in Arabic, *Ibn Sina*), who lived in the country of Persia (today's Iran) from 980 to 1037, wrote medical books that influenced doctors for generations.

The Crusades

Three different religions considered Palestine, the land that included Jerusalem, a Holy Land. It was the home of David, an ancient leader of the Jewish people, and the place where the ancient Jewish king Solomon had built his temple. Thus the Jews considered Jerusalem a holy city. Since Christians believed that Jesus was crucified, buried, and resurrected in Jerusalem, they also considered it a holy city in their religion. Muhammad had visited the city as well and, according to Islamic belief, rose up into the heavens during that visit. Therefore, Muslims considered Jerusalem a holy city, second in importance only to Mecca in their religion.

Muslims took over Jerusalem as early as the seventh century. There they lived peacefully with those of other religions until about A.D. 1000, when their leader encouraged his people to destroy the Holy Sepulcher [SEPP-uhl-ker], considered by Christians to be the tomb of Jesus. In 1095 the pope, or leader of the Christian church, declared that Christians should go to war to reclaim the city of Jerusalem and the important Christian monuments in it. He called for a crusade, a war to win the Holy Land for Christianity.

Christians from all over Europe armed themselves and started on the long journey east. To capture Jerusalem in 1099, Christian soldiers killed every Muslim they could find. Over the next 200 years, many passionate Christians traveled to Jerusalem. Some entered the

> The word *crusade* comes from the Latin word for cross. The Christian soldiers fighting in these wars were called Crusaders. The Muslims called these wars the Frankish invasions. *Frankish* is another word for French, but the Muslims used it to refer to all Western Europeans, whom they saw as invading their territory.

city peacefully, but some attacked. This long series of conflicts over the Holy Land and the city of Jerusalem is called the Crusades.

One of the most famous meetings during the Crusades took place in 1192, when King Richard I of England (called Richard the Lion-hearted) met Saladin of Egypt, a mighty Muslim leader. Richard won his name lion-hearted because of his bravery and eagerness to fight. He joined with the king of France to lead a Crusade to the Holy Land.

Saladin had become the most powerful Muslim of his time by conquering territory in North Africa. In 1187, he had captured Jerusalem. As Richard's small army approached the city, Saladin's troops surprised them outside the city gates. Even after his horse was killed beneath him, Richard the Lion-hearted kept fighting. Saladin, admiring Richard's courage, sent more horses. Saladin had such respect for Richard the Lion-hearted that, even though he won the war, he agreed not to destroy things sacred to Christians and agreed to let Christians make safe pilgrimages to Jerusalem.

The Crusades involved long and bloody battles and cost many lives, but they also opened up communication between Europe and the Middle East. More trade and travel happened between these two parts of the world than ever before, and the geography, culture, and learning of the Middle East became more widely known.

Saladin.

African Kingdoms

The Geography of Africa

Africa is a continent of amazing geographical variety. It contains the largest desert in the world, the Sahara. But just north of the western Sahara are the Atlas Mountains, whose peaks are covered with snow for much of the year. And just south of the Sahara is the Sahel, a broad band of short grassland and scrub vegetation that stretches from the Atlantic Ocean to the Indian Ocean. Further south, more moisture helps create a savanna landscape of tall grasses and scattered trees. This is Africa's big game country, home of lions, leopards, elephants, and rhinos. South of the savanna, the Congo River cuts

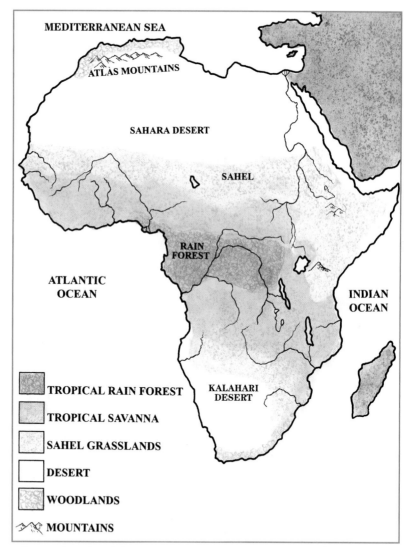

MEDITERRANEAN SEA

ATLAS MOUNTAINS

SAHARA DESERT

SAHEL

RAIN FOREST

ATLANTIC OCEAN

INDIAN OCEAN

KALAHARI DESERT

TROPICAL RAIN FOREST
TROPICAL SAVANNA
SAHEL GRASSLANDS
DESERT
WOODLANDS
MOUNTAINS

through a lush tropical rainforest. South of the rainforests, the savanna resumes, eventually giving way to a southern desert, the Kalahari, which stretches nearly to the southern tip of the continent. Desert, grassland, rainforest, mountains, rivers, and abundant wildlife—Africa has it all!

Egypt and Kush

Africa also has a rich history. You may know about the ancient Egyptians, who lived and farmed along the Nile River, and whose rulers, the pharaohs, built massive pyramids.

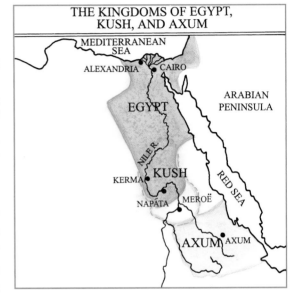

THE KINGDOMS OF EGYPT, KUSH, AND AXUM

The Egyptian civilization clustered at the downriver (or northern) portion of the river. Further upriver, a civilization called the kingdom of Kush lasted for almost 1,500 years, from about 1000 B.C. to A.D. 300.

The people of Kush established a succession of important trading cities. The first great city was Kerma, a walled city near the Nile. Trade with Central Africa and Egypt made Kerma rich—but Egypt also wanted to control that trade. Around 1500 B.C., the Egyptians invaded Kerma and destroyed the city.

Kushite pyramids at Meroë.

Hundreds of years later, around 1000 B.C., a second Kushite kingdom arose. The town of Napata was its major city. This Kushite kingdom grew strong enough to conquer Egypt, and it lasted nearly twelve centuries. The Kushites of Napata built pyramids, the ruins of which still stand today.

The third great Kushite city, Meroë [mehr-OH-way], was famous for making and selling iron weapons. Kushites in Meroë developed a language of their own. They wrote inscriptions on temples and tombs. But no one yet has cracked the code to learn how to read the ancient Kushite language. Since we can't read the inscriptions the Kushites left behind, we have to use other clues to learn how these people lived and what they believed. Pictures on Meroë's temple walls show the queens and kings who ruled Meroë. These pictures suggest that in Kush, the powerful people considered it good to be fat. Magnificent golden jewelry belonging to one Kushite queen has been found, showing the wealth and artistic skill that the later Kushites achieved

Meroë stayed wealthy as long as trade continued with Egypt. When the Romans conquered Egypt and sent their traders along the Red Sea coast instead of down the Nile, trade slowed down and Meroë lost its chief way of making money. Around A.D. 340 another ancient African kingdom, Axum, invaded Meroë. That invasion marked the decline of the kingdom of Kush.

Axum

In the part of Africa that we now call Ethiopia, there was an ancient kingdom called Axum. Axum was a major trading empire. It was a place where traders brought iron, tortoise shells, animal hides, rhinoceros horn, gold, and slaves from the lands in the interior of Africa. These goods were traded for iron tools and weapons, copper implements, cloth, and wine.

Thanks to all this trade, Axum became wealthy and attracted people from Italy, Greece, Egypt, and Persia. Huge granite monuments still exist in this part of Africa, evidence that the Axumites were skilled architects and stonemasons. Ancient coins made of bronze, silver, and gold have also been found.

Axum grew more powerful by gaining control of land in Africa and on the Arabian Peninsula. The kings of Axum also converted to Christianity and made it the official religion of the kingdom.

In the fourth century, Axum invaded Meroë. For a while after that, Axum was the most powerful kingdom in eastern Africa. Then, in the late sixth century, a severe drought made it impossible to grow enough food to feed the people. At the same time, the Persians took over much of the trade between Africa and the Middle East. That was the end of the kingdom of Axum.

Trading Caravans

The Nile River and the Red Sea are natural routes for travelers to follow, but Africa presents other geographic features that are more challenging, like the vast Sahara Desert. Nevertheless, trade across the Sahara has been going on for at least 2,000 years. Around A.D. 400, traders brought camels from Arabia. These sturdy animals made crossing the Sahara easier. Camels carry heavy loads, can go for days without water, and are able to cover ground rapidly. It took three months for a caravan to cross the Sahara. The journey was long and difficult, but the rewards made it worth the effort.

Just what did these camel caravans carry across the desert? One answer is *salt*. With salt so cheap today, it is hard to imagine a time when salt was almost worth its weight in gold. In a world without refrigerators, salt was one of the best ways to preserve meat and fish. Salt can be harvested from salt water or dug from mines. But not all areas of the world had easy access to salt. For that reason, the salt that came from the Sahara was valued highly in other parts of Africa and the Middle East.

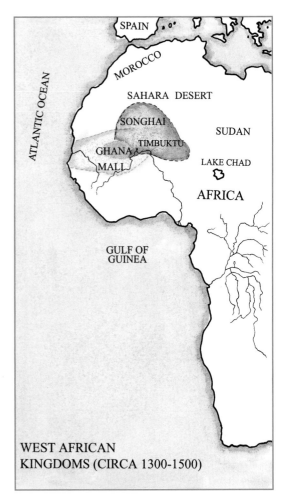

WEST AFRICAN KINGDOMS (CIRCA 1300-1500)

Those who lived where salt was plentiful had things they wanted in trade. People in western Africa had discovered how to separate gold nuggets from the other rocks and pebbles in their rivers. People living farther south hunted wild elephants for their tusks. Tusks are made of ivory, which was highly prized for making carvings and jewelry. Traders brought gold and ivory from western African to trade for salt from the north. Sadly, these caravans also carried human beings who were sold as slaves.

West African Kingdoms

Traders who crossed the Sahara came to know the people living in western Africa. One group, located amid the Sahel grasslands south of the Sahara, called their land *Ouagadou* (wa-ga-DOO). But outsiders called it *Ghana* (GAH-nah), the word in *Ouagadou* for warrior king.

Ghana was the first of West Africa's great trading kingdoms. *Ghana* was most powerful from about A.D. 800 until A.D. 1100. Then another kingdom, called *Mali* (MAH-lee) gained in strength, especially from about A.D. 1235 to A.D. 1400. A third West African trading kingdom, *Songhai* (SONG-high), became the region's strongest power by A.D. 1450 and maintained its power until about 1600.

Mali

Ancient Africans loved to listen to story-tellers, whom they called *griots* [GREE-ohs]. *Griots* would play the drum, sing songs, and dance to tell stories about the ancestors of their people. Here is a verse from one *griot's* song:

A modern-day griot.

> *Listen, then, sons of Mali, children of the*
> *black people, listen to my word, for I am*
> *going to tell you of Sundiata, the father of*
> *the bright country, of the savanna land,*
> *the ancestor of those who draw the bow.*
> *. . . He was great among kings; he was*
> *peerless among men; he was beloved*
> *of God because he was the last of the*
> *great conquerors.*

This *griot's* song tells of the great leader of *Mali*, named *Sundiata Keita* [SUN-dee-ah-tah KAY-tah] and known also as "the Lion King." Much of what we know about *Sundiata Keita* comes through legend and story, which tell us that he ruled *Mali* from A.D. 1230 to 1255 and helped his country gain wealth, land, and power. *Sundiata's* armies conquered gold mines in the south. *Sundiata* also built a new capital city, which became a rich trading center. *Mali* became one of the richest farming regions in West Africa. As he conquered more land, *Sundiata* brought many separate villages together into one country. The people respected *Sundiata* for his leadership and his religion.

While many West Africans worshiped a collection of local gods, *Sundiata* learned about Muhammad and the *Qur'an* and decided to become a Muslim. His devotion to Islam made an impression on his people, who mourned his death in 1255.

If you look on a map of the world today, you will find countries in Africa called Ghana and Mali, but these countries aren't in the same places as the ancient kingdoms of the same name.

Mali's next great ruler, *Mansa Musa*, reigned from 1312 to 1336. (*Mansa* means ruler, or king.) Like *Sundiata*, *Mansa Musa* was a devout Muslim. In 1324, he decided to fulfill the important responsibility of Muslims and to make a pilgrimage, or *hajj*, to Mecca. It was no small feat to travel from *Mali* to Mecca. *Mansa Musa* had a 3000-mile journey to make, crossing the Sahara, and he did it in the grandest Malian style. His wife and children, servants, cooks, and *griots*, all went with him—thousands of people. One hundred camels carried supplies, salt, and gold. Wherever he stopped on Friday, Islam's holy day, he left behind gold in order to build a mosque.

This pilgrimage gained at-

Mansa Musa and his wealth were so legendary that he was shown, seated and holding a nugget of gold, on the first European map of North Africa. The map was made about A.D. 1375.

tention throughout the Muslim world. It was not, however, the last of *Mansa Musa's* efforts on behalf of his religion. Back home in *Mali*, he built more mosques and Islamic schools. His armies conquered the small trading town of Timbuktu, which *Mansa Musa* transformed into a great center of Islamic learning. He brought Muslim architects to the city to design magnificent buildings. He hired Muslim professors to teach in the new schools. Thanks to him, and to many of the traders and travelers coming from the Middle East, Islam became an important religion in that part of Africa.

Ibn Batuta: World Traveler

We know more about the kingdom of *Mali* thanks to a man from Morocco named *Ibn Batuta* [IB-un bah-TOOT-ah]. *Ibn Batuta* was a man who loved to travel. As a Muslim, he made his pilgrimage to Mecca in 1325, at the age of twenty-one. But he didn't stop there. He pressed further into Asia and also traveled around the Mediterranean. He visited kings and governors, especially those in Muslim countries. He visited Timbuktu in 1352, fifteen years after the death of *Mansa Musa*. Later in his life, *Ibn Batuta* wrote a book about his travels.

Ibn Batuta wrote with great excitement about the palace in Timbuktu. He described how the *mansa*, or ruler, received visitors, stepping out of the palace in a red velvet tunic and a golden cap. Before him strolled his court musicians. Three hundred armed slaves marched behind. The *mansa* walked to a platform under a tree, where he sat upon a silk carpet, shaded by a silk umbrella with a golden bird on top. "As he takes his seat, the drums, trumpets, and bugles are sounded," wrote *Ibn Batuta*.

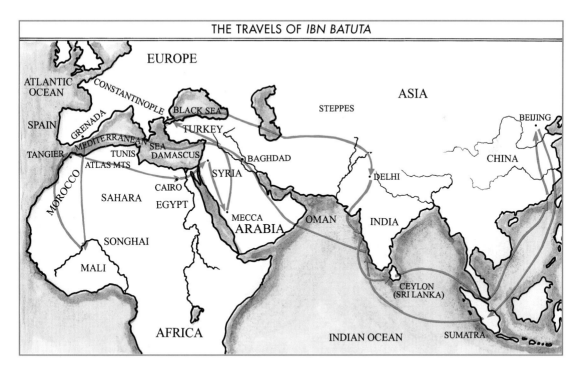

THE TRAVELS OF *IBN BATUTA*

Songhai

Soon after the time of *Ibn Batuta's* visit to Timbuktu, the kingdom of *Mali* began to lose power. Local *mansas* began fighting among themselves and broke away from the larger kingdom. Foreign raiders captured and destroyed the great city of Timbuktu.

As *Mali* declined, the power of nearby *Songhai* began to increase. Many of the people of *Songhai* had embraced Islam. In 1493 (just a year after Christopher Columbus set sail on his voyage of discovery) they chose as their leader an army general who was a deeply religious Muslim. His name was *Askia Muhammad*. The first word in his name, *Askia* [AHS-kee-ah], means general. The second word in his name indicates his faith in the Islamic prophet Muhammad. That combination of features—a fiercely religious warrior—sums up the character of *Askia Muhammad* and his rule, which lasted from 1493 to 1528. *Askia Muhammad* led a *jihad*, or holy war, against nearby people who did not believe in Islam. His efforts increased the power of *Songhai* and spread Islam throughout West Africa.

Songhai's wealth and culture attracted many traders. In the early 1500s, one visitor wrote about all the things being traded in one of *Songhai*'s markets: meat and bread, melons and cucumbers, pottery, and many fine items crafted of gold, leather, or iron. Traders from other lands brought

A man stands before a Mosque in modern-day Timbuktu.

things that the *Songhai* people wanted, like salt, horses, swords, and woven cloth. Slaves were also bought and sold at the market. Many of those sold as slaves were prisoners captured during intertribal wars. Traders would transport slaves across the Sahara. Not long after this time, European traders began to arrive by boat along the Atlantic coast of West Africa. They were looking for slaves to bring back to work on plantations in the Americas.

In 1591, the kingdom of *Songhai* was attacked by Morocco, a country to the north. The Moroccans had muskets and cannons. *Songhai*'s soldiers had only spears and swords. "Everything changed," wrote a historian of the time. "Danger took the place of security; poverty of wealth. Peace gave way to distress, disasters, and violence." Soon *Songhai* disappeared, and with it the golden days of West Africa.

China: Dynasties and Conquerors

Historians use different ways to divide up time. They talk about decades or centuries, the reign of a king, or a presidency. Historians who study China divide time into dynasties [DIE-nah-stees]. A dynasty is a family or group of people that governs a country through several generations.

In 221 B.C., a ruler from the region known as Qin [cheen] conquered all the surrounding regions and founded the Qin Dynasty. He gave himself the title of Qin Shihuangdi [cheen shih-hwahng-dee], which means First Emperor of the Qin Dynasty. It is from the word *Qin* that we get today's name for China.

Qin Shihuangdi

After he came to power in 221 B.C., Qin Shihuangdi created an empire. His deputies laid out provinces, set up a central government, formed an army, and improved roads and

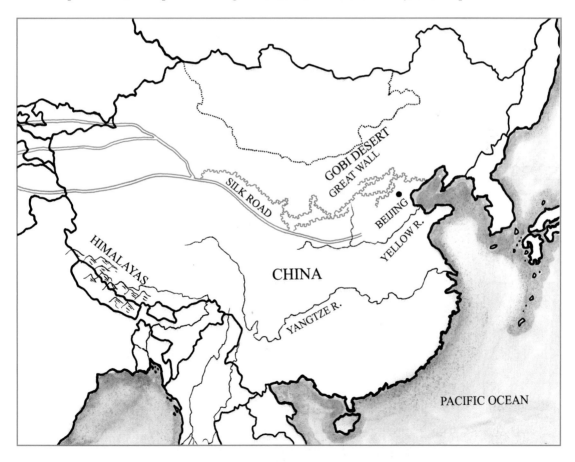

irrigation systems. He made sure that everyone used the same written language. He forced people to work hard, pay taxes, and obey his government.

Qin Shihuangdi worried that his territory might be attacked by armies from the north. He had workers connect some old forts along the border of his empire into a wall many miles long. Almost a million people were put to work to build this wall. Later rulers added new sections to the wall and connected existing sections. Today this gigantic wall is known as The Great Wall of China.

The Chinese people paid taxes to pay to build the wall, as well as a magnificent palace for Qin Shihuangdi. Many people were unhappy with the emperor; some even wanted to kill him. To protect himself Qin Shihuangdi slept in a different bedroom every night.

The Han Dynasty

After Qin Shihuangdi died, people looked for relief from his harsh rule. The next period of Chinese history, the Han Dynasty, lasted 400 years, from 206 B.C. to A.D. 209. During this time, the ideas of Confucius [con-FYOO-shus] became the official philosophy of the government.

Confucius was a philosopher and scholar who had lived many years earlier, around 500 B.C. Confucius came up with many rules for good behavior, including a version of the Golden Rule: always treat others with the greatest respect. Confucius wanted this rule to guide the personal behavior of everyone in society, including the rulers. Although the ideas of Confucius were not widely accepted in his own day, they won official acceptance during the Han Dynasty and have played an important part in Chinese life ever since.

Under the Han Dynasty education was considered important, and a Confucian school opened in the capital city. China grew in every direction. Trade routes connected China to India, the Middle East, and Rome.

What sorts of things did people carry on these trade caravans between China and the West? For starters, they carried silk, a fabric that was then made only in China. Silk was such an important trade item that the network of trails that led from China to the Near East and the Mediterranean came to be known as the Silk Road.

The arts flourished during the Han Dynasty. Artists made beautiful bronze and clay sculptures and paintings on silk cloth. Paper was invented in China during

Confucius.

Silk is made in a remarkable way. Caterpillars called silkworms spin cocoons. Then people unwind their cocoons. With that thread, they weave silk cloth. For hundreds of years, only the Chinese knew how to raise silkworms and make silk.

the Han Dynasty, around A.D. 105. At first, paper was made from silk rags, which were pounded into a pulp and moistened with water. Later, plant materials, like tree bark or bamboo stalks, were also used to make pulp. It would be another thousand years before Europeans learned to make paper.

This silk painting shows a Chinese woodcutter (*on the left*) and a printer (*on the right*).

During the Han Dynasty, many Chinese people began to follow the Indian religion called Buddhism [BOOD-izm]. Buddhism is a religion based upon the life and teachings of Siddhartha Gautama [sid-ARTH-a gow-TAH-ma], who lived around 500 B.C. He did not care for wealth or possessions and used meditation to become good in heart and pure in mind, and he persuaded his followers to do the same. Buddhism differs from Confucianism because Buddhists concentrate on inner enlightenment rather than on rules of external behavior.

The Tang Dynasty

The Tang Dynasty (A.D. 618—906) was a period of bustling trade. Chinese products, especially silk, were in great demand in Europe. Many caravans traveled the Silk Road, and many ships sailed in and out of China's southern ports, such as Canton.

During the Tang Dynasty, the Chinese developed printing. Images were cut into blocks of wood. Then the woodblocks were inked and pressed against paper. The world's first printed book, a sewn-together collection of block-printed pages, was made in China in the year 868. It would be almost 600 years before Europeans mastered the art of printing.

During the Tang Dynasty, Chinese merchants began using printed certificates to stand for money when they were trading with people from far away. These certificates worked something like our dollar bills today.

Also during the Tang Dynasty, inventors discovered the formula for gunpowder: a combination of chemicals that explodes when lit. Just think how many things depend on the invention of gunpowder: guns and grenades, rockets and bombs—not to mention fireworks, which the Chinese of the Tang Dynasty enjoyed just as much as we do today.

The Song Dynasty

Leaders during the Song Dynasty, which lasted from 960 to 1279, presided over another great age of artistry and invention. The Chinese are thought to have invented the compass during this period. Thanks to inventions like the iron plow, improved irrigation methods, and new types of seeds and fertilizers, farmers could grow more food. China's population grew to about 120 million people.

More and more books were printed in China. People learned to carve individual words on small blocks, then combine blocks to print a whole page of words. They could break up the blocks, rearrange them, and print another page—a process known as movable type. This big step in printing technology meant the Chinese could print more books—which encouraged more Chinese people to read.

The Mongol Invasions

The land north of China, on the other side of the Great Wall, is called Mongolia. Mongolia is a cold, dry land that includes the huge Gobi Desert. From the first century on, fierce Mongol warriors had attacked China, trying to move south and take over territory.

Around 1200, a mighty leader united all the Mongol territories and created an army of soldiers so strong, the Chinese could not keep them out. That leader was called Chinggis Khan [JENG-giss KAHN]. His men attacked on horseback and fought ferociously. Around 1279 one of Chinggis Khan's grandsons, Khubilai [KOO-blye] Khan, attacked China. Khubilai Khan defeated the emperor and became the new ruler of China. He chose a northern city, Beijing, as his home. That city is still the capital of China today.

Eight other Mongol emperors succeeded Khubilai Khan. Their combined reign is called the Yuan [ywahn] Dynasty. The Yuan Dynasty lasted from 1279 to 1368. During this period, the Mongol rulers opened China's doors to traders. Traders poured in by land and sea, carrying out China's silk, pearls, spices, gems, and fine porcelains, and bringing new ideas. One of those traders was a man named Marco Polo.

Marco Polo

In the 1260s, Marco Polo and some of his relatives left the city of Venice, Italy, to make their fortunes by traveling between Europe and China and trading valuables, such as gold, jewels, and lamp oil. Marco Polo and his relatives crossed the Mediterranean Sea and landed in the Middle East. They rode camels past Mount Ararat, where people believed Noah's ark had landed after the flood. They traveled to the waters we now call the Persian Gulf, then through the steep, difficult terrain of Afghanistan and on to the Gobi Desert. Altogether, it took the Polos three years to travel from Venice to the khan's palace in China.

And that was just the beginning of Marco Polo's travels! In all, Marco Polo spent twenty-four years traveling throughout China and other lands. We still can read his book, *The Travels of Marco Polo*, which was published in 1298—and we still can wonder (as people in his day did, too) how many of his stories are true and how many have been spiced up by his vivid imagination.

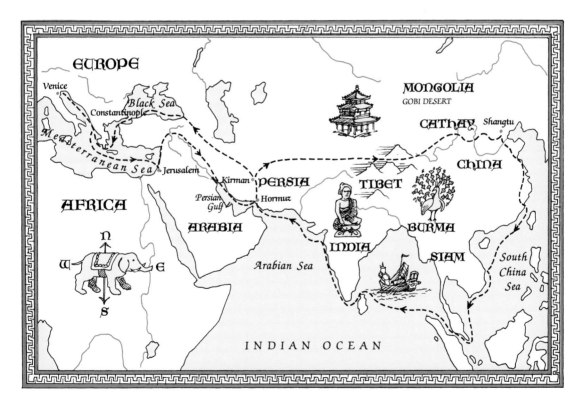

Marco Polo's travels.

The Ming Dynasty

The Ming Dynasty lasted three centuries, from 1368 to 1644. It began when a man named Zhu, an orphaned son of poor parents, proclaimed himself emperor and led an army against the Mongols, driving them out of China. Zhu and his descendants reaffirmed the Chinese way of life for the country and its people. Many great works of art, especially fine porcelain pottery, date from the Ming Dynasty. (You can see an example in the Visual Arts section of this book.)

In Beijing, the emperors built an elaborate imperial palace where they could live and govern without being disturbed. Known as the Forbidden City, it contains fantastic buildings, temples painted with dragons, and palaces ornamented with gold, all encircled by a wall. The Forbidden City still exists today, but it is not forbidden anymore, and if you go to China you can see it.

The Forbidden City.

The Voyages of Zheng He

In the early 1400s, the Chinese launched a mighty fleet, commanded by Admiral Zheng He [jung huh]. During his twenty-odd years of exploring, Zheng He sailed through the Indian Ocean, to Persia and Africa, and around the tip of Africa into the Atlantic Ocean. According to one estimate, his navy contained more than 300 ships and more than 30,000 sailors. Zheng He's flagship was longer than a football field, with both end zones added in—more than four times as large as Columbus's flagship, the *Santa Maria*. Everywhere Zheng He went, foreign powers were amazed. They realized that China must be a mighty empire if it had such a navy.

There is no telling where the ships of the Chinese navy might have sailed and what they might have discovered if they had followed up on the discoveries of Zheng He. If the great Chinese navy had sailed on, America might have been discovered by the Chinese instead of the Europeans! But it was not to be: shortly after Zheng He's death, China's rulers decided to disband the fleet and China entered a period of isolation.

The American Revolution

Our Country in 1750

If you had lived in the American colonies in 1750, you would have been a loyal subject of the British king. You would have lived by the laws made by the British Parliament and shared some rights with British citizens. American colonists and British citizens both gained from this peaceful partnership.

But all that was about to change. A war broke out in 1754, and the consequences of the war would eventually lead colonists to break away from Britain and form a new country: the United States of America.

The French and Indian War

In 1754, France and Britain went to war because both countries claimed the same land in the Ohio Valley. France convinced some of its Native American allies to take arms against the British. Because the French and the Indians fought on the same side, this war is known as the French and Indian War.

The British government sent soldiers to defend its colonies, and American colonists fought side by side with them. Young George Washington acquired his first military experience in this war.

The war lasted from 1754 until 1763. Many battles were fought, and many soldiers killed on both sides. Finally, in 1759, the British launched a daring attack on the French city of Québec, in Canada. The attack succeeded, and the treaty that ended the war gave Britain almost all of France's territory in North America.

Taxation without Representation

The French and Indian War cost a lot of money. The British needed to get out of debt, so King George III and his Parliament decided to make the colonies pay more taxes.

This decision made the colonists angry. They protested, held meetings, and cried out against what they saw as an injustice. They believed that no one should take their money unless they or their elected representatives agreed to it. But the British

King George III ruled the American colonies until 1776.

Parliament, which decreed that Americans would be taxed, was elected in Britain. The American colonists had no say in who became a member of Parliament. The Americans felt this was unfair. "No taxation without representation" became their rallying cry.

The British government did not listen. In 1765 Parliament passed the Stamp Act, which said that all American newspapers, court documents, and other important papers had to be printed on special paper, marked with an official stamp. Every time colonists used a sheet of stamped paper, they had to pay a tax. The colonies exploded with anger. Americans formed groups they called the Sons of Liberty to oppose the tax.

A Stamp Act stamp.

By the spring of 1766, Britain repealed the Stamp Act. The colonies thought their troubles were over. But the very next year Parliament passed a new set of tax laws, called the Townshend Acts, which made the American colonists even angrier than before. The British government began to worry that the colonies might rebel. Parliament sent an army to Boston, Massachusetts, in 1768.

A Massacre and a Tea Party in Boston

In March 1770, violence broke out on the streets of Boston. A small group of Americans taunted and threatened some British troops. The soldiers shot into the crowd, killing five colonists. This event became known as the Boston Massacre, and news of it spread quickly throughout the colonies.

In 1773, the British Parliament made a new law saying that only one company, the British East India Company, could sell tea in America. The company planned to sell tea at a very high price. Boston's Sons of Liberty responded with what they called a tea party—but it was like

This famous but one-sided depiction of the Boston Massacre was made by the American patriot Paul Revere.

no other tea party that had been held before! They dressed up like Native Americans and boarded ships in Boston Harbor. Then they smashed open the crates of tea on board and dumped the tea into the water, leaving behind nothing for the East India Company to sell.

The Boston Tea Party made King George III and the British Parliament furious. Parliament passed more laws, limiting the rights and freedoms of the colonists. One law ordered Boston Harbor closed to colonists' boats, putting almost half of the men of Boston out of work. Another law forced Americans to pay for housing for British troops. Colonists called the new laws the Intolerable Acts, because they could not tolerate them.

The First Continental Congress

In 1774, men from twelve of the colonies met in Philadelphia to decide how they could work together to oppose harsh British laws. They called themselves the First Continental Congress, because it was the first meeting, or congress, among representatives of the colonies. A delegate named Patrick Henry impressed everyone by declaring, "I am not a Virginian but an American!" Most Americans still thought of themselves as being from a particular colony—from Massachusetts, or New York, or Virginia—but Henry's remark showed that this was beginning to change.

The representatives to the First Continental Congress did two important things. First, they advised their fellow colonists to form small volunteer armies, called militias. They also wrote to King George, asking him to consider their complaints. Unfortunately, the harsh laws remained in place.

The War of Words

At first the colonists only waged a war of words against Parliament and King George, but, gradually, more and more colonists began to call for open rebellion. In 1775 Virginia's House of Burgesses held a secret meeting at which Patrick Henry challenged his fellow Virginians to join the people of Massachusetts and resist the British. Some members still hoped for peace, but Henry insisted that there were no grounds for hope. The British were already preparing for war by sending armies and fleets to America, and there had already been skirmishes in Massachusetts:

I have but one lamp by which my feet are guided, and that is the lamp of experience. I know of no way of judging of the future but by the past. And judging by the past, I wish to know what there has been in the conduct of the British ministry for the last ten years to justify those hopes [for peace] . . .

Are fleets and armies necessary to a work of love and reconciliation? . . . Let us not deceive ourselves . . . These are the implements of war. . . . Has Great Britain any enemy, in this quarter of the world, to call for all this accumulation of navies and armies? No, she has none. They are meant for us: they can be meant for no other. They are sent over to bind and rivet upon us those chains which the British ministry have been so long forging. And what have we to oppose to them? Shall we try argument? . . . We have been trying that for the last ten years. Have we anything new to offer upon the subject? Nothing. We have held the subject up in every light of which it is capable; but it has been all in vain. . . .

Gentlemen may cry, Peace, Peace—but there is no peace. The war is actually begun! The next gale that sweeps from the north will bring to our ears the clash of resounding arms! Our brethren are already in the field! Why stand we here idle? What is it that gentlemen wish? What would they have? Is life so dear, or peace so sweet, as to be purchased at the price of chains and slavery? Forbid it, Almighty God! I know not what course others may take; but as for me, give me liberty or give me death!

Patrick Henry delivering his "Give me liberty or give me death" speech.

While Patrick Henry's speech inspired colonial leaders, Thomas Paine addressed the common man. In 1776, he published a pamphlet called *Common Sense*, urging the colonies to declare independence. Over 150,000 copies of *Common Sense* were printed. People read the pamphlet and then passed it on to their friends. In six months' time, 1 million colonists had read the words of Thomas Paine. He had convinced them. They were ready for independence.

The Redcoats Are Coming!

In the New England colonies, men who wanted independence began preparing for war. They began gathering weapons and ammunition. In Massachusetts, they hid the guns and ammunition near the towns of Concord and Lexington, north of Boston. British spies learned of these secret stores. The British planned to raid the towns and seize the weapons. But the Americans had spies, too, who learned—just in time—of the British plans.

Paul Revere, a silversmith in Boston, and his friend, William Dawes, learned that the

British would soon be marching to Concord and Lexington. Revere and Dawes rode through the night, telling everyone, "The redcoats are coming! The redcoats are coming!" (Redcoat was a common nickname for British troops, who wore bright red uniforms.)

An artist's rendition of Paul Revere's famous ride.

Lexington and Concord

When the British arrived in Lexington, American militia men were ready to meet them. These men called themselves Minute Men because they could be ready for duty on a minute's notice. They were not trained soldiers like the British troops. They were volunteers with little or no training in warfare. They drilled only now and then and wore everyday clothing. But they were skilled marksmen, with much hunting experience. One Minute Man bragged that he could "shoot the acorn from a squirrel's mouth"!

As the British drew near somebody fired a shot. Nobody knows if it was a Minute Man or a redcoat. Eight American farmers were killed in the first exchange of fire.

The American Revolution later became so famous, that this first shot became known as "the shot heard round the world." The phrase comes from a poem by Ralph Waldo Emerson, which you can read on page 16.

Later that day, in the nearby town of Concord, the British again fought hard, but the Minute Men outdid them, killing two redcoats for every American lost. It was April 19, 1775, and the Americans had won their first victory!

Yankee Doodles Are Dandy!

As the redcoats marched toward Lexington, English army musicians played the song "Yankee Doodle" on their flutes. They meant it as an insult to the Americans: "yankee" was an insulting name for a man from New England, and a "doodle" was a fool. But after Lexington and Concord, the Americans wrote new words and sang the song, proudly calling themselves Yankee Doodle!

Bunker Hill

After the battles of Lexington and Concord, colonial militiamen stayed at the ready. They knew the British would strike back. On the night of June 16, 1775, some 1,200 Americans dug in on Bunker and Breed's Hills, the best high ground in the town of Charleston, across a narrow inlet from Boston. All night they worked without food, drink, or sleep. By morning, they had a good start on forts, built of mud and rock, at the top of both hills. British troops fired cannons from ships and from the ground below. By afternoon, barges brought even more British soldiers. They marched up Bunker Hill to fight the Americans.

The British failed in their first attempt to take Bunker Hill. Later in the day they tried again, and again they failed. The frustrated general sent his troops up Bunker Hill one more time. The exhausted Americans did their best to hold out but finally ran out of ammunition and had to retreat.

The British claimed victory, but they had suffered almost four times as many casualties

One of the heroes of the Battle of Bunker Hill was a freed slave named Peter Salem. At a crucial point in the battle, when the colonists were on the verge of defeat, Salem shot the British commander. This stunned the British and helped the colonists rally.

as the Americans. A British general remarked that another victory of this kind would ruin him. Many soldiers, American and British, died at Bunker Hill—but the other important thing that died there was the British confidence that they could easily defeat the Americans.

The Second Continental Congress

The Second Continental Congress had been meeting since May 1775. Delegates from all thirteen colonies attended. After the battles around Boston, the delegates had new decisions to make. Now they were engaged in war. They needed to gather together an army to defend themselves, and they needed a general to take command.

They chose General George Washington, who had served during the French and Indian War. Washington had also served in the House of Burgesses in Virginia and was one of the most respected leaders in the colonies. In June 1775, he was appointed commander-in-chief of the Continental Army.

Who Had the Advantage?

George Washington was an experienced military leader, but the Continental Army was made up of ordinary citizens with few

A British soldier (*left*) and an American soldier (*right*).

weapons. Commanding them wouldn't be easy—and fighting against Britain, the greatest military power in the world, seemed an almost impossible task. Washington worried that he and the Continental Army would be crushed.

On paper, the British had a great advantage. They had about 30,000 professional soldiers, including hired soldiers from Germany. The Americans could only field about 15,000 volunteers. The British soldiers were well armed, well trained, and well paid. The Americans were short on ammunition and even shorter on money.

Most alarming of all was the imbalance between the two navies. The British had 270 mighty warships. The Americans had only eight small ships.

Although the British army and navy were bigger, richer, and more experienced, the Americans did have some advantages. The Americans knew the land they were fighting on, and British troops and supplies would have to cross the Atlantic Ocean on slow boats before they could be deployed.

The Americans were also motivated by powerful ideas—ideas of liberty and independence. One foreign observer described the American fighting spirit: "It is incredible that soldiers composed of men of every age, even of children of fifteen, of whites and blacks, almost naked, unpaid, and rather poorly fed, can march so well and withstand fire so steadfastly."

A recruiting poster for the Continental Army.

African Americans in the Revolution

About 5,000 black Americans served in the Continental Army. Others joined the navy, and some did dangerous work as spies. About 300 blacks joined the British, who promised to free them from slavery if they helped fight the Americans.

Breaking Ties: The Declaration of Independence

After appointing George Washington to head the Continental Army, the Second Continental Congress declared independence from Britain. The Congress appointed a committee to write the official letter that the colonies would send to England. Thomas Jefferson of

Signing the Declaration of Independence.

Virginia wrote the first draft of that letter, America's Declaration of Independence. Benjamin Franklin and others changed words and sections. The final document was approved by the Second Continental Congress on July 4, 1776. Today we still celebrate our independence on the Fourth of July.

The Words of the Declaration

Here is a famous section from the Declaration of Independence:

We hold these truths to be self-evident, that all men are created equal, that they are endowed by their Creator with

The Declaration of Independence.

certain unalienable rights, that among these are life, liberty, and the pursuit of happiness—that to secure these rights, governments are instituted among men, deriving their just powers from the consent of the governed, that whenever any form of government becomes destructive of those ends, it is the right of the people to alter or to abolish it.

The final sentence expresses one of the most radical ideas in the Declaration. It says that people can not only form governments, but also change or replace them when they do not work well anymore.

The Declaration went on to list the actions of the king that made Americans break from British rule, then boldly stated that America would rule itself. It concluded with these last, stirring words:

We, therefore, the Representatives of the UNITED STATES OF AMERICA, in GENERAL CONGRESS Assembled, [do declare] That these United Colonies are, and by Right ought to be, FREE AND INDEPENDENT STATES; that they are absolved from all Allegiance to the British Crown, and that all political Connection between them and the State of Great-Britain, is and ought to be totally dissolved; and that as FREE AND INDEPENDENT STATES they have full Power to levy War, conclude Peace, contract Alliances, establish Commerce, and to do all other Acts and Things which INDEPENDENT STATES may of right do. And for the support of this Declaration, with a firm Reliance on the Protection of divine Providence, we mutually pledge to each other our Lives, our Fortunes, and our sacred Honor.

In other words, the Declaration of Independence stated that America was a new, free country on its own, able to make friends and enemies, wage war, and do business with other countries. The men who signed the Declaration promised that they were willing to risk everything, including their lives and their honor, to start a new country—the United States of America.

America's Most Famous Signature

John Hancock was president of the Second Continental Congress and added the first and most famous signature to the Declaration of Independence. Hancock's signature has become so famous that his name is a slang term for signature. When someone says, "Put your John Hancock here," it means you should sign your name.

"The Times That Try Men's Souls"

The Americans had declared their independence, but they still had to fight for it. Unless they could win the war, the Declaration of Independence would not mean anything.

The first months of war were difficult. Many American soldiers were killed, wounded, or captured in early battles. Others simply gave up and went home.

Some Americans began to wonder if they had made a mistake by declaring indepen-

First money coined by the United States.

dence. But others kept up hope. Thomas Paine, the author of *Common Sense*, wrote another pamphlet, called *The Crisis*. "These are the times that try men's souls," he wrote. By "try,"

Paine meant "test." He was saying that the Revolutionary War was testing the strength of America's spirit. Did Americans have enough determination to keep going? Paine wrote, "The summer soldier and the sunshine patriot will, in this crisis, shrink from the service of his country, but he that stands it *now* deserves the love and thanks of man and woman."

By December 1776, General Washington had barely 3,000 soldiers left. The British troops were right on their heels, forcing them to retreat from New York into New Jersey, then farther south into Pennsylvania. It was cold, and the soldiers were feeling weary and discouraged. On Christmas Eve, Washington gave the order to cross the icy Delaware River once again and march nine miles north to Trenton, New Jersey, under cover of darkness. There they

Thomas Paine.

surprised a company of German soldiers fighting for the British and took 1,000 prisoners.

Surprise victories such as this one encouraged the Americans, but Washington needed more soldiers. Congress offered twenty dollars and one hundred acres of free land in the west to each new volunteer. By the spring of 1777, Washington had 9,000 men. But the next major battles, in Pennsylvania, didn't go well for the American troops. The British army captured Philadelphia and chased the Continental Congress out of town.

Saratoga

Things changed for the better after the Battle of Saratoga, in New York. The British planned to send thousands of troops, under the command of General John Burgoyne, down from Canada to capture territory in New England. While many American soldiers were ragged

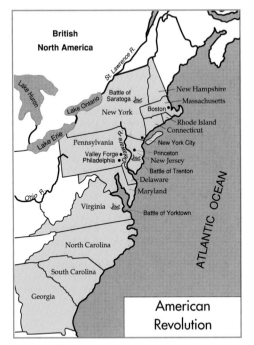

British
North America

St. Lawrence R.

Lake Huron

Lake Ontario

Lake Erie

Battle of Saratoga

New York

Boston

New Hampshire

Massachusetts

Rhode Island

Connecticut

Pennsylvania

Valley Forge
Philadelphia

New York City

Princeton
New Jersey

Battle of Trenton

Delaware

Maryland

Ohio R.

Virginia

Battle of Yorktown

North Carolina

South Carolina

Georgia

ATLANTIC OCEAN

American
Revolution

and half-starved, General Burgoyne traveled with his personal supply of champagne and silver cups in which to drink it!

But the determined Americans made things hard for Burgoyne. Sometimes the British general found his way blocked by huge trees laid across the roads. His troops began to run out of food. They wrote to Britain for supplies and reinforcements, but help never arrived. As Burgoyne's troops grew weaker, the Continental Army grew stronger. In a series of battles, Burgoyne's forces were finally defeated at Saratoga in October 1777. The British general surrendered almost 6,000 soldiers to the Americans.

Saratoga was more than just a major victory for the Americans. It was an event that made America—and the world—realize that the newly declared nation was capable of winning the Revolution. Now Ben Franklin could convince the king of France and his government to help America, and this proved to be a major turning point. Soon the French were shipping arms, ammunition, and troops to America.

The French Enter the War

To win the war, America needed to win on the sea. America had no navy to speak of, but the French navy came to American aid, starting in 1778.

The French sent twenty-four great ships to America, carrying 1,700 guns and 19,000 seamen. The French ships attacked British ships and set up a blockade that prevented the British from delivering supplies and troops.

The French also sent soldiers and generals to help with the war effort. The most famous of these was the Marquis de Lafayette. When he was only nineteen, Lafayette became inspired by the American cause. In 1777, a year before the French officially decided to support the Americans, Lafayette outfitted a ship at his own expense, planning to sail to America.

Lafayette.

French authorities tried to stop him, but he escaped and reached Philadelphia in the summer of 1777. He met George Washington, who was so impressed with the brilliant young Lafayette that he treated him as if he were his own son and made him a major general in the Continental Army.

More European Friends

The French were not the only Europeans who helped the American cause. Baron Friedrich von Steuben [STOO-ben] was a soldier from Prussia who couldn't speak a word of English when he first volunteered to help the Americans. At first, he had to use an interpreter to speak. Once Washington appointed him inspector-general, he taught the Americans military discipline and skills.

The Polish military engineer Thaddeus Kościuszko [kosh-CHOO-shko] came to America in 1776, drawn by the American ideal of freedom. He advised the Americans on battle plans and taught them how to build strong forts. His military know-how also helped the Americans win the Battle of Saratoga.

Women in the Revolution

Many women helped in army camps and on the battlefields during the Revolution. They cooked for the soldiers in camp, tended the wounded, and carried pitchers of water to thirsty soldiers during battles. One brave woman, nicknamed Molly Pitcher, was married to an artilleryman. He was responsible for loading and firing a cannon. When he fell wounded, Molly Pitcher stepped in and took his place.

Molly Pitcher.

Deborah Sampson was another female war hero. Sampson was so eager to fight for independence that she disguised herself as a man so she could join the Continental Army. When she was wounded, she tended her own wounds so no one would discover her secret. Finally she came down with a fever and had to go to the field hospital, where a surprised doctor found out the truth. By that time, she had served in the army for three years!

Heroes and Villains

Nathan Hale just before his execution.

The American Revolution produced famous heroes and notorious villains. One of the great heroes was Nathan Hale, a daring young American spy. In 1776, British soldiers captured Hale and gave orders for his execution. But Hale wasn't frightened. As he waited to be hanged he calmly told those nearby, "I only regret that I have but one life to lose for my country."

Another brave hero was sea captain John Paul Jones. In 1779, Jones and his men attacked a British ship. The Americans were outgunned and seemed to be losing the battle. The British captain called to Jones, asking if he was ready to surrender. Jones called back, "I have not yet begun to fight!" Then Jones pulled alongside the British ship and ordered his men to board it. The sailors fought by moonlight for two hours, with both ships in flames. At last the British captain surrendered. Jones's brave and defiant words became a rallying cry for patriotic Americans.

John Paul Jones.

For most of the Revolution, Benedict Arnold was an important American leader. He helped the Americans win several battles, including the Battle of Saratoga. But Arnold, a proud man, felt unappreciated. So he secretly started working for the British. He tried to send the British advice on how to attack the important American fort at West Point. But his plot was discovered and he fled to England. Benedict Arnold has been a synonym for traitor ever since.

Valley Forge

For the Americans, the low point of the Revolutionary War was the long, bitterly cold winter of 1777. While the British troops relaxed in Philadelphia, the Americans barely survived in tiny log huts in Valley Forge, twenty miles away. They were cold, hungry, and sick. They fought no battles that winter, but 2,000 men died from sickness. One soldier wrote in his diary: "I am sick—discontented—and out of humor. Poor food—hard lodging—cold weather —fatigue—nasty clothes—nasty cookery—vomit half my time—smoked out of my senses."

But that hard winter in Valley Forge brought new discipline and order to the Continental Army, thanks to training from Baron Steuben. Under his expert guidance, the soldiers sharpened their fighting skills and renewed their confidence. After Valley Forge, things began to improve.

Washington and Lafayette inspect their shivering army at Valley Forge, 1777.

War's End: "The World Turned Upside Down"

In 1781, the British general Cornwallis marched most of the British army to Yorktown, Virginia. George Washington knew this part of Virginia well, and he knew that the British had camped at a spot where they could be surrounded. Washington sent a message to the leader of the French fleet, asking him to sail to Yorktown. Then Washington marched his army south from New Jersey.

When Washington heard that the French fleet had arrived, he was so happy he tossed his hat into the air. The Americans encircled the British army on land while French ships sailed into the bay, cutting off their chances to escape by sea.

American and French guns pounded away at Cornwallis's troops. Finally, on October 19, 1781, the British army surrendered. The Redcoats marched in a long line, turning their weapons over to the Americans, while their band played a tune called "The World Turned Upside Down."

They must have felt that their world had turned upside down on that day in history. A small and unprepared nation of disunited colonies had beaten the mightiest nation on earth! Although the peace treaty between America and Britain wasn't signed until 1783, the Americans clinched their independence at the Battle of Yorktown.

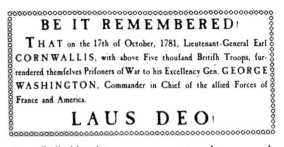

BE IT REMEMBERED!

THAT on the 17th of October, 1781, Lieutenant-General Earl CORNWALLIS, with above Five thousand British Troops, surrendered themselves Prisoners of War to his Excellency Gen. GEORGE WASHINGTON, Commander in Chief of the allied Forces of France and America.

LAUS DEO!

Handbills like this one were printed to spread the news of the British surrender. "Laus Deo" is Latin for "Praise Be to God."

Making a Constitutional Government

Starting Over

Once the Americans declared their independence, they had to develop their own government. The Declaration of Independence had laid down some ideas about government, such as the idea that a government should protect people's inalienable rights, but the Declaration did not explain how a government based on such ideas should be organized, and Americans in different states had different ideas.

During the Revolutionary War and early 1780s, the most important decisions about government were left to the individual states. Each state created its own constitution, or written plan of government. Each set up its own government, raised its own money, and formed its own trading partnerships with foreign nations and with other states. Each state printed its own paper money, too.

The Articles of Confederation

The members of the Continental Congress believed that the states should make their own arrangements, but they also believed that a central government would be necessary to allow the states to cooperate. After adopting the Declaration of Independence, delegates presented a written plan for a central government. This plan called for a strong central government, but many Americans worried that a strong national government might boss them around the way the British king and parliament had.

The Continental Congress argued over many other questions. How would states be represented in the central government? How much money would each state contribute to the national treasury?

The members of the Continental Congress argued for a year and a half, until November 1777. In the end they approved a document called the "Articles of Confederation," which described a loose union of states with a weak central government. There was no president and no court system. The central government couldn't make people pay taxes or regulate trade among the states and foreign nations.

Getting the states to agree to the Articles of Confederation was even harder than writing them. Each of the thirteen states had to ratify, or vote their approval of, every one of the Articles. That took almost four more years! At last, in 1781, all thirteen states agreed, and the Articles of Confederation became our first constitution.

Shays' Rebellion

As it turned out, the Articles of Confederation didn't work all that well. The articles left too much power in the hands of the states and limited what the central government could do. The event that showed the weakness of the Articles of Confederation was Shays' Rebellion.

In 1786, farmers in Massachusetts were having a hard time paying their taxes. They tried to get help from the state. When their requests were denied, a farmer named Daniel Shays led an attack on a U.S. arsenal, to seize the weapons in it. Congress was too weak to defend the arsenal and had to rely on troops from the state of Massachusetts to end the violence.

Shays' Rebellion showed Americans that if the national government was going to keep the country united, stable, and at peace, it needed more power. John Adams said that the Articles were like a "rope of sand" that didn't bind the states together.

During Shays' Rebellion angry citizens attacked tax collectors and government officials.

Drafting the Constitution

In May 1787, leaders of the Continental Congress asked representatives from every state to assemble in Philadelphia. The purpose of their meeting was to improve the Articles of Confederation. But that's not what happened.

The delegates from Virginia arrived one week ahead of the rest and, meeting by themselves, decided that what was really needed was a new constitution, not just a revision of the Articles. They sat down and did the job on their own, before any other delegates arrived. The result was called the Virginia Plan. It was presented to the other state representatives when they got to Philadelphia, and many of its ideas eventually became part of the U.S. Constitution.

James Madison: Father of the Constitution

The previous year a man from Virginia named James Madison had begun to plan a new system of government for America. He started by studying histories of Greece and Rome, and he borrowed ideas about government from many civilizations, ancient and modern. He read the

James Madison.

writings of great philosophers who wrote about ideal governments. When Madison had read all the books he could find in America, he wrote to his friends in Europe, asking them to send more books.

Madison wanted to create a government strong enough to put down rebellions and prevent states from ignoring federal laws. But he also wanted a government that would not interfere with people's basic rights. Madison's ideas became the basis for the Virginia Plan.

Madison is called the Father of the Constitution for many reasons:

1. He researched and prepared a model government plan in advance of the Constitutional Convention.
2. He urged delegates to attend the Convention and sent letters to leaders in all states.
3. He arrived early and prepared the Virginia Plan before other delegates arrived.
4. He was among the most vocal, hardworking, and influential of the debaters at the Convention—he made over 150 speeches!
5. He took down detailed notes, our only thorough record of the debates at the Convention.
6. He wrote a set of important newspaper articles, called the Federalist Papers, to promote adoption of the Constitution among the states.
7. He composed the first ten amendments to the Constitution, which we call the Bill of Rights.

Debates and Compromises: The Constitutional Convention of 1787

When delegates arrived at the Constitutional Convention in May 1787, they began by talking about Madison's Virginia Plan. Much discussion and debate centered on Madison's plan to structure the government into three branches: executive, legislative, and judicial. Those three branches still form the basic structure of our United States government today.

The executive branch. Executives are the people who execute or carry out the laws of the country. The executive branch is in charge of running the government and the president is the leader of the executive branch.

The legislative branch. To legislate means to make laws. The legislative branch, also called Congress, is in charge of making the laws that people must follow. Congress is made up of two houses, the Senate and the House of Representatives.

The judicial branch. Judicial comes from a Latin word for judgment. The judicial branch includes the courts and judges, who oversee the laws of the nation and settle disagreements about those laws. The Supreme Court is the highest American court.

Madison's plan to divide the government caused disagreements between the large and the small states. If the number of representatives each state sent to Congress were determined by the number of people that lived in that state, larger states would have an advantage. The smaller states, with fewer people (such as Maryland, New Hampshire, and Delaware) were afraid that larger states would have more power, because they would have more representatives in the legislative branch. The states with larger populations (such as New York, Pennsylvania, and Virginia) thought it unfair that a state with only 5,000 people could have as much say in the government as a state with half a million.

A delegate from Connecticut came up with a solution. Divide the legislative branch in two, he suggested. Establish a Senate and a House of Representatives. Every state, no matter the size, would elect two Senate representatives; but the number of elected officials sent by a state to the House of Representatives would be determined by that state's population. This idea, called the Connecticut Compromise, solved the problem and created a legislative structure that is still in place today.

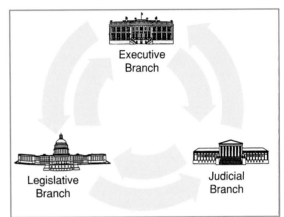

The three branches of the government.

Slavery and the "Three-Fifths Compromise"

Delegates to the Constitutional Convention also argued about slavery. Wealthy Southerners owned plantations on which slaves planted and harvested crops like rice, tobacco, and cotton. In 1787, about 750,000 black people with roots in Africa lived in America. These black Africans made up about one-fifth of the population. Ninety percent of those black Americans were slaves.

Northerners did not generally grow their crops on large plantations, so they did not depend as heavily on slavery. During the Revolution two states, Pennsylvania and Massachusetts, even made slavery illegal. Some northern delegates came to the Constitutional Convention with the hope that slavery would be outlawed everywhere.

Angry debates went on for weeks. Although slaves could not vote, they did have an influence on the House of Representatives. Delegates argued whether a population count should include slaves. If it did, it would increase the number of representatives Southern states sent to Congress. Southern states wanted every slave counted; Northerners did not want slaves counted at all. Finally, the delegates came up with a "Three-Fifths Compromise," agreeing to count every five slaves as three people in a state's population.

The delegates wrote other clauses regarding slavery. Congress was not allowed to pass any

Slaves at work, with a plantation house in the background.

laws to control or regulate the slave trade for twenty years. Northern delegates reluctantly accepted a clause that allowed slave owners to recapture runaway slaves and bring them back from other states. Southern delegates unhappily allowed Congress to collect tax money from plantation owners for every slave they owned.

In the end, all the delegates accepted these compromises, but many were unhappy with them. George Washington (who owned slaves in Virginia) wrote Thomas Jefferson (who also owned slaves in Virginia) that it was his strong wish "to see some plan adopted by which slavery in this country might be abolished by law."

The United States finally did abolish slavery, but not for many years. All the states in the North had abolished slavery by the 1820s, but slavery was not prohibited in the South until after the Civil War.

What Does the Constitution Say and Do?

The Constitution that was drafted by the Constitutional Convention in 1787 is the same Constitution we use today. It has changed over the years only by the addition of amendments, or changes. Its words are the supreme law of our country.

The Constitution begins with a long introduction, called the preamble, which states the goals of the new United States government:

> *We the People of the United States, in order to form a more perfect Union, establish justice, insure domestic tranquility, provide for the common defense, promote the general welfare, and secure the blessings of liberty to ourselves and our posterity, do ordain and establish this Constitution for the United States of America.*

Of the 170 constitutions used by countries around the world today, the United States Constitution is the oldest.

Let's take a look at what this preamble means.

We the People . . . This famous opening phrase reminds us that this Constitution was written and agreed to by American citizens. It was not the act of a king handing down the law to everyone else. Planning a government in this way was entirely new among the nations of the world in 1787, and so it was important to announce that at the beginning.

Also, by saying "we the people" instead of "we the states" or "we the representatives of New York, New Jersey, etc.," the preamble makes the point that this Constitution is a binding agreement among all the people of the country—not just among the leaders of the various states.

. . . to form a more perfect Union . . . The United States was already a union of states under the Articles of Confederation, but the Constitution's goal was an even better system of government.

. . . establish justice . . . This phrase refers to the strong authority of the Constitution and the judicial branch of the newly created government. It is a clear reminder that the law of the land is the same law for all states.

. . . insure domestic tranquility . . . Tranquility means peace. Domestic means at home. One of the purposes of the Constitution is to ensure that peace is not disrupted, as it was in Shays' Rebellion.

. . . provide for the common defense. . . This phrase states that the government can create

and maintain a national army to defend all the states, offering common defense, or protection for everyone.

. . . *promote the general welfare* . . . The Constitution guarantees that the central government will make decisions about trade and money issues for the benefit of all states and all people. No state will be allowed to let its individual interests harm the welfare of another state.

. . . *secure the blessings of liberty to ourselves and our posterity* . . . This phrase recalls the fragile peace that existed in the years following the Revolution. At the time this was written, several foreign nations—including Britain and Spain—were in a position to attack the United States. Pirates raided American merchant vessels on the open seas, and Native Americans were still allies with foreign nations. War might break out at any time. The freedom that had been won through the Revolution had to be secured, or kept safe, by the new government.

At the same time, freedom could be threatened when citizens or groups tried to get too much power. Enemies from within the nation could do as much damage as enemies from without, and the Constitution was designed to protect against either. "Posterity" refers to the people of the future. The Constitution is an attempt to guarantee liberty not only for those who wrote it and voted for it but also for all generations to come.

Checks and Balances

The founding fathers who wrote the Constitution wanted to make sure that no single branch of government could take too much power for itself, so they devised a system of checks and balances. The checks are ways in which each branch keeps the other branches from becoming too powerful. The balances are ways that the branches equal one another in power and responsibilities.

In this system, one branch has the authority to overrule certain decisions of the other branches. For example, the president can veto (or reject) a bill passed by Congress, but Congress can override the president's veto with a two-thirds majority vote in each house. For another example, the president appoints justices to the Supreme Court, but the Senate must approve the appointments.

The Bill of Rights

Finally, the delegates came to an agreement on the rules describing the new government of the United States of America, and they were ready to share the document—the United States Constitution—with others. But the states had to ratify (or approve) the Constitution before it became the law of the land.

That process took three more years of debating, but finally the U.S. Constitution was rat-ified in 1790. Many states asked for certain changes, or amendments, that guaranteed the rights of individual citizens—rights such as the freedom to speak, the freedom to publish newspapers and books, the freedom to choose a religion, and the freedom to get together in a peaceful assembly. In 1791, ten amendments were added to the Constitution. We still call those first ten amendments the Bill of Rights. They promise important liberties to all Amer-ican citizens.

For example, the First Amendment states that Americans can worship as they choose (this is called freedom of religion), can speak freely as long as they are not unfairly harming oth-ers (freedom of speech), and can publish opinions freely, again as long as they do not unfairly harm or lie about others (freedom of the press). The Fourth Amendment promises that the armed services and the police will treat Americans fairly and prohibits unreasonable search and seizure. Other Amendments promise that all Americans have the right to due process of law. They will be judged through fair trials, with decisions made by a jury of fellow Ameri-cans. And even when they are found guilty of crimes, Americans are protected by the Bill of Rights from cruel and unusual punishments.

National, State, and Local Governments

The Constitution describes the government of our nation. But states have constitutions, too. State governments, just like the national government, are divided into three branches—executive, legislative, and judicial—in a system of checks and balances. Just as the president leads the nation, so a governor leads the state, helped by representatives in the state legisla-ture. States are divided into cities and counties, which have their own local governments as well. Most city governments are led by a mayor, elected by the people and assisted by mem-bers of a city council.

In the United States, we believe in a government "of the people, by the people, and for the people," as President Abraham Lincoln said in 1863. How do Americans participate in their national, state, and local governments?

They vote in elections to choose their leaders and representatives. Often they volunteer or run for office themselves. They write letters to the editor of their local newspaper and let-ters to their government representatives, explaining what they believe the government should be doing. They pay taxes, which is money that goes to help run governments and all that they help to make happen. Tax money helps build schools and auditoriums, parks and roads. It pays to keep the streets clean and light the street lamps. It pays the salaries of sol-diers and policemen, teachers and librarians.

Early Presidents and Politics

Our First President: George Washington

Americans were pleased when George Washington took office as the United States' first president in 1789. He had a hard job because he had no model to follow. The Constitution didn't spell out all the details of the president's job.

Congress decided to create a cabinet, a group of advisors to help the president make decisions. Washington's first job was to pick the best men he could find to fill these positions. The cabinet members were called secretaries, and each cabinet member oversaw one part of the government. The secretary of state worked on relationships with other countries. The secretary of the treasury worked on the nation's money. We still have these jobs and others like them in the government today. Together these people are called the president's administration.

George Washington.

Another member of Washington's administration was his vice president. In the country's first years, the presidential candidate who received the second-largest number of votes became vice president.

According to the Constitution, presidents were elected for four-year terms. George Washington served as president for two terms, or eight years—and those eight years were not easy ones. In 1793, war broke out between France and Great Britain. Washington made sure that his young nation, barely recovered from its own Revolutionary War, stayed out of the war in Europe.

There were wars of words and ideas in his own cabinet, though, especially between Thomas Jefferson, his secretary of state, and Alexander Hamilton, his secretary of the treasury. When Washington's second term ended, he had had enough of their arguing. Besides, he felt that no president should serve for more than two terms. He feared that if he died while he was still president, it would look like later presidents should serve for the rest of their lives, which would make them seem like kings. Washington retired to his beloved home in Mount Vernon, Virginia, and lived only two more years.

The Beginning of Political Parties

When people run for president today, they run as candidates from a political party, as a Democrat or a Republican, for example. People who belong to the same political party agree on a lot of things and disagree with those in other parties. Political parties are a way people with common beliefs work together.

But when George Washington was elected, there were no political parties. Political parties as we know them began with those disagreements between Jefferson and Hamilton. These two men held very different beliefs about who should rule the country and what kind of government the United States should have.

Jefferson saw the United States as a nation of small farmers. He trusted the American people to make many decisions for themselves and thought a strong central government might get in the way of freedom. He thought it was better for the state and local governments to have more power than the central government.

Hamilton thought it was a bad idea to give Americans that much freedom. While Jefferson championed the common people, Hamilton was suspicious of them. Hamilton once shouted at Jefferson: "Your people, sir, is a great beast!" Hamilton favored a stronger central government and also tended to favor merchants and tradesmen over farmers. He believed that if people running businesses worked closely with people running the government, that partnership would strengthen the nation. He argued that the United States should run a national bank that could help businesses.

Jefferson opposed Hamilton's bank. It would be dangerous, he argued, to have so much money under the control of one big bank. He feared that by following Hamilton's policies, a small number of Americans would become rich and powerful.

Jefferson's followers called themselves Republicans, because

Thomas Jefferson.

they believed that in a republic, the common man should play a big part in the government. Hamilton's followers called themselves Federalists, because they believed in a strong federal (or national) government. People took sides, and soon the Republicans and the Federalists became the nation's first political parties.

At that time, most Americans did not think that parties would be a permanent part of the political system. But, little by little, it became clear that parties were here to stay.

Today, we realize that political parties are an important part of our democratic system of government. People will always disagree about what should be done, even though they all sincerely want to do what is best for the country. Political parties allow people with similar views to join together to campaign for the ideas that seem right to them.

The two major parties today are the Democrats and the Republicans (although not the same Republicans as in Jefferson's day). In elections, Democrats run against Republicans; sometimes one party wins, and sometimes the other one does, but the losing party keeps an eye on what the winning party does and tries to convince the voters that it should win next time. Meanwhile, other people who hold beliefs different from the two main parties are called

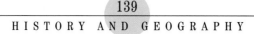

independents. Both parties try hard to get the independents' votes. And if both parties fail to satisfy voters, anyone who gets enough supporters can start a new party! That has happened several times in American history.

A New Capital City

For a while New York was the capital of the United States. But Southern representatives had to travel far from home to get there, so Congress decided to build another city, halfway between the North and the South. They founded the city we now call Washington, and they made sure that the land around it wasn't part of any state. They called the area the District of Columbia. Now we call our capital Washington, D.C.

The plan for the new capital was drawn up by a French mapmaker and artist named Pierre L'Enfant [pee-AYR lahn-FAHN]. L'Enfant worked together with a talented African-American surveyor named Benjamin Banneker to lay out the streets and buildings for the new city.

It took many years to build the house for the president and his family, now called the White House, and the new office building for Congress, called the Capitol. John Adams, who was elected president after Washington, was the first to live in the President's House. In 1800, when he and his wife moved in, the building still had no stairs to the second floor and many of its walls were still unfinished.

The White House.

Our Second President: John Adams

John Adams was one of the hardest-working, most vocal, and most influential of all the Founding Fathers. He had taken part in almost every important action that helped to form our new country. During the Revolutionary War, Adams served without pay as a leader of the Continental Congress. Later, he served as the country's first vice president.

When Washington stepped down, Adams ran against Thomas Jefferson for president. Adams just barely won the election, which meant that Jefferson became his vice president. Then the arguments between Federalists and Republicans got even worse. Adams was a Federalist, which

John Adams.

meant that the Republicans did not agree with him, but many people in his own party disagreed with him, too.

Like Washington, Adams wanted to keep America out of the war in Europe. But plenty of Americans wanted their country to join in the war, and they got angry at Adams. Tired of all the criticism, John Adams approved laws that placed a stiff penalty on anyone who criticized the government. These laws limited the rights of free speech and a free press promised in the Bill of Rights. A huge storm of protest developed. During his years as president, Adams grew bitter. He once groused that he felt he lived in "an enemy country."

Abigail Adams, the wife of John Adams, wrote letters to her husband when he was a delegate to the Continental Congress. She noted that some of the rights granted to men did not apply equally to women, and she tried to convince her husband to do something about this:

March 31, 1776. I long to hear that you have declared an independency—and, by the way, in the new code of laws, which I suppose it will be necessary for you to make, I desire you would remember the ladies, and be more generous and favorable to them than [were] your ancestors.

Best of Friends, Worst of Enemies

John Adams and Thomas Jefferson started out as friends. They worked together on the Declaration of Independence. After the Revolution, John Adams represented the United States in Great Britain while Thomas Jefferson represented the country in France. They wrote letters to each other and shared many hopes for their new nation.

The troubles between these two great men began when Washington became president. Adams was vice president, and he leaned in favor of Hamilton's Federalist party. Jefferson was secretary of state, and he was the leader of the Republican party. The two men became fierce political enemies and eventually ran against each other for president. When Adams became president, with Jefferson his vice president, their friendship broke down.

But this sad story has a happy ending. Both Adams and Jefferson lived long lives. Near the end of their lives, they became friends once again and started writing letters back and forth. As he lay dying, John Adams thought of his friend Thomas Jefferson. His last words were, "Thomas Jefferson still survives." On the very same day, hundreds of miles away, Jefferson died as well, thinking of his friend John Adams. By a spooky twist of fate, both men died on the very same day: July 4, 1826, the fiftieth anniversary of the signing of the Declaration of Independence!

Our Third President: Thomas Jefferson

Thomas Jefferson was one of the most extraordinary men in an age full of extraordinary men. Like George Washington, Jefferson was a Virginia plantation owner. But he was interested in many subjects besides farming. He studied literature, foreign languages, philosophy, politics, astronomy, geography, medicine, music, and architecture. He always bought books when he traveled. His library grew and grew until he contributed the books he owned to help start the Library of Congress, the official library of the United States. He wrote the Declaration of Independence and designed many beautiful buildings, such as his home in Virginia called Monticello.

Mr. Jefferson's Big Purchase

Jefferson was a man of vision. He could imagine a time when the population of the United States would have grown so that it needed more territory. He also feared that if foreign powers controlled surrounding areas, they could make trade and travel difficult.

In those days, France owned most of the land west of the Mississippi, from Canada to Mexico, and controlled all trade down the Mississippi River through the port of New Orleans. This vast French territory was

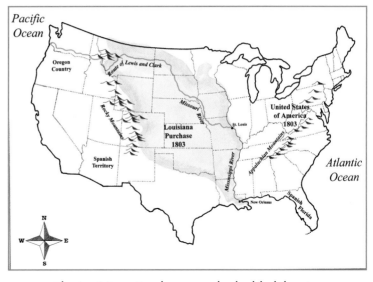

The Louisiana Purchase nearly doubled the size of the United States.

called Louisiana, after France's King Louis XIV. Jefferson sent James Monroe, his secretary of state, to France to ask the French leader, Napoleon, to sell the city of New Orleans. As it turned out, Napoleon offered to sell the entire territory of Louisiana!

So in 1803, for $15 million, Jefferson bought the entire Louisiana territory, an area of about 828,000 square miles, which now includes Iowa, Missouri, Arkansas, Nebraska, Kansas, Oklahoma, most of South Dakota, and parts of seven other states. Overnight, Jefferson doubled the size of the United States and gained control of the Mississippi River. The deal he struck came to be called the Louisiana Purchase.

Lewis and Clark

With the curiosity of a scientist, Thomas Jefferson wanted to learn all he could about the new, unexplored lands to the west. So the next year, in 1804, he sent an expedition to explore and map the land west of the Mississippi. In the years 1804 to 1806, a group of explorers led by two men, Meriwether Lewis and William Clark, walked and canoed all the way to the Pacific Ocean and then back to Virginia.

Lewis and Clark asked a young Shoshone Indian woman, Sacajawea, to help them cross the plains and mountains and talk with the Native

Sacagawea helped Lewis and Clark explore the Louisiana Territory.

Americans they met. They made maps and wrote down their observations concerning weather patterns, rocks and soil types, plants, and animals. They found the bones of a forty-five-foot dinosaur. They recorded 200 new species of plants. They brought back the skull of a prehistoric mastodon, which Jefferson proudly displayed at Monticello.

Our Fourth President: James Madison

James Madison was more of a scholar and a philosopher than he was a politician. Not as strong in his peacekeeping resolve as Jefferson and Adams had been, Madison allowed the United States to be drawn into the war in Europe.

There were good reasons why the Americans would consider fighting. Both Britain and France were searching American ships at sea. The British would kidnap American sailors and force them to fight against France.

The British were doing something else that made Americans angry. Some British officials and troops still lived in forts at the western edge of American territory. They made friends with Native Americans nearby and encouraged them to attack American settlers.

Even so, not all Americans agreed as to which side they supported in the European war. Some wanted the United States to go to war with Britain; some wanted to fight France; most didn't want the United States to go to war at all. In 1812, those who supported a war with Britain were called the war hawks. They convinced Madison to declare war on Britain.

The War of 1812

So the United States went back to fighting with Britain, in a two-year-long series of battles we now call the War of 1812. Afraid that the British would capture Washington, President Madison left the capital and took command of a fort in Maryland.

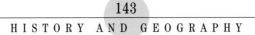
The British sailed into the Chesapeake Bay. They did invade Washington, but they found the town deserted. All the members of Congress, even the army had fled. Brave Dolley Madison, the wife of the president, stayed in Washington until the last minute, gathering up important papers and valuables. The British started fires in the President's House, the Capitol, and other government buildings. They worried that the empty town was a trap, though, so they returned to their ships before they had completely destroyed Washington. The President's House was later rebuilt, and—to cover up the fire damage—painted white. That's how it got its modern name, the White House.

The War of 1812 dragged on for two years. Finally the two tired countries signed a peace treaty on Christmas Eve, 1814. The War of 1812 was the last time Britain and America ever went to war against each other.

During the War of 1812, Francis Scott Key witnessed the British bombardment of Fort McHenry and wrote "The Star-Spangled Banner," which later became the national anthem.

The biggest battle of the War of 1812 wasn't fought until after the peace treaty was signed. Word of the treaty had not yet reached the city of New Orleans. American troops led by General Andrew Jackson took a well-protected position. British troops attacked. The Americans fired their rifles and the British, marching in the open, didn't have a chance. Many died in the Battle of New Orleans, but the battle created a new national hero—Andrew Jackson.

Our Fifth President: James Monroe

James Monroe had joined George Washington's Revolutionary Army at the age of eighteen. In one battle, a bullet lodged in his shoulder and stayed there the rest of his life. He studied law with his friend Thomas Jefferson, and represented the United States as an ambassador to France. He was elected governor of Virginia and appointed secretary of state by James Madison. Monroe was elected president in 1816 and re-elected by an overwhelming majority in 1820.

The Problem of Slavery

In 1820, Missouri was ready to become a state. That made some people worried. As the country grew, the states argued more and more about slavery. The big plantation owners of the South depended on the work done by slaves to make money. In the North, people made money on smaller farms and, more and more, by working in factories. By 1820, almost no one in the North owned slaves. In fact, a few people in the North had begun to argue loudly against slavery.

Those who wanted to abolish slavery throughout the United States came to be called abolitionists. Abolitionists fought against slavery in many ways: by publishing books, delivering speeches, helping runaway slaves escape, and convincing states to pass laws forbidding slavery.

Arguments about slavery went on constantly in Congress. But since there were equal numbers of free states (in the North, without slavery) and slave states (in the South, where slaves were held), the arguments almost always ended in a draw. If Missouri were to become a state— a slave state—it would tip the balance, and there would be more slave states than free states.

The answer? A compromise. Missouri was admitted into the Union, but so was Maine: one slave state and one free state, bringing the number of states to twenty-four and preserving the delicate balance. This decision was called the Missouri Compromise.

The Monroe Doctrine

In a presidential message in 1823, Monroe proclaimed what we now call the Monroe Doctrine. A doctrine is an official statement of policy. In this case, Monroe made an official statement about how the United States would interact with other nations. He was especially concerned about the way that European nations continued to try to exert their power in North America, South America, and the Caribbean—in other words, in the Western Hemisphere. One hundred years before, that territory was a New World being explored by many different European countries. Now, Monroe wanted Europe to understand, the United States of America could take care of itself—and its neighbors.

The new policy was essentially a warning to European powers. The United States would consider its own security threatened if a nation from elsewhere in the world tried to establish a new colony or interfere with any government in the Western Hemisphere. Monroe stated that the United States had no plans to interfere in Europe or conquer any of its lands. In other words, he sent this message to Europe: "You stay out of our affairs, and we'll stay out of yours."

Our Sixth President: John Quincy Adams

The son of John and Abigail Adams, John Quincy Adams was practically raised to be president. When he was ten, he accompanied his father on a diplomatic mission abroad. At fourteen, he became secretary to the American ambassador to Russia. He studied in private schools in Europe and at Harvard University in Massachusetts.

John Quincy Adams became president, but he was never popular with the people. He left the White House after four years. Later Adams served in the House of Representatives, where he worked hard to abolish slavery. He was replaced as president by the much more popular Andrew Jackson.

Our Seventh President: Andrew Jackson

President Andrew Jackson, elected in 1828, was a different kind of president from those who came before him. He was sometimes called the president of the common man. Born in the backwoods on the border between North and South Carolina, he was described by a neighbor as "the most roaring, rollicking, game-cocking, horse-racing, card-playing, mischievous fellow that ever lived."

Andrew Jackson.

Jackson had fought against the British during the Revolution and against the Indians siding with the British in the War of 1812. By leading the American army to victory in the Battle of New Orleans, he became one of that war's heroes. He was a man of the frontier and a man of action, and a huge majority of voters elected him. People poured into Washington, D.C., for his inauguration. Crowds swarmed through the White House, making a mess, standing on satin chairs in their muddy boots, and knocking over punch bowls.

Jackson worked to make the United States more democratic than it had been. Up to this time, only white men who owned a certain amount of property had the right to vote. Jackson supported the right of *all* white men to vote, regardless of their wealth, property, or education. He was a populist, which means he believed in the wisdom of the people. He was suspicious of anything that gave rich people more power in the government.

Before he became president, Jackson had led troops in battle against Native Americans. As president, Jackson continued his efforts to turn Indian land into U.S. territory. He urged Congress to pass the Indian Removal Bill, which allowed the American government to force Native American tribes to move from their lands and homes, sometimes more than a thousand miles away. Many were moved to what was called Indian Territory, now the state of Oklahoma.

One southeastern tribe, the Cherokee, refused to go, but American soldiers forced them to walk 800 miles to Indian Territory. Many of them died along this Trail of Tears.

This painting captures the hardships endured by the Cherokee people along the Trail of Tears.

Reformers

Making a More Perfect Nation

Throughout the 1800s, brave men and women worked to make America a nation where all people had the liberty promised by the Declaration of Independence. Reformers started schools, organized meetings, gave speeches and published articles to convince other people to believe in their causes. The abolitionists represented one of the biggest reform movements, but there were many others.

Dorothea Dix fought for the rights of the mentally ill. In the early 1800s, people with mental illnesses were imprisoned with people who had committed terrible crimes like murder. Dix believed that people who were mentally ill needed special care in hospitals, not prisons. She encouraged state governments to run mental hospitals, worked to improve conditions in those hospitals, and convinced doctors to treat mentally ill people with more kindness and understanding.

Horace Mann was a pioneering reformer of American education. In the nineteenth century, the few people who finished high school or college were the sons of rich families. Some schools stayed open only a few months a year. Mann believed that more people—men and women, rich and poor—deserved a good education. He worked to make public schools, run by state governments, provide education for most children at least half of the year.

Dorothea Dix worked for better treatment for the mentally ill.

Women's Rights

Lucretia Mott and Elizabeth Cady Stanton believed that America's promise of liberty for all would not be fulfilled until women's rights equaled men's. In July 1848, Mott and Stanton organized a meeting in Seneca Falls, New York, inviting people to talk about how to promote the cause of women's rights. One hundred people attended, and they shocked many Americans by demanding that women be given the right to vote. In a document called the Declaration of Sentiments and Resolutions, modeled after the Declaration of Independence, they wrote that men seemed to desire "an absolute tyranny" over women. But the women countered: "We hold these truths to be self-evident: that all men and women are created equal."

Amelia Bloomer attended the convention at Seneca Falls. She was the editor of a magazine that supported equal rights for women. Bloomer also wanted to see reforms in the way women dressed. She believed that women should be free to wear comfortable clothes that allowed them to live a more active life. The loose-fitting, comfortable pants worn under a short skirt are still called bloomers in her honor.

Sojourner Truth

Sojourner Truth was an African-American woman born into slavery in New York in 1795. She gained her freedom in 1827, when New York freed its slaves. At that time she stopped using her given name and began calling herself Sojourner Truth. A sojourner is someone who visits a place for a while, then moves on, and Sojourner Truth saw herself as someone who traveled from place to place, helping people see the truth. She began to speak publicly in support of abolition and women's rights. Although she never learned to read and write, she was a powerful speaker.

Sojourner Truth.

In 1851, Sojourner Truth attended a women's convention in Ohio. Many convention participants did not support her attendance. They were afraid that their cause, the rights of women, would be damaged if it were linked with the rights of blacks. During the meeting, a clergyman argued against women's rights. He said that Jesus Christ was a man and described how Eve in the Bible had tempted Adam to disobey God's orders. He also argued that women were inferior in intellect, or brainpower, to men. The atmosphere of the convention thickened with hostility.

Then Sojourner Truth rose from her seat and approached the platform. Several women whispered: "For God's sake, don't let her speak!" But the president of the convention allowed Sojourner Truth to speak and later wrote down her recollection of what Sojourner Truth said:

Well, children, where there's so much racket there must be something out o' kilter. I think that 'twixt the negroes of the South and the women of the North, all talkin' about rights, the white men will be in a fix pretty soon. But what's all this talking about?

That man over there says that women need to be helped into carriages, and lifted over ditches, and to have the best place everywhere. Nobody helps me into carriages, or over mud-puddles, or gives me any best place! And ain't I a woman?

Sojourner Truth pulled back her sleeve to show her right arm. Then, in a voice "like rolling thunder," she continued:

> Look at me! Look at my arm! I have ploughed and planted, and gathered into barns, and no man could head me! And ain't I a woman? I could work as much and eat as much as man—when I could get it—and bear the lash as well! And ain't I a woman? I have borne thirteen children, and seen them most all sold off to slavery, and when I cried out with my mother's grief, none but Jesus heard me! And ain't I a woman?
>   Then they talk about this thing in my head; what's this they call it?

Someone in the audience whispered the word she was looking for—intellect. And Sojourner Truth continued:

> That's it, honey. What's that got to do with women's rights or negros' rights? If my cup won't hold but a pint, and yours holds a quart, wouldn't you be mean not to let me have my half-measure full?

The crowd cheered. Then Sojourner Truth pointed her finger and sent a sharp, fiery glance at the ministers who had argued against women's rights:

> Then that little man in black there, he says women can't have as much rights as men, 'cause Christ wasn't a woman! Where did your Christ come from? From God and woman! Man had nothing to do with Him!
>   If the first woman God ever made was strong enough to turn the world upside down all alone, these women together ought to be able to turn it back, and get it right side up again! And now that they is asking to do it, the men better let them.

By this point the applause was so enthusiastic and loud that Sojourner Truth had to pause before speaking her final words:

> Obliged to you for hearing me, and now old Sojourner Truth ain't got nothing more to say.

Sojourner Truth's speech had turned the tide in favor of women's rights and "turned the sneers and jeers of an excited crowd into notes of respect and admiration." Hundreds rushed up to shake hands with her and bid her good luck in her continuing quest to help America live up to its ideas of justice and equality.

III.

Visual Arts

Introduction

This chapter complements the history and geography chapters by discussing examples of medieval, Islamic, African, Chinese, and American art. Parents and teachers can build on the brief treatment offered here by exposing children to additional books and pictures and by taking them to visit museums and interesting buildings. Although books are delightful and informative, there is no substitute for the experience of seeing works of art in person. Many museums make this experience possible for all by offering free admission once a week.

Children should experience art not only as viewers but also as creators. They should be encouraged to draw, cut, paste, and mold with clay, to imitate styles and artists they have encountered and develop a style of their own.

Art of the Middle Ages

Cathedrals

In the Middle Ages, a church was built in the center of almost every town in Europe, and magnificent Gothic cathedrals were created in the larger towns and cities.

These cathedrals were designed to suggest the majesty of God and to inspire prayer. Outside, towers and spires emphasize height and grandeur. Inside, tall ceilings create awe-inspiring spaces, sometimes one hundred-feet high. Throughout the building, statues, paintings, and stained-glass windows depict stories from the Bible and the lives of the saints.

Here are some stained-glass windows from the cathedral in Chartres, France. The circular window is called a rose window. It is high up in the cathedral and very big, so it casts colored light through much of the building.

One of the most beautiful Gothic cathedrals was built in Chartres [SHAR-truh], France. Walking into Chartres Cathedral is like walking inside a rainbow. Standing inside this enormous space, you feel very small, but the soft light and colorful windows make you feel warm and protected, too. Light filters through large stained-glass windows, casting colors on the floor.

Chartres Cathedral is still in the very center of the town. Can you

Chartres Cathedral.

This is the front of Paris's famous Gothic cathedral, Notre Dame. How many Gothic arches you can find?

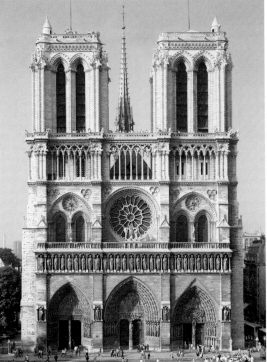

see the spiderlike stone supports sticking out the back of the cathedral? They help hold up the building. Because Gothic cathedrals are so tall and have such large windows, stone braces called buttresses strengthen the walls. When they stick out beyond the wall, like these do, they are called flying buttresses.

Often Gothic cathedrals look symmetrical, with each side a perfect reflection of the other, but in Chartres Cathedral the two main towers look very different. That is because it took so long to build this cathedral. The south tower of the cathedral, on the left in the picture on page 152, was built in the thirteenth century, around 1200, but the north tower, on the right, wasn't finished until after 1400. Architectural styles had changed in those 200 years. The designer of the north tower wanted to be up to date more than he wanted matching towers!

In France's capital city of Paris, there is another great medieval cathedral called Notre Dame [NO-truh DAHM]. (Notre Dame means our lady in French, which is another name for Mary, the mother of Jesus.) Notre Dame provides many examples of the Gothic arch, an arching shape with a point on top that makes doorways and windows look tall and elegant.

At the top of Notre Dame's two large

The soaring interior of the Cathedral of Notre Dame, in Paris.

Gargoyles, sculptures in the shape of imaginary creatures, peer down from the heights of Notre Dame Cathedral.

stone towers sit statues of make-believe demons called gargoyles. People hoped these scary creatures would keep evil away from their church. Notre Dame's gargoyles had another job, too. These sculptures sit at the ends of drain spouts. When it rains, water runs through the roof gutters and drains out through the mouths of gargoyles.

Inside Notre Dame, the ceiling is made of tall pointed arches, crisscrossed by stone spines. Like the buttresses on the outside of a cathedral, these rib vaults were designed to help support the weight of all that stone in such a tall building. The rib vaults work like a skeleton, holding up the weight of the stone roof and ceiling.

Books of Silver and Gold

During the Middle Ages, books were not printed; they were copied by hand. Few books existed, so they were highly valued.

We still have some of the beautiful books made by monks in the Middle Ages. These books are called illuminated manuscripts. A manuscript is a book written by hand. Many of the pages were illuminated, which means that color and sparkle were added to them with paint and bits of real gold and silver.

Around A.D. 900, monks in Great Britain

This page from the Book of Kells shows Mary, the mother of Jesus, with the baby Jesus. Angels surround Mary and Jesus. Does the infant Jesus look realistic to you?

created one of the most famous illuminated manuscripts in the world, *The Book of Kells*. *The Book of Kells* contains the four Gospels —the first four books in the New Testament, which tell about the life of Jesus. *The Book of Kells* is written in a special, ornate handwriting. Paintings decorate many of its pages, including the one shown on page 154.

The monks did not use paper for *The Book of Kells*. They used parchment, made from the skin of sheep or calves. Velvety smooth sheets of parchment were cut and stitched together to make a book. The monks used pens made of goose quills and paintbrushes made of animal fur to apply colored paint, gold, and silver to the parchment pages.

Medieval Tapestries

Churches and monasteries were not the only places where art was found in the Middle Ages. Kings and queens, lords and ladies wanted beautiful art objects around them. They enjoyed seeing pictures of their favorite stories woven into tapestries, or large cloth wall hangings.

In the Middle Ages, people told stories about unicorns, saying that only a pure and lovely maiden could see this magical beast. Some of the most famous tapestries from the Middle Ages show a story called "The Hunt of the Unicorn." We do not know who designed or wove these tapestries, but we do know that they hung in a castle in Cluny, France, during the 1400s.

The detail of this tapestry, part of a series created to tell a mythic story about hunting a unicorn, shows the unicorn after it has been captured.

Islamic Art and Architecture

The Alhambra

During the Middle Ages, Muslim people from northern Africa conquered much of Spain. They developed an architectural style very different from the Gothic style.

On a hill overlooking the town of Granada [grah-NAH-dah], Spain, one Muslim leader built a palace that became known as the Alhambra [ahl-HAHM-bra]. Completed in the 1300s, the Alhambra was a home for the royal family. It included an enormous bath, more like an indoor pool than the bathtubs and showers we have today.

Europeans called the style of the Alhambra Moorish, because they called the Muslim people from North Africa Moors.

From as early as 100 B.C., Spain was part of the Roman Empire. When the Muslims took over in Spain, in the eighth century, they changed the design of buildings to suit their needs and their sense of beauty. They replaced thick Roman columns with slim, delicate ones. They smoothed the walls of buildings with plaster and drew designs on them before it dried. These designs give the walls a delicate appearance, very different from the solid, bare walls of Roman buildings. You can see this in the photo of the Court of the Lions at the Alhambra.

The Alhambra includes a courtyard called the Court of the Lions, so named because its large central fountain is ringed by twelve fountains shaped like lions.

The Dome of the Rock

The Dome of the Rock, sometimes called the Mosque of Omar, was built for Muslims in Jerusalem in 691. Muslims believe that the prophet Muhammad journeyed up to heaven from this spot (see page 95).

One of the first things you notice when you look at the Dome of the Rock is the golden dome on top of the

Here is how the Dome of the Rock in Jerusalem looks today.

mosque. When Muhammad met someone who didn't believe in God, he would point to the sky and ask who had made the stars and planets. Islamic mosques are built with domed ceilings, to remind the people inside of God's power. Some ceilings are decorated to shine like a starry night sky.

The Taj Mahal

One of the world's most famous buildings is the Taj Mahal in India. The Taj Mahal was built in the 1600s as a tomb for a Muslim emperor's beloved wife. Many people consider it one of the world's most beautiful buildings.

The Taj Mahal in India, one of the world's most famous buildings, was built in the 1600s. Its domes and minarets make it a good example of Islamic architecture.

Built at the end of a very long, narrow pool of still water, the Taj Mahal appears to float. When you look at it from a distance, the pool reflects its perfect symmetry, or balance. As you walk closer, the gleaming white building looms bigger and bigger. Slender minarets, or towers, stand at the four corners.

The Word of Allah, Decorated

The *Qur'an* is the holy book of Islam, just as the Bible is the holy book of Christianity. Muslims believe that the *Qur'an* holds the actual words of God.

Muslims believe only God can create living things. They are not permitted to paint images of living things, including people, in their religious books or buildings. So Muslim artists and architects decorate holy books and mosques with geometric patterns instead. Over the centuries, Muslims have made beautiful copies of the *Qur'an*. Some are so beautiful they are considered works of art, with elegant Arabic lettering and touches of real gold.

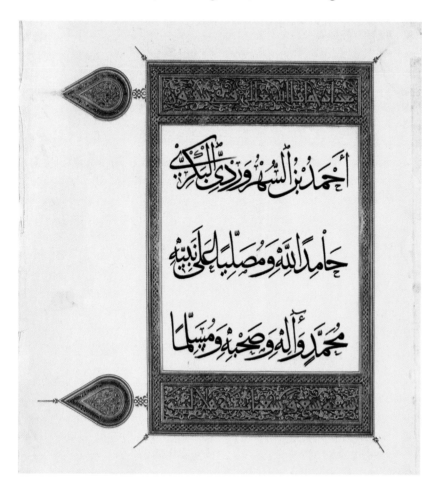

This illuminated page from the *Qur'an*, painted in the 1300s, has Arabic writing in the center and complicated decorations painted along its edges.

Art of Africa

In this photograph from Mali, two dancers (*left*) wear antelope headdresses while three drummers make music for their dance.

Dancing Antelopes

Long ago many African people did not write down their histories. They remembered things from the past by singing songs, dancing, acting, and telling stories—and by making works of art.

In Mali, a group of people called the Bamana [bah-MAH-nah] believed that long ago, a special being called Chiwara [chee-WAH-rah] used magical powers to teach the people to farm. To remember their ancestors and to honor the powers of Chiwara, Bamana artists carved tall wooden figures shaped like antelopes, designed to be worn on top of the head. During planting and harvest festivals, young men hid their bodies under costumes made of fiber, wore these tall headdresses, and performed a dance like leaping antelopes. The dance told the story of Chiwara.

Bamana artists didn't try to make their sculptures look exactly like real antelopes. Instead, they suggested the shape of the antelope's body with big, bold curves.

Portraits in Clay and Bronze

The Yoruba [YO-roo-bah] people of West Africa lived in the city of Ife [EE-fay]. From about A.D. 1000 to 1500, artists in Ife carved beautiful sculptures.

This brass sculpture probably represents the head of an Ife king.

Ife sculptures are made of brass (a metal) and terra cotta (red clay baked in a hot fire). Ife sculptors made sculptures that looked like real people, with delicate features, dignified expressions, and eyes that stare straight ahead.

To make this brass head, the sculptor molded the head, using a mixture of sand and clay. He covered it with a thin layer of beeswax. Next, using a knife made of bone, he molded the details of the face into the beeswax, then covered it all with a thin layer of clay. When he put the sculpture on a hot fire, what do you think happened? The beeswax melted and drained out, leaving a thin hollow space between two face-shaped shells of clay. The sculptor then poured hot melted brass into the space. After the brass cooled, he broke the clay shells. What remained was this brass sculpture.

A Portrait Mask of an African Queen

The Edo [EH-doe] people lived in Benin [ben-EEN], a kingdom southeast of Ife, in the area of today's Nigeria. The Edo people considered the king and his ancestors to be like gods, and they created sculptures to show their respect. The mask on this page, carved out of ivory, is a portrait of Idia [id-EE-a], the mother of a king who lived in Benin in the sixteenth century. The king may have worn this mask on his belt for important occasions.

In Benin, every time a hunter killed an elephant, one tusk was given to the king. Ivory carvers lived near the palace and worked for the king.

Like the brass and terra cotta heads made by the Yoruba, Benin masks represented real people. The artist did not make an exact copy of the person's facial features, though. We can say that he idealized the portrait, or made it closer to perfect than any one person can be.

This ivory mask was created to represent a queen of the Edo people in Benin (now part of the country of Nigeria). The queen's head is surrounded by bearded men, representing soldiers.

Art of China

Paintings on Silk

The people of ancient China believed that the spirit of nature breathes life into all things. For them, the artist's job was to capture this spirit in art.

By the end of the sixth century, Chinese artists were capturing the spirit of nature by making paintings on scrolls—long bands of paper or silk. Chinese artists painted pictures of children, birds, flowers, and animals. By the tenth century, Chinese artists painted entire landscapes, or pictures of natural scenery, on silk scrolls.

The image of a five-colored parakeet, sitting on a flowering cherry tree branch, was painted on silk by Emperor Hui-tsung [hwee-soong] early in the twelfth century. Alongside the painting, you can see red ink stamps and fancy Chinese handwriting. The red stamps are like a signature, showing who owned this silk scroll over time. The handwriting is a poem. Sometimes the artist wrote a poem on his painting, or sometimes friends would add comments to a painting, writing in Chinese characters.

This lovely picture of a parakeet on branches in bloom was painted on a silk scroll by the Emperor Hui-tsung, who lived in the early 1100s, during the Zhou Dynasty.

The Art of Handwriting

In China beautiful handwriting became an art form. Chinese people appreciated calligraphy (the art of beautiful handwriting) for its beauty, and for the shape and pictures in its symbols.

The Chinese language is different from English, both in the way it sounds and in the way it looks. Instead of letters, the Chinese use characters that stand for words. Many Chinese characters are little pictures that look something like the things they stand for. Chinese calligraphers worked hard to make their characters look beautiful.

Choose one character in this example of Chinese calligraphy, made in the eleventh century by a man named Huang T'ing-chien [wong ting-CHEN]. Imagine making it with a paintbrush. Where would you start? What direction would you move the paintbrush? You would

Can you guess which Chinese character here means tiger? The tiger has a long tail that swerves around. (It's the top character in the fifth column.)

have to decide how hard to press down, whether to make the lines thick or thin, and how much ink to put on your brush. Calligraphers think carefully about all these things, but finally they dip their brushes into the ink and, quick as lightning, paint the characters without stopping.

Why Are Cups and Saucers Called China?

The Chinese started making porcelain [POR-suh-luhn], or fine white pottery, during the Tang Dynasty, which lasted from A.D. 618 to 907. Nobody in Europe was making such lovely pottery at that time, so the Europeans traded with the Chinese for their porcelain and simply called it china. It would be another 700 years before the Europeans learned the recipe for porcelain. During China's Ming Dynasty, which lasted from 1368 to 1644, artists got so good at making porcelain, they made porcelain sculptures six feet tall!

Potters in the Ming Dynasty developed glazes, or shiny paints, for decorating their pottery. Their favorite colored glaze was this brilliant blue, made from a chemical called cobalt.

American Art

Portraits of Patriots

How would you paint a picture of the president of the United States? In a suit, or in work clothes? Smiling or looking very serious? Would you paint a richly detailed background or decide to focus on your subject's face? Would you paint exactly what you saw, or leave out physical imperfections? After you decided these basic questions, you would need to decide how to use color, line, form, light, and shadows. These are the choices portrait painters have to consider. Different artists make different decisions.

Copley's portrait of the silversmith and American patriot, Paul Revere.

A detail of one of Gilbert Stuart's many portraits of George Washington. Another of Stuart's portraits of Washington became the model for the picture on our one-dollar bill.

One of the first great American painters, John Singleton Copley, painted a portrait of Paul Revere, the famous patriot. In the portrait, Revere, a silversmith and engraver, is dressed in his work clothes. He holds a silver teapot. On the table are the engraving tools he will use to decorate the teapot.

Wealthy Americans loved to have portraits painted of themselves and their families, especially by artists who had studied art with great European masters. Gilbert Stuart was one such artist. Stuart took art lessons from British painters when he was still a child. Later he studied painting in London.

By 1795, Stuart was considered the premier portrait painter in America. Martha Washington hired him to paint portraits of herself and her husband. George Washington grumbled about sitting for his portrait. Later Stuart remembered that Washington was "grave" and "sullen" while sitting for his portrait. What expression do you think Gilbert Stuart captured in his portrait of Washington?

Unlike Copley, who carefully painted clothes, settings, and personal belongings, Stuart chose to concentrate on Washington's face. Notice the way Stuart uses the color red in Washington's cheeks, to draw our eyes there. With quick, sketchy brushstrokes and softly blended colors, Stuart creates a warm, fuzzy background that frames Washington's head.

People who knew Washington said the portrait looked like him. But Stuart also idealized this portrait in some ways. He left out scars caused by smallpox and a mole under Washington's left ear. By painting Washington without physical flaws, Stuart emphasized his heroic qualities—and this is the image most of us remember when we think of George Washington today.

Painting Revolutionary History

Every so often a painting captures a moment in history so perfectly that it becomes a famous symbol of the event. *Washington Crossing the Delaware*, by Emanuel Leutze, is that kind of painting.

On the day after Christmas in 1776, Washington led his half-starved and freezing troops

Here is the German artist Leutze's painting of Washington crossing the Delaware. The actual painting is more than twelve feet high and twenty-one feet wide!

across the Delaware River for a surprise attack on enemy troops camped at Trenton, New Jersey. The revolutionaries' victory, one of the most important events in the war, inspired them to keep fighting. Leutze chose to paint not the actual battle, but the river crossing that preceded it.

Notice that only Washington is standing. His profile juts into the sky, while his soldiers hunch over the oars. His face is one of the few in the picture above the horizon. The bright sky illuminates his profile, highlighting it more dramatically than any other. All of these decisions allowed the painter to turn General George Washington into a larger-than-life figure, symbolic of patriotic devotion and bravery in support of the American cause.

Little Mountain, Great Architect

When he was a boy, Thomas Jefferson had a secret hideaway at the top of a mountain on his father's estate in Albemarle County, Virginia. Many years later, he built a house there. Jefferson designed, built, and rebuilt Monticello [mont-i-CHELL-oh, Italian for little mountain] over more than forty years, through the years he helped lead the Revolution, write the Declaration of Independence, and served as vice president and president. "Architecture is my delight, and putting up and pulling down one of my favorite amusements," he once said.

Jefferson learned about architecture from books. His favorite book showed buildings that

Jane Pitford Braddick, a friend of Thomas Jefferson and his family, painted this watercolor of Monticello in 1825. If you want to see another image of Monticello, look on a nickel.

looked like ancient Greek and Roman temples. Monticello, and other buildings Jefferson designed, have wide, open porches with white columns and triangular pediments above them, elements borrowed from classical temples. This classical style of architecture reminded Jefferson of another gift from ancient Greece and Rome—democracy, or government of the people, the central idea that inspired the American Revolution.

Jefferson constructed Monticello almost entirely of American materials. The timber was cut from his forests and the stone was cut right out of the mountain. The nails and bricks were made by workers at Monticello. A plantation as big as Monticello required the work of many people. More than one hundred slaves lived in houses built near Monticello.

The watercolor on page 165 shows Jefferson's house, Monticello, in 1825, the year before Jefferson died. The painter, Jane Pitford Braddick, was a friend of Jefferson's granddaughters. Eleven of Jefferson's grandchildren lived with him at Monticello, and Braddick chose to include three of them in her picture. She also included another person in the painting—an artist, doing another drawing of Monticello!

IV.

Music

Introduction

This chapter introduces some vocabulary, symbols, and concepts that will help children understand and appreciate music. It offers basic information about musical notation, the orchestra, vocal ranges, and Gregorian chants (a topic that ties in with the medieval history section). It also profiles a few composers and prints the lyrics to some popular songs.

The value and delightfulness of this chapter will be greatly enhanced if children are able to listen to the classical selections described. To facilitate such listening, the foundation has assembled CD collections of the works discussed here. These are available on our Web site (www.coreknowledge.org).

In music, as in art, students benefit from learning by doing. Singing, playing instruments, and dancing all sharpen a child's sense of how music works. We encourage you to share good music with children by singing some of the songs presented here, attending concerts, listening to the radio, and playing CDs and tapes.

The Elements of Music

Make a Note of It!

Long ago, people shared music by singing to each other and playing musical instruments. Later, when they wanted to remember more complicated music or share music with people far away, musicians developed *musical notation*—a way to write down music so that different people, no matter what language they spoke, could read that music and sing or play it.

When composers write music down, they use special marks called *notes*, and they arrange the notes on a set of parallel lines called a *staff*. The notes on the staff below give the music for the beginning of "Twinkle, Twinkle, Little Star."

When you are learning a piece of music, you can follow the notes across the staff from left to right, just as you follow words across the page when you read.

The position of notes on the staff tells you how high or low the notes are. The higher the note sits on the staff, the higher your voice goes when you sing that note. Can you hear how your voice goes up to a higher pitch as you move from the first "twinkle" to the second one, and then up again as you sing "little"? Then the pitch of your voice comes steadily downward until you sing "are" at the same pitch as the first note.

The shape of the note tells you how long to hold each note. Did you notice that when you sing "Twinkle, Twinkle, Little Star," you hold the notes for "star" and "are" longer than the other notes? That's because these notes are half notes, while the other notes in the song are quarter notes. A half note is held twice as long as a quarter note.

Shorter and Longer Notes

The music for "Twinkle, Twinkle, Little Star" contains only half notes and quarter notes, but musicians also use other notes, some shorter and some longer. An eighth note is like a quarter note with a little flag on top.

♪

An eighth note is held for half as long as a quarter note. When two or more eighth notes are written side by side, they are sometimes connected with a bar, like this:

A whole note is held twice as long as a half note. That means it's held for as long as four quarter notes, or eight eighth notes. It looks like this:

If a composer wants to make a note last longer than a half note but not as long as a whole note, he or she just adds a little black dot to the right of the note. That dot tells performers to hold the note half again as long.

Another special symbol can be used to show that a note should be held for a long time. Composers use a *tie*, or a curved line that ties the notes together, to tell the musician to continue to hold the first note through the time of the second.

Look at the sample above. Can you find the tied notes? The dotted notes? How many of each do you see?

Give It a Rest!

Composers also need to tell musicians when to be quiet. When a composer wants silence, he writes a mark called a rest. A whole rest lasts as long as a whole note, a half rest as long as a half note, and a quarter rest as long as a quarter note. This chart shows notes and rests of the same length.

whole whole   half   half   quarter quarter
note   rest   note   rest   note   rest

Measures and Time Signatures

Look again at the music for "Twinkle, Twinkle, Little Star." Do you see the vertical (up-and-down) lines that separate the notes into groups? These lines are called *bar lines*. They divide the music into *measures*. How many measures of "Twinkle, Twinkle, Little Star" are shown?

Composers use a single bar line to mark the end of a measure. They use a double bar line to mark the end of a piece of music.

See the two numbers sitting on top of one another at the beginning of the music—the ones that look like a fraction? Those numbers make up the time signature. The top number tells you how many beats there are in each measure, and the bottom number tells you what kind of note represents one beat. For "Twinkle, Twinkle, Little Star," the time signature is 4/4. The 4 on the top means that there are four beats per measure, and the 4 on the bottom means each beat lasts as long as a quarter (1/4) note.

You can see that the first measure of "Twinkle, Twinkle, Little Star" is made up of four quarter notes, each of which is held for one beat: "twin-kle, twin-kle." But the second measure is a little different. It only contains three notes. But one of these notes—the one that goes with the word "star"—is held for twice as long—for two beats. So there are still four beats in this measure, even though there are only three notes.

When the time signature is 4/4, we say that the song is written in four-four time. Many popular songs are written in 4/4 time. But you will also see songs in 2/4 time and 3/4 time. How many quarter notes fill a measure in 2/4 time? How many eighth notes will fit in a measure in 3/4 time? As you can see, math skills are important for understanding music.

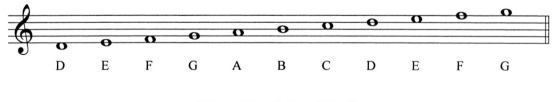

The Treble Clef

Musical pitches are named after the first seven letters of the alphabet: A B C D E F G. Each line and each space on the staff corresponds with one of these letters.

Do you see how the letters repeat themselves as you go from low to high? At the bottom of the staff, just below the bottom line, is D. Then you move up to E, F, and G. But there's no H. Instead the letters start over again, with A.

How can you remember which positions on the staff correspond with which letters? Here's one way. Notice that the letters that are located on the lines, from bottom to top are E, G,

B, D, and F. You can remember these letters by memorizing this sentence: "**E**very **g**ood **b**oy **d**oes **f**ine."

Another way to remember which letters go where on the staff is to look at the treble clef. The treble clef is the fancy, curlicue symbol located at the beginning of the music. The treble clef is also known as the G clef because the innermost circle of the clef circles around the second line in the staff—the line that stands for G. If you remember this, you can figure out all the other pitches above and below G.

The lowest note shown on the music above is D. What would happen if the composer wanted to write a note one note lower than D? He or she would just draw a short line segment below the staff and place the note on the line segment. This particular note actually has a special name. It is called middle C, because the key that sounds this note is located in the middle of a piano keyboard.

Middle C

The music for "Twinkle, Twinkle, Little Star" begins and ends at middle C. See if you can identify the other notes in the first few measures of the song by letter.

The Composer's Language

Composers place notes on a staff to show how they want their music to be performed, but sometimes they give even more specifics.

When the composer wants the music to be played smoothly, without breaks between the notes, he or she writes *legato* in the music. In Italian, *legato* means tied together. In a piece sung *legato*, there's little breath between notes. When the composer wants the music to be played in the opposite way, with short, bouncy sounds, he or she writes the Italian word *staccato*. Staccato means detached or "separated."

Other notations, written in Italian words or their abbreviations, tell musicians how loud or soft to play a piece of music.

mp mezzo piano (moderately soft)
p piano (soft)
pp pianissimo (very soft)

mf mezzo forte (moderately loud)
f forte (loud)
ff fortissimo (very loud)

Another instruction you may see written on music is Da capo al fine. Da capo means from the beginning. Al fine [ahl FEE-nay] means to the end. This instruction is often used when the composer wants the beginning of a piece repeated.

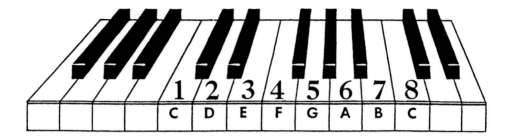

Sharps and Flats

The notes in a piece of music match the notes on a piano keyboard. The white keys on the piano all have letter names. Can you match the piano keys with the keys written on the staff?

The black keys on a piano are important, too. They don't get their own names, though. They get named according to the keys on either side.

Find D on the piano keyboard. The black key just to the right of D is called D-sharp, which can be written D♯ for short. D♯ is a little bit higher in pitch than D.

Now go back to D on the piano keyboard. The black key just to the left of D is called D-flat, or D♭ for short. D♭ is a little bit lower in pitch than D.

A black key can have two names. It can be called the sharp of a note to the left or the flat of a note to the right. No matter which name you call that note, it always sounds the same.

Listening and Understanding

The Orchestra

Half an hour before a performance, the concert hall is quiet. The stage lights shine on empty chairs, arranged in the shape of a fan, all pointing toward a platform at the edge of the stage. Ushers lead the first audience arrivals to their seats, and the hall begins to stir with quiet conversation. Soon, the musicians enter from backstage, carrying their instruments and walking to their places. They settle in and, just as athletes stretch and move their bodies before a big event, the musicians begin to warm up. The concert hall soon fills with high-pitched toots, deep rumbles, and plucked strings. To the audience it sounds a little chaotic, but soon the musicians will be ready for the concert.

From out of all the noise, an oboe sounds the note A. Soon all the other musicians are playing the same note. Violinists draw their bows lightly across all four strings of their instruments; the A is one of them. If any string sounds off-pitch, a violinist turns the tuning pegs to adjust it.

The musicians have spent many hours practicing for the concert, and now they are ready to perform. The conductor crosses the stage, steps up on the platform, bows to the audience, turns to the orchestra, lifts his baton, and signals for the music to begin.

Fanning out in front of the conductor, the orchestra includes four major families of instruments. The strings are played with a bow or plucked with a finger; the woodwind and the brass instruments are blown; the percussion instruments are struck with sticks or mallets.

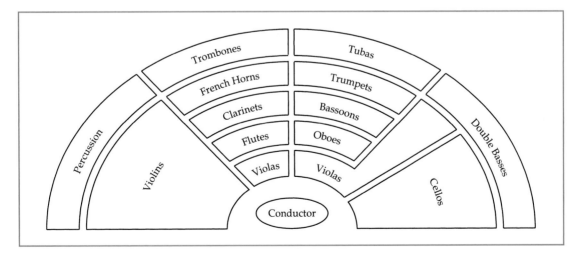

The orchestra is divided into groups for different kinds of instruments.

The conductor knows the music and every instrument's part. Even when all the instruments are playing, the conductor can hear if a note is played too high or low, too loud or soft, or out of rhythm. The conductor's job is to help all the instruments blend into a beautiful and well-balanced whole and to make sure the music is played the way the composer meant it to be played. The conductor is like a coach who tries to get all the members of the team to work together to ensure a winning performance.

Leonard Bernstein conducting the New York Philharmonic Orchestra.

A Magical Musical Tour

At first, it can be difficult to figure out how an orchestra works. That's why the English composer Benjamin Britten wrote *The Young Person's Guide to the Orchestra*. In this piece of music, you'll hear the same melody, or theme, played a number of times, by different instruments of the orchestra. This makes it easier to identify each of the instrument families, as they take turns. When a piece of music plays the same theme in different ways, it is called a theme and variations.

The Young Person's Guide to the Orchestra begins as the whole orchestra plays the main theme. The four major families—woodwinds, strings, brass, and percussion instruments—play the theme and variations, then the whole orchestra plays together. If you can, listen to Britten's piece and begin to identify instruments by their sounds.

The **woodwinds** begin with the high notes of the piccolo and the sweet, clear sound of two flutes, accompanied by violins and a harp. The thoughtful-sounding oboe comes in next, followed by the smooth and athletic clarinets, which make sounds that seem to loop all around. The bassoons, next, make the deepest, fullest sounds.

The family of **strings** then comes in, led by the violins.

These men are playing string instruments: from the left, two violins, a viola, and a cello.

Their sound is so important to the orchestra that there are more of them than any other instrument. Violas, a bit larger in size, have a deeper, often somber-sounding tone. Both the violin and the viola are held against the musician's chin while he or she draws a bow across the strings.

Cellos, much larger than the violas, are held upright on the floor, between the knees of the players. Cellos have a rich, warm sound. The double bass, largest member of the string family, rumbles when it plays its lowest notes. The harp belongs in this instrument family, too. A harpist plucks its forty-seven strings while seated beside it.

Among the **brasses,** the horns lead the way. The trumpets come in with higher, bright sounds. The trombone, played by sliding one metal tube in and out of another, adds a deep voice. The bass tuba has an even deeper, heavier sound.

The **percussion instruments** take their turn as the kettle drums, or timpani [TIM-pahn-ee], make deep, vibrating sounds you can feel as well as hear. There are many rhythmic noisemakers in this family, including bass drum, cymbals, tambourine, and triangle. Wooden blocks clapped together make a sound like the crack of a whip, commanding the whole orchestra to play together again.

The tuba makes a deep, low sound.

Benjamin Britten ends his tour of the orchestra with a fugue, in which the instruments play one after another as if singing a round. This gives us another chance to hear the distinctive qualities of each family of instruments. Now we can appreciate the role each has in the full orchestra sound. The brass instruments sing out at the end of the piece, celebrating the sounds of the orchestra. Each time you listen to this piece, you will be able to distinguish more clearly the instruments of the orchestra by the sounds that they make.

The Instrument We All Can Play

Even without music lessons, you already play the oldest, most universal, and most expressive musical instrument of all—the human voice. Babies seem to discover this instrument all on their own. Before they walk, they experiment with making all kinds of sounds. You can practice all the basic elements of music—rhythm, melody, harmony—simply by singing.

Everyone has a high note, a low note, and notes in between that he or she can sing comfortably. The highest note and the lowest note that you can sing define your *range*.

Can you think of a popular American song that has such a big range from its highest to its lowest note that it's a challenge to sing every note? Many people would name "The Star-Spangled Banner," the national anthem of the United States. Think of how low your voice goes when you sing the word say in "O-oh say can you see?" Think of how high you have to go to sing "and the rockets' red glare, the bombs bursting in air."

Voices, High and Low

Have you noticed that among the people you know, some sing high and some sing low? The voices of women and men are divided into three main categories of singers.

Women's voices
    High: soprano
    Middle: mezzo [MET-so] soprano
    Low: alto

Men's voices
    High: tenor
    Middle: baritone
    Low: bass

Composers write music with these vocal ranges in mind, and their choices can have dramatic effects.

Music of the Middle Ages

In the world history and art sections of this book, you learned about Europe in the Middle Ages. During the Middle Ages, groups of men lived in religious communities, devoting all their time and work to their religion. They were called monks, and their homes were called monasteries. Monasteries were quiet, protected places where monks could concentrate on their faith. The monks wore plain robes, gave up their personal possessions, and promised never to marry. They went to bed early and woke up before sunrise. They did a lot of physical labor, much of it to help the poor.

During the Middle Ages, few people knew how to read and write. Monks could read music as well as words, and they spent many hours carefully copying music and Latin texts by hand. (They lived in a time before computers and printing presses, when every book had to be copied by hand.)

Every day, the monks came together to pray and sing. The songs they sang are called Gregorian chants, in honor of Pope Gregory the Great, who was the head

A monk copying music.

of the Roman Catholic Church from 590 to 604 A.D. Gregorian chants are still sung today by monks.

The words in the chants were mostly taken from the Bible and usually they were sung in Latin, with no instruments playing along. Sometimes two choirs sat across from each other, taking turns at singing.

When you first hear Gregorian chants, they may sound monotonous. There are similar sounds over and over again without much variation. Modern music sounds much more complicated, with more contrast in rhythm and harmony. But strong voices singing in a candlelit church echo and blend into one bigger voice, sounding beautiful, powerful, and even a bit mysterious. Try to find a recording of Gregorian chants to hear for yourself.

George Frideric Handel (1685–1759)

George Frideric Handel (HAN-del) was born in Germany in 1685. He was interested in music as a young boy, but his father wanted him to be a lawyer, not a musician, and would not let him have an instrument. Handel smuggled a small keyboard instrument called a clavichord [CLA-vi-cord] into his house. He wanted to play music so much, he played his clavichord in secret. Later, when he was older, he studied music full time, no longer having to keep it a secret.

Handel.

Handel is best known for his compositions based on stories from the Bible. One of these pieces, called *Messiah* [mes-SYE-ya], is performed by an orchestra and a chorus, with soloists in all the vocal ranges singing special parts. Each part of *Messiah* tells a different episode in the life of Jesus. For words, Handel used verses from the English Bible and a prayer book. The most famous part of *Messiah* is the thrilling "Hallelujah Chorus," in which voices proclaim the everlasting glory of God.

There is a story that when Handel's *Messiah* was performed the first time for King George of England, the king was so moved by the "Hallelujah Chorus" that he stood up to hear it. Whether the story is true or not, audiences have been standing up to hear that chorus ever since, such is the inspiring effect of Handel's music.

Franz Joseph Haydn (1732–1809)

When he was very young, Franz Joseph Haydn (HIGH-dun) delighted his family with his singing. He soon became a church choirboy, and by the time he was eight, he was singing in the choir of the cathedral in Vienna, Austria. He also learned to play the violin, the organ, and other instruments.

As he grew older Haydn wrote music, played the piano to accompany singing lessons, and taught music to others. Word of his talent spread, and eventually a prince in Hungary brought him to live in his palace. There Haydn's job was to teach, write music, and direct concerts for the prince and his many guests. He lived in the palace for nearly thirty years, where he produced music that made him famous throughout Europe.

At the prince's palace, Haydn often conducted symphonies after dinner. He composed more than one hundred symphonies altogether, and many other works besides. His symphonies are considered so important in the history of music, he is sometimes called the Father of the Symphony.

Haydn.

A *symphony* is a musical composition performed by an orchestra. The word comes from the Greek *sym*, meaning together and *phonos*, meaning sound. Usually a symphony is divided into four movements, or sections, each distinctly different from the others.

As Haydn conducted the palace orchestra, he noticed that the quieter passages in his music actually lulled some guests to sleep. He decided to play a musical joke on the prince and his guests. In one symphony, the second movement begins with a gentle melody—the kind that might put a drowsy person to sleep—then suddenly the sound of a great chord unexpectedly bursts in, breaking the quiet. Ever since, people have called Haydn's Symphony No. 94 in G the "Surprise Symphony." Have a listen!

Wolfgang Amadeus Mozart (1756–1791)

Wolfgang Amadeus Mozart (MOTE-sart) was also born in Austria. His father was a professional musician who could tell from very early on that his son had remarkable musical skills. By the age of four, Mozart played the piano and the violin very well. By the time he was eight, he was composing symphonies!

Through much of his childhood, Mozart toured Europe with his father and older sister, playing music. Everywhere he went, the young boy amazed audiences. When the emperor of Austria heard Mozart play, he called him a "little wizard."

Mozart as a young man.

Mozart wrote musical compositions of all kinds—for the piano and for small groups of instruments, for orchestras, and for singers. He wrote several famous operas, which are plays in which the actors sing rather than speak their lines.

One of Mozart's most famous operas is *The Magic Flute*. *The Magic Flute* is a strange and beautiful love story, full of dragons, sorcerers, and spells. It tells the story of the young prince Tamino [tah-MEE-no], who sets out to rescue the beautiful princess Pamina [pah-MEE-na]. Tamino has to pass many tests, some in the company of a silly birdcatcher named Papageno [pa-pa-GAY-no]. In the end, Tamino passes all his tests and is united with Pamina.

Sarastro (*right*) sings one of the arias in Mozart's *Magic Flute* during a performance in San Francisco, California. Tamino stands in the center of the picture with his arms at his side.

Mozart followed the rules for composing different types of music, but he always added a twist, so that each piece included new, bold musical ideas. For example, Mozart wrote twelve variations of an old French song called "Ah, vous dirai-je Maman" for the piano. The song has the same tune as "Twinkle, Twinkle, Little Star." Mozart begins with the simple melody; then he changes it around. He changes the *tempo*, or speed of the music. He changes the dynamics, or the intensity with which the music is played, so some versions are loud and some are quiet. Some sound proper and formal; some sound exuberant and full of fun; one even sounds a little spooky.

Mozart said that his music came to him in a kind of "lively dream." He heard all the parts at once and kept them in his head until he could write them all down. Haydn once said that Mozart was "the greatest composer known to me," and many people agree with him to this day.

Some Songs for Fourth Graders

Auld Lang Syne

"Auld Lang Syne" is an old Scottish song, often sung on New Year's Eve. "Auld lang syne" means old long since, or the old times. In the song two old friends are talking. One asks, "Should old friends and old times be forgotten?" Then he answers his own question, saying "No, let's have a drink —'a cup of kindness'—for old times' sake!"

Should auld acquaintance be forgot
And never brought to mind?
Should auld acquaintance be forgot
And days of Auld Lang Syne?

For Auld Lang Syne, my dear,
For Auld Lang Syne,
We'll take a cup o' kindness yet,
For Auld Lang Syne!

Cockles and Mussels

In Dublin's fair city
    Where girls are so pretty,
'Twas there I first met with
    Sweet Molly Malone.

She drove a wheelbarrow
    Through streets broad and narrow,
Crying, "Cockles and mussels,
    Alive, all alive."

Chorus:
"Alive, alive-o! Alive, alive-o!"
Crying, "Cockles and mussels,
Alive, all alive."

She was a fishmonger,
    But that was no wonder:
Her father and mother
    Were fishmongers, too.

They drove wheelbarrows
    Through streets broad and narrow,
Crying, "Cockles and mussels,
    Alive, all alive!"
Chorus.

She died of the fever,
    And nothing could save her
And that was the end
    Of sweet Molly Malone.

But her ghost wheels her barrow,
    Through streets broad and narrow,
Crying, "Cockles and mussels,
    Alive, all alive!"
Chorus.

Comin' Through the Rye

If a body meet a body
    Comin' through the rye,
If a body kiss a body,
    Need a body cry?

Every lassie has her laddie.
    None, they say, have I;
Yet all the lads they smile on me,
    When comin' through the rye.

Loch Lomond

Oh! you take the high road and
I'll take the low road,
And I'll be in Scotland afore ye;
But me and my true love
Will never meet again
On the bonnie, bonnie banks of Loch Lomond.

'Twas there that we parted,
In yon shady glen,
On the steep, steep side of Ben Lomond,
Where purple in hue,
The Highland hills we view,
And the moon coming out in the gloaming.

My Grandfather's Clock

My grandfather's clock was too large for the shelf,
So it stood ninety years on the floor.
It was taller by half than the old man himself,
Though it weighed not a pennyweight more.
It was bought on the morn of the day that he was born,
And was always his treasure and pride.
But it stopped short—never to go again,
When the old man died.

In watching its pendulum swing to and fro,
Many hours he spent while a boy;
And in childhood and manhood the clock seemed to know
And to share both his grief and his joy.
For it struck twenty-four when he entered at the door,
With a blooming and beautiful bride.
But it stopped short—never to go again,
When the old man died.

My grandfather said that of those he could hire,
Not a servant so faithful he found;
For it wasted no time, and had but one desire—
At the close of each week to be wound.
And it kept in its place—not a frown upon its face,
And its hands never hung by its side.
But it stopped short—never to go again,
When the old man died.

It rang an alarm in the dead of the night—
An alarm that for years had been dumb;
And we knew that his spirit was pluming for flight—
That his hour of departure had come.
Still the clock kept the time, with a soft and muffled chime,
As we silently stood by his side.
But it stopped short—never to go again,
When the old man died.

Waltzing Matilda

Once a jolly swagman camped by a billabong,
Under the shade of a coolibah tree,
And he sang as he watched and waited till his billy boiled,
"You'll come a-waltzing matilda with me.

Waltzing matilda, waltzing matilda,
You'll come a-waltzing matilda with me."
And he sang as he watched and waited till his billy boiled,
"You'll come a-waltzing matilda with me."

Down came a jumbuck to drink at that billabong.
Up jumped the swagman and grabbed him with glee.
And he sang as he stuffed that jumbuck in his tucker bag,
"You'll come a-waltzing matilda with me.

Waltzing matilda, waltzing matilda,
You'll come a-waltzing matilda with me."
And he sang as he stuffed that jumbuck in his tucker bag,
"You'll come a-waltzing matilda with me."

Up rode the squatter, mounted on his thoroughbred;
Down came the troopers, one, two, three.
"Where's that jolly jumbuck you've got in your tucker bag?
"You'll come a' waltzing Matilda with me."

Waltzing matilda, waltzing matilda,
You'll come a-waltzing matilda with me,
Where's that jolly jumbuck you've got in your tucker bag?
"You'll come a-waltzing Matilda with me."

Up jumped the swagman and sprang into that billabong.
"You'll never take me alive," said he.
And his ghost may be heard as you pass by that billabong
"You'll come a' waltzing Matilda with me."

This Australian song isn't about a woman named Matilda who liked to waltz. A "matilda" is a knapsack that Australian hobos carried in the late 1800s. To go "waltzing matilda" meant to walk around, looking for work, with all your belongings in your knapsack. In this song, a "swagman," or hobo, stuffs a farmer's sheep into his knapsack and gets caught in the act.

The Yellow Rose of Texas

There's a yellow rose in Texas
That I am going to see.
No other soldier knows her—
No soldier, only me.
She cried so when I left her,
It like to broke my heart,
And if I ever find her,
We never more will part.

She's the sweetest rose of color
This soldier ever knew.
Her eyes are bright as diamonds;
They sparkle like the dew.
You may talk about your dearest May
And sing of Rosa Lee,
But the Yellow Rose of Texas
Beats the belles of Tennessee.

Songs of the U.S. Armed Forces

The Army Goes Rolling Along

Valley Forge, Custer's ranks,
San Juan Hill and Patton's tanks,
And the Army went rolling along.
Minute men, from the start,
Always fighting from the heart,
And the Army keeps rolling along.

The Marine's Hymn

From the halls of Montezuma
To the shores of Tripoli,
We fight our country's battles
In air, on land, and sea.
First to fight for right and freedom,
And to keep our honor clean,
We are proud to claim the title
Of United States Marines!

Air Force Song

Off we go into the wild blue yonder,
Climbing high into the sun;
Here they come zooming to meet our thunder,
At 'em boys, Give 'er the gun!

V.

Mathematics

Introduction

This chapter offers a brief overview of essential math topics for fourth grade, including number sense, fractions and decimals, computation, measurement, and geometry.

Success in learning math comes through practice: not mindless, repetitive practice but thoughtful practice, with a variety of problems. While it is important to work toward the development of higher-order problem-solving skills, such skills depend on a sound grasp of basic facts and an automatic mastery of fundamental operations. Since practice is the secret to mastery, practice is a prerequisite for more advanced problem-solving.

Some well-meaning people fear that practice in mathematics—memorizing arithmetic facts or doing timed worksheets, for example—constitutes joyless, soul-killing drudgery for children. Nothing could be further from the truth. It is not practice but *anxiety* that kills the joy in mathematics. And one way of overcoming anxiety is by practicing until the procedures become so easy and automatic that anxiety evaporates.

One effective way to practice is to have children talk out loud while doing problems, explaining computational steps along the way. In this way the child's mental process becomes visible to you, and you can correct misunderstandings as they happen.

This brief outline presented here *does not constitute a complete math program*, since it does not include as many practice problems as a child ought to do while learning this material. To learn math thoroughly, children need to be shown these concepts and then encouraged to practice, practice, practice. We therefore urge that parents and teachers select a math program that allows plenty of opportunities to practice.

The best math programs incorporate the principle of incremental review: once a concept or skill is introduced, it is practiced again and again through exercises of gradually increasing difficulty (including story problems). One result of this approach is that a child's arithmetic skills become automatic. Only when children achieve automatic command of basic facts—when they can tell you instantly what 6 times 6 equals, for example—are they prepared to tackle more challenging problems. Math learning programs that offer both incremental review and varied opportunities for problem solving get the best results.

Numbers and Number Sense

Place Value

Can you read this number?

329,425,278

When you read numbers with this many digits, you have to pay attention to the place value of each digit.

millions			thousands			ones		
hundreds	tens	ones	hundreds	tens	ones	hundreds	tens	ones

(Fill in boxes above with 462,977,003.)

Beginning at the right, the values of the places are: ones, tens, hundreds; thousands, ten thousands, hundred thousands; millions, ten millions, hundred millions. Each place has a value 10 times greater than the place to its right. This system of writing numbers is called the decimal system.

"Decimal" means having to do with 10. In the decimal system, the place values are based on groups of 10. In the decimal system, whenever we have 10 of a certain place value, we write it as 1 in the next highest place value. For example, there are *10* tens in *1* hundred. There are *10* hundreds in *1* thousand.

When you read a number, always begin with the largest place value.

4,315,825

The four is one digit to the left of the millions' comma. It is in the millions' place. 4,315,825 is read, "four million, three hundred fifteen thousand, eight hundred twenty-five."

462,977,003

The 4 is 3 digits to the left of the millions' comma. It is in the hundred millions' place. 462,977,003 is read, "four hundred sixty-two million, nine hundred seventy-seven thousand, three." Notice how the commas make the number easier to read, by dividing the digits up into groups of three?

The Value of Digits

In the number 9<u>3</u>6,<u>4</u>55,171, the underlined 3 is in the ten millions' place. Its value is 30,000,000. The underlined 4 is in the hundred thousands' place. Its value is 400,000.

Another useful way to look at place value is to see how many of each place value a number has. For example, take 43,289. You can write the number in terms of how many ten thousands, thousands, hundreds, tens, and ones it has. It has 4 ten thousands, 43 thousands, 432 hundreds, 4,328 tens, or 43,289 ones in it. Learning to use place value in this way is very useful in both subtraction and division.

Commas and Place Value

You can write the numbers from 1000 to 9999 with a comma or without a comma: 9,672 or 9672. However, whenever you write numbers ten thousand or greater, always write them with commas, to mark off each period. Always 10,403; never 10403.

Comparing Numbers

When you compare numbers always begin by comparing the digits with the largest place values. For example, to compare 286,563 and 97,800, you begin at the left, with the largest places.

Think: 286,563 ? 97,800

               200,000 > 90,000

               so, 286,563 > 97,800

Remember that the sign > stands for is greater than. The sign < stands for is less than. A statement like "286,563 > 97,800" is called an inequality because it shows how the numbers are *not* equal.

Another way to practice comparing numbers is to first write a double inequality: find a number that fits between the two numbers in order to compare them. 286,563 is greater than 200,000. 200,000 is greater than 97,800. You write:

286,563 > 200,000 > 97,800

so, 286,563 > 97,800.

Standard Form and Expanded Form

The standard way to write a number is to express it as a single number with digits. For example, 8,532,706 is in standard form.

You can also write the number in expanded form, separating the digits in each place. There are two ways to write the same number in its expanded form. You can write 8,532,706 = 8,000,000 + 500,000 + 30,000 + 2,000 + 700 + 6. Or, you can multiply each digit by its place value, like this: 8,532,706 = $(8 \times 1,000,000) + (5 \times 100,000) + (3 \times 10,000) + (2 \times 1,000) + (7 \times 100) + (6 \times 1)$.

Using a Number Line

You can also compare numbers using a number line. Suppose your friends have been selling lemonade. They sold 7 glasses on Monday, 5 on Tuesday, 1 on Wednesday, 16 on Thursday, and 10 on Friday.

By placing these numbers on a number line, you can see which day was the best for sales. The farther to the right a number is on the number line, the larger it is. The farther left, the smaller the number.

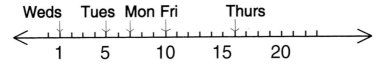

Negative Numbers

Positive numbers are numbers greater than 0. There is also another set of numbers that are less than 0. They are called negative numbers. Negative numbers are written with a minus sign.

Negative numbers are a bit harder to understand than positive numbers, but they can be very useful. For instance, suppose you were keeping track of how much money your friend Jerome owed you. Let's say at first Jerome owes you 5 dollars. Then Jerome buys you a hot dog that costs 2 dollars. Subtract 2 from 5 by moving your finger two notches to the left on the number line below.

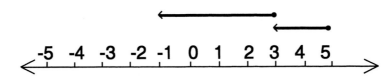

Now Jerome only owes you 3 dollars. Suppose he buys you a big ice cream sundae for 4 dollars. If you move four more ticks to the left, you move past zero to -1. What does it mean to say Jerome owes you -1 dollar? It means you owe him a dollar! How much would you owe him if he loaned you 3 more dollars?

See if you can put these numbers in order from the least to the greatest: 1, -3, 2, 0, -5. By using the number line, you can see that the order would be -5, -3, 0, 1, 2. Don't be fooled into thinking that -5 must be larger than -3 because 5 is larger than 3. The number line shows you that -5 is farther to the left of zero than -2, which means it is smaller.

Rounding

Sometimes you do not need to know an exact value for a number: you can use "round" numbers. Let's practice rounding.

To decide which way to round, always look at the digit in the place just to the right of the one to which you are rounding. If you are rounding to the nearest ten, you look at the digit in the ones' place. If you are rounding to the nearest hundred, you look at the digit in the tens' place.

If the digit to the right is 4 or less, you round down. If the digit to the right is 5 or greater, you round up. Here are three examples:

14 rounded to the nearest 10 → 10
(because 14 is closer to 10 than to 20)

18 rounded to the nearest 10 → 20
(because 18 is closer to 20 than to 10)

15 rounded to the nearest 10 → 20
(15 is halfway between 10 and 20, but when a number is halfway
between two numbers, you always round up.)

Now let's round 3,417 to the nearest thousand. When you look in the thousands' place, you see 3. Your choice is to round the number up to 4,000 or round it down to 3,000. Because the digit in the place just to the right is a 4, you should round down to 3,000. Notice that when you round a number to a certain place value, all the digits to the right of that place become zeros.

Perfect Squares

When you take a number and multiply it by itself, you "square" the number. If you square a whole number, the resulting product is called a perfect square. Here are some examples of perfect squares:

$$1 \times 1 = 1 \qquad\qquad 7 \times 7 = 49$$
$$2 \times 2 = 4 \qquad\qquad 8 \times 8 = 64$$
$$3 \times 3 = 9 \qquad\qquad 9 \times 9 = 81$$
$$4 \times 4 = 16 \qquad\qquad 10 \times 10 = 100$$
$$5 \times 5 = 25 \qquad\qquad 11 \times 11 = 121$$
$$6 \times 6 = 36 \qquad\qquad 12 \times 12 = 144$$

You can see why 9, 16, 25, and the other products above are called perfect squares if you draw pictures that stand for the numbers.

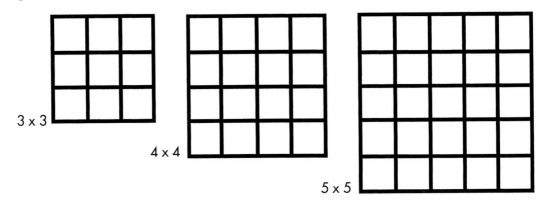

You can read the equation "5 × 5 = 25" as "5 times 5 equals 25." Or you can say, "5 squared equals 25."

Square Roots

When we take the square root of 25, we ask what number multiplied by itself equals 25. The answer is 5: 5 × 5 = 25. So the square root of 25 is 5.

Let's try that again. What number multiplied by itself equals 81? 9 × 9 = 81. So the square root of 81 is 9.

We use a special symbol to mean "square root of": $\sqrt{\ }$. We read $\sqrt{64}$ as "the square root of 64." What does $\sqrt{64}$ equal? How about $\sqrt{100}$? $\sqrt{144}$?

Roman Numerals

The numerals we use most often—the digits 0,1,2,3,4,5,6,7,8,9—are called Arabic numerals. But you may also encounter Roman numerals.

Here are the Roman numerals from 1 to 10. Look at them carefully, especially the numerals for 4 and 9.

I II III IV V VI VII VIII IX X

Here are the Roman numerals from 10 to 100, counting by tens:

X XX XXX XL L LX LXX LXXX XC C

If you learn the values of the following Roman numerals, you can use these symbols to write numbers into the thousands.

I is 1.   V is 5.   X is 10.   L is 50.

C is 100.   D is 500.   M is 1000.

Here are two rules:

1. When a Roman numeral that is the same size or smaller comes after another Roman numeral, you add their values together.

XV is (10 + 5), or 15

XXX is (10 + 10 + 10), or 30.

2. When a Roman numeral that is smaller comes right before one that is larger, you subtract the smaller one from the larger one.

IV is (5 – 1), or 4

IX is (10 – 1), or 9

XL is (50 – 10), or 40

Often, you need to use both these rules to write numbers in Roman numerals. The example below shows you how grouping numbers within a long Roman numeral helps you read it:

$$CDXLVIII$$
$$= CD + XL + VIII$$
$$= (500\text{-}100) + (50\text{-}10) + (5+3)$$
$$= 400 + 40 + 8$$
$$= 448$$

Sometimes people still use Roman numerals for years. For example, you might find a book published in the year MCMLXXXVII:

$$M + CM + LXXX + VII$$
$$= 1000 + (1000\text{-}100) + (50+30) + (5+2)$$
$$= 1000 + 900 + 80 + 7$$
$$= 1987$$

What year is it now? Can you write the year in Roman numerals? What famous historical event happened in MDCCLXXVI? How about MCDXCII?

Graphs

Information, or data, is often given to us in numbers. Sometimes those numbers are used to make pictures, called graphs, that can help us understand the numbers.

A bar graph is a good way to show different amounts. Here is a table of data we will use to make a bar graph.

Along the bottom of the graph we write the days of the week. Along the side of the graph we choose a convenient way to show the millimeters of rain: in intervals of 2 millimeters. We title the

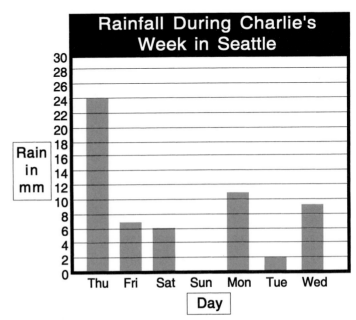

graph, label the information along the bottom and the sides, and draw a bar to show each day's rainfall.

You can see right away from this graph that there was far more rain on Thursday than on any other day.

A line graph can show how amounts or numbers change. At the end of each week for five weeks, Mrs. Sinclair found the average price per share of the stock she owned. Here is her table of data:

To make a line graph, we put the dates along the bottom of the graph. Along the side, we choose money amounts in intervals that will make the graph a reasonable size and show the data clearly. We give the graph a title and labels along the bottom and side.

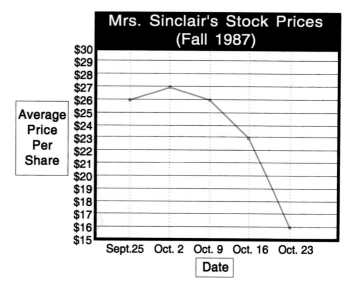

Plotting Points on a Grid

The location of a point on a grid is named by a pair of numbers, called an ordered pair. For example, the location of point A is named by the ordered pair (2,1). The first number of the ordered pair tells you how many units to the right a point is from zero. The second number tells you how many units up a point is from zero. Point A is at (2,1): you get to point A from zero by going 2 units to the right, then 1 unit up. Point B is at (5,3): 5 units to the right of zero and 3 units up.

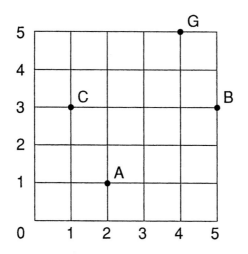

Multiplication

Multiplication Review

Remember that multiplication is a quick way of adding the same number over and over again. You can solve $4 + 4 + 4 + 4 + 4$ in two ways. You can write the numbers in a column and add them, or you can multiply 4×5. $4 \times 5 = 20$. In this equation, 4 and 5 are the *factors*, and 20 is the *product*.

Do you know the basic multiplication facts, from 1×1 to 10×10? Can you fill in the blanks in the following equations?

$$4 \times 8 = \underline{\quad} \qquad\qquad \underline{\quad} \times 7 = 35$$

$$7 \times 6 = \underline{\quad} \qquad\qquad \underline{\quad} \times 9 = 63$$

If it takes you more than a second or two to solve any of these, you should practice your multiplication facts.

A Property of Multiplication

Remember also that multiplication has a special property. This property allows you to find a product by first multiplying with one part of a number and then multiplying with the other part, then adding the two partial products together, to find the whole product. Here is an example with 9×4. If you didn't remember that $9 \times 4 = 36$, you could figure it out this way:

$$9 \times 4$$
$$= (6 + 3) \times 4$$
$$= (6 \times 4) + (3 \times 4)$$
$$= 24 + 12$$
$$= 36$$

Because of this property of multiplication, there is an easy way to multiply numbers of more than one digit in your head. You can multiply the value in each digit separately, and then add to find the whole product. Here's an example:

$$3 \times 17$$
$$= 3 \times (10 + 7)$$
$$= (3 \times 10) + (3 \times 7)$$
$$= 30 + 21$$
$$= 51$$

To multiply 3624×5: first you multiply $5 \times$ the ones, then by the tens, then by the hundreds, then by the thousands. Then you add those numbers together.

$$3,624 \times 5 =$$
$$(4 \text{ ones} \times 5) + (2 \text{ tens} \times 5) + (6 \text{ hundreds} \times 5) +$$
$$(3 \text{ thousands} \times 5) =$$
$$(4 \times 5) + (20 \times 5) + (600 \times 5) + (3,000 \times 5)$$
$$= 20 + 100 + 3,000 + 15,000$$
$$= 18,120$$

There is a quicker way to work through these same stages of multiplication. First, write the two numbers to be multiplied one on top of another. Then multiply the ones', tens', hundreds', and thousands' columns, "carrying" numbers to the next column, as needed.

$$\begin{array}{r} {\scriptstyle 3\ 1\ 2} \\ 3,624 \\ \times\, 5 \\ \hline 18,120 \end{array}$$

First multiply 4×5. $4 \times 5 = 20$, or 2 tens, 0 ones. Write zero in the ones' place and *carry the two tens by writing a small 2 over the ten's column.* Now move to the tens' place. 5×2 tens $= 10$ tens, plus 2 tens carried over from the ones' column $= 12$ tens. Write 2 in the tens' column and carry the 1 hundred for the hundreds column. Continue to multiply and add in this way until you have multiplied each digit by the 5 and added in the numbers carried over from the last place.

Multiples

24 is a multiple of 6, because $6 \times 4 = 24$. A multiple of a number is the product of that number and any whole number. 36 is also a multiple of 6 because $6 \times 6 = 36$.

Here are some multiples of 6: 6, 12, 18, 24, 30 . . .

Here are some multiples of 7: 7, 14, 21, 28, 35 . . .

Here are some multiples of 10: 10, 20, 30, 40, 50 . . .

Notice that all multiples of 10 end in zero. All whole numbers that end in zero are multiples of 10.

Here are some multiples of 2: 2, 4, 6, 8, 10, 12, 14 . . .

Notice that all the multiples of 2 are even. You can define even numbers this way—even numbers are numbers that are multiples of 2.

Common Multiples

18 is a multiple of 6, because $6 \times 3 = 18$. But 18 is also a multiple of 9, because $9 \times 2 = 18$. We say that 18 is a common multiple of 6 and 9. Another common multiple of 6 and 9 is 36, because $6 \times 6 = 36$ and $9 \times 4 = 36$. Can you find three common multiples for 4 and 6?

Multiplying by Tens

Whenever you multiply a number by ten, you make it ten times as large. In the decimal system, you make a whole number ten times as large just by adding an extra zero to it. So it is easy to multiply by ten—just add an extra zero to the number you're multiplying by.

4	54	184
$\times 10$	$\times 10$	$\times 10$
40	540	1,840

You can use this knowledge to multiply by any multiple of ten. Suppose you wanted to multiply 23×60. You already know how to multiply 23×6, and you know how to multiply by ten. By combining these two skills you can get your answer:

$$23 \times 60$$

$$= 23 \times (6 \times 10)$$

$$= (23 \times 6) \times 10$$

So, the product of 23×60 is equal to the product of 23 times 6, times ten:

$$\begin{array}{r} ^{1} \\ 23 \\ \times\,6 \\ \hline 138 \end{array}$$

Then multiply 138×10, which is as easy as adding a zero: $138 \times 10 = 1,380$. So 23×60 = 1,380. Try multiplying 14×70.

Multiplying by Two-Digit Numbers

Once you know how to multiply by tens, you can multiply by any two-digit number. You just break the problem down into two parts: First you multiply by ones, and then you multiply by tens. After this, you add. Here's how you would find the product of 23×58.

Think: 23×58 is $(20 \times 58) + (3 \times 58)$

$$\begin{array}{r} 58 \\ \times\,23 \\ \hline 174 \end{array}$$ Multiply 58 by 3 ones.

Multiply 58 by 2 tens. Make sure to write a zero in the ones' place.

$$\begin{array}{r} 58 \\ \times\,23 \\ \hline 174 \\ 1,160 \end{array}$$

Then add.

$$\begin{array}{r} 58 \\ \times\,23 \\ \hline 174 \\ +\,1,160 \\ \hline 1,334 \end{array}$$

You can multiply larger numbers by two-digit numbers in the same way. Here's an example.

$$372 \times 48 = 372 \times (40 + 8)$$
$$= (372 \times 40) + (372 \times 8)$$

$$
\begin{array}{r}
372 \\
\times\ 48 \\
\hline
2{,}976 \\
14{,}880 \\
\hline
17{,}856 \\
\end{array}
\begin{array}{l}
\\
\\
=\ 372 \times 8 \\
=\ 372 \times 40 \\
=\ 372 \times 48 \\
\end{array}
$$

Multiplying by Hundreds

When you multiply a whole number by 100, you add *two* zeros to it. Multiplying by 100 is like multiplying by 10 twice.

$$100 \times 6 = (10 \times 10) \times 6 = 10 \times (10 \times 6) = 10 \times 60 = 600$$

$$
\begin{array}{r}
6 \\
\times\ 100 \\
\hline
600 \\
\end{array}
\qquad
\begin{array}{r}
87 \\
\times\ 100 \\
\hline
8{,}700 \\
\end{array}
\qquad
\begin{array}{r}
942 \\
\times\ 100 \\
\hline
94{,}200 \\
\end{array}
$$

To multiply by any multiple of 100, write zeros in the ones' place and the tens' place of the product, because you are multiplying by 100. Then multiply using the digit in the hundred's place.

Write zeros in the ones' place and the tens' place.

$$
\begin{array}{r}
487 \\
\times\ 300 \\
\hline
\end{array}
$$

Multiply

$$
\begin{array}{r}
487 \\
\times\,300 \\
\hline
146{,}100
\end{array}
$$

Multiplying by Three-Digit Numbers

Once you know how to multiply by hundreds, you can multiply by three-digit numbers. First multiply by the ones, then by the tens, then by the hundreds. Then add. Here is an example.

Multiply by 4 ones.

$$
\begin{array}{r}
565 \\
\times\,394 \\
\hline
2{,}260
\end{array} = 4 \times 565
$$

Multiply by 9 tens.

$$
\begin{array}{r}
565 \\
\times\,394 \\
\hline
2{,}260 \\
50{,}850
\end{array} = 90 \times 565
$$

Multiply by 3 hundreds.

$$
\begin{array}{r}
565 \\
\times\,394 \\
\hline
2{,}260 \\
50{,}850 \\
169{,}500 \\
\hline
222{,}610
\end{array}
\begin{array}{l}
\\
\\
\\
= 300 \times 565 \\
= 394 \times 565
\end{array}
$$

Multiplying by Thousands

When multiplying a whole number by 10, you add one zero. When multiplying by 100, you add two zeros. How many zeros do you suppose you will add when multiplying a whole number by 1,000? Did you say three zeros? If so, you picked up on the pattern. Multiplying by 1,000 is like multiplying by 10 three times.

$$
\begin{array}{r} 7 \\ \times\ 1{,}000 \\ \hline 7{,}000 \end{array}
\qquad
\begin{array}{r} 23 \\ \times\ 1{,}000 \\ \hline 23{,}000 \end{array}
\qquad
\begin{array}{r} 981 \\ \times\ 1{,}000 \\ \hline 981{,}000 \end{array}
$$

To multiply by any thousand, write zeros in the ones', tens', and hundreds' place of product. Then multiply by the digit in the thousands' place:

Write zeros in the ones', tens', and hundreds' place.

$$
\begin{array}{r} 64 \\ \times\ 2{,}000 \\ \hline 000 \end{array}
$$

Multiply.

$$
\begin{array}{r} 64 \\ \times\ 2{,}000 \\ \hline 128{,}000 \end{array}
$$

Multiplication with Zeros

Sometimes you need to multiply numbers that end in several zeros. There is a handy shortcut for multiplying numbers that end in zeros.

Let's say you wanted to multiply 300×500. You can do this as you would normally. Write two zeros in the product. Multiply 500 by 3.

$$
\begin{array}{r} 500 \\ \times\ 300 \\ \hline 00 \end{array}
\qquad\qquad
\begin{array}{r} 500 \\ \times\ 300 \\ \hline 150{,}000 \end{array}
$$

Or you can take a shortcut. You can rule off all the zeros at the ends of the numbers, and write *all four* of the zeros in the product right away. Then multiply 5 by 3.

$$5 \mid 00$$
$$\times 3 \mid 00$$
$$\overline{\qquad 0000}$$

$$5 \mid 00$$
$$\times 3 \mid 00$$
$$\overline{15 \mid 0,000}$$

Use this strategy to multiply 2000×600 and 600×800.

Checking Multiplication

There are two different ways of checking multiplication: by estimation or by changing the order of the factors you are multiplying. Estimation lets you know if your answer is about right. Changing the order of the factors gives you an exact check.

To check a multiplication problem by estimation, round each factor to the nearest ten, hundred, or thousand. (You do not need to round one-digit factors.) Then multiply and check to be sure the estimate is close to the answer you came up with.

To check this problem:

$$254$$
$$\times 49$$
$$\overline{2,286}$$
$$10,200$$
$$\overline{12,446}$$

Round both factors to the nearest ten and multiply:

$$254 \quad \rightarrow \quad 250$$
$$\times 49 \quad \rightarrow \quad \times 50$$
$$\overline{\qquad\qquad\qquad 12,500}$$

See if the original product is close to the estimate. If it's not go back and multiply again.

12,446 is close to 12,500 ✔

Based on this check, you can't say that your multiplication is absolutely correct, but you know you are in the ballpark.

You can also check multiplication by changing the order of the factors and multiplying again.

To check this problem,

$$
\begin{array}{r}
68 \\
\times\ 37 \\
\hline
476 \\
2{,}040 \\
\hline
2{,}516
\end{array}
$$

reverse the order of the factors and multiply.

$$
\begin{array}{r}
37 \\
\times\ 68 \\
\hline
296 \\
2{,}220 \\
\hline
2{,}516
\end{array}
$$

If your answer is correct, the product will be the same both times.

Multiplying Three Factors

You've just seen how you can check a multiplication problem by changing the order of the two factors to be multiplied. You can also do this when multiplying three factors. When you multiply three numbers, you can multiply them in any order, but one particular order may be easiest.

Look at $879 \times 5 \times 6$, for example. In this problem, you can save time if you multiply 5×6 in your head to get 30, and then multiply 30×879.

Division

Division Review

Division and multiplication are inverse operations. That means that one inverts, or reverses, the other. Take the equation $10 \times 10 = 100$. You could invert this by dividing: $100 \div 10 = 10$. The first equation says if you combine ten groups, each containing ten items, you'll have a hundred items all told. The second says, if you break that collection of a hundred items into ten equal groups, each group will have ten items.

Before you learn more complicated division, check to be sure you know the facts of simple division. For example, since you know that $8 \times 4 = 32$, you should also know that $32 \div 4 = 8$, and $32 \div 8 = 4$.

Finally, remember two important rules about division: You cannot divide by 0, and any number divided by 1 equals that number.

Factors

A factor is a number that divides another number evenly, without leaving a remainder. What are the factors of 4?

$$4 \div 1 = 4$$

$$4 \div 2 = 2$$

$$4 \div 3 = \text{DOES NOT DIVIDE EVENLY}$$

$$4 \div 4 = 1$$

So the factors of 4 are 1, 2, and 4 because they all divide 4 evenly. 3 does not divide 4 evenly and so is not a factor of 4.

Common Factors

The factors of 20 are 1, 2, 4, 5, 10, 20. The factors of 24 are 1, 2, 3, 4, 6, 8, 12, 24. How many factors do 20 and 24 have in common? There are three: 1, 2, and 4. Factors shared by two or more numbers are called common factors.

What are the common factors of 28 and 42? of 30 and 45?

Prime Numbers

Every whole number larger than 1 has at least two factors. The number can be divided evenly by itself and it can be divided evenly by 1. If a number has *only* two factors, it is called a prime number. 11 is a good example of a prime number. You can divide 11 evenly by 1 (11 ÷ 1 = 11) and you can divide it by 11 (11 ÷ 11 = 1). But you cannot divide 11 evenly by 3 or 4 or 6, or any other whole number. So 11 is a prime number.

2 is considered the first prime number (1 is a special case.) Can you pick out the other prime numbers between 2 and 20? Hint: there are seven of them, not counting 2.

Composite Numbers

What do we call a number that's not prime? We call it a composite number. A composite number is a number that is divisible by at least one other number besides itself and 1. 6 is a good example. 6 is evenly divisible by 1, 2, 3, and 6. So it is a composite number. Is 21 composite? How about 37?

Dividend, Divisor, Quotient

In the equation 32 ÷ 8 = 4, 32 is the *dividend*, 8 is the *divisor*, and 4 is the *quotient*. The dividend is the number you are dividing, the divisor is the number you are dividing by, and the quotient is the answer.

Three Ways of Writing Division Problems

You can write a division problem in three ways. 28 divided by 7 can be written:

$$28 \div 7 \qquad 7\overline{)28} \qquad \frac{28}{7}$$

All three ways mean the same thing: 28 divided by 7.

Divide and Conquer

Let's divide 33 by 5.

$$
\begin{array}{r}
6 \ \ \text{R.3} \\
5\overline{)33} \\
-30 \\
\hline
3
\end{array}
$$

First we look to see if the divisor is smaller than the first digit of the dividend. It's not (5>3), so we have to look at the next digit of the dividend and divide 5 into 33. $5 \times 6 = 30$. 33 - 30 leaves a remainder of 3. So 33 divided by 5 is 6 with a remainder of 3. We abbreviate this quotient "6 R3."

Because multiplication and division are inverse operations, you can use your multiplication skills to check your division. To check a division problem, you multiply the quotient by the divisor and add the remainder (if there is one). Your answer should equal the dividend.

$$(\text{quotient} \times \text{divisor}) + \text{remainder} = \text{dividend}$$
$$(6 \times 5) + 3 =$$
$$30 + 3 = 33 \; \checkmark$$

You can begin to use this same form—a multiplication and an addition—as a way of writing division answers.

$$33 = (6 \times 5) + 3 \qquad 3 < 5$$

You write the inequality 3<5 to show that the remainder is less than the divisor. Remember that if the remainder is *not* less than the divisor, the quotient is too small and you need to go back and redo your division.

Understanding Remainders

When you do division word problems, you may need to think about your remainders in different ways. Suppose that 31 students are going on a trip in some school vans. Each van can hold 7 students. How many vans are needed?

When you divide 31 by 7, you get ($7 \times 4 = 28$) with a remainder of 3. Does the answer 4 with a remainder of 3 mean you only need 4 vans? No. If you only had 4 vans, 3 people would not be able to go on the trip. In this problem the remainder tells us an extra van will be needed. Altogether, 5 vans will be needed for the trip.

Now try the following problem: Mrs. Pauli is making surprise baskets for a fair. She has 6 baskets and 52 treats to place in them. If she wants all the baskets to have the same number of surprises, how many treats should go in each basket, and how many will be left over for her grandchildren?

Zeros in Quotients

Sometimes when you divide, you need to write a zero as one of the digits of the quotient. Consider $922 \div 3$.

First divide the hundreds.

$$
\begin{array}{r}
3 \\
3\,\overline{)\,922} \\
-\,9 \\
\hline
0
\end{array}
$$

Think: $0 < 3$

Divide the tens. Since you cannot divide 2 by 3, write a zero
in the tens' place of the quotient, and bring down the tens.

$$
\begin{array}{r}
3\,0 \\
3\,\overline{)\,9\,2\,2} \\
-\,9\,\downarrow \\
\hline
0 \\
0\,2
\end{array}
$$

Bring down the ones. Divide 22 by 3.

$$
\begin{array}{r}
3\,0\,7 \ \text{R1} \\
3\,\overline{)\,9\,2\,2} \\
-\,9\,\downarrow\downarrow \\
\hline
0 \\
0\,2\,2 \\
-\,2\,1 \\
\hline
1
\end{array}
$$

Think: $1 < 3$

[Check by multiplying the quotient by the divisor and adding the remainder.]

$$
\begin{array}{r}
307 \\
\times\,3 \\
\hline
921 \\
+\,1 \\
\hline
922
\end{array}
$$

Practice writing your answer as a multiplication and an addition, followed by an inequality.

$$922 = (3 \times 307) + 1 \qquad 1 < 3$$

The Number of Digits in a Quotient

Before you begin solving a division problem, figure out first how many digits there will be in the quotient. For example, in the problem $496 \div 3$, you know right away that there will be three digits in the quotient, because you can divide 4 hundreds by 3. Another way to think of this is that $496 > 3 \times 100$. You know the quotient will be at least 100, which is the smallest possible three-digit number.

In the problem $519 \div 6$, you know right away that the quotient will have two digits. You cannot divide the 5 in the hundreds place by 6 but you can divide 51 tens by 6. Another way to think of this is that $519 < 6 \times 100$. You know the quotient will be less than 100.

Dividing Larger Numbers

You can use the same method to divide larger numbers by one-digit numbers. Here is an example of dividing a number in the thousands.

$$8 \overline{)8254}$$

You can divide 8 thousands by 8. Begin by dividing the thousands. The quotient will have four digits.

$$
\begin{array}{r}
1\,0\,3\,1 \text{ R.6} \\
8\,\overline{)8\,2\,5\,4} \\
-8\downarrow\downarrow\downarrow \\
\hline
2\,5\downarrow \\
-2\,4\downarrow \\
\hline
1\,4 \\
-8 \\
\hline
6
\end{array}
$$

In this problem notice that you cannot divide 2 in the hundreds' place by 8. So you write a zero in the hundreds' place, bring down the 5, and divide 8 into 25 tens.

Mental Division

Sometimes you can do a division problem in your head, without writing out all the steps. Here's an example.

$$3 \overline{)\,936}$$

To solve this problem, **Think:**

9 hundreds ÷ 3 = 3 hundreds

3 tens ÷ 3 = 1 ten

6 ones ÷ 3 = 2 ones

so, $3 \overline{)\,936}^{\,312}$

Try solving $8 \overline{)\,1{,}866}^{\,233 \ R2}$ and $7 \overline{)\,749}$ in your head.

Dividing by Tens

When dividing by tens, remember that division is the opposite of multiplication. Here's an example:

$$30 \overline{)\,90}$$

To solve this problem, **think:** what times 30 = 90?

Try different numbers.

2 × 30 = 60

3 × 30 = 90

$$\begin{array}{r} 3 \\ 30 \overline{)\,90} \\ -\,90 \quad \text{(Subtract } 30 \times 3) \\ \hline 0 \end{array}$$

Think: 0 < 30

Now try 60.

Dividing by Two-Digit Numbers

When the divisor is a two-digit number, but not an even ten, round it to the nearest ten to estimate what the quotient will be. Here is an example.

$$28\,\overline{)\,640}$$

To divide the 64 tens by 28,

Round 28 to 30.

Think: what $\times$ 30 is about 64?

$2 \times 30 = 60.$

$$\begin{array}{r} 2 \\ 28\,\overline{)\,640} \\ -56 \\ \hline 8 \end{array}$$

Think: $8 < 28$

To divide the 80 ones by 28.

Think: what $\times$ 30 is about 80?

$2 \times 30 = 60$

$3 \times 30 = 90$

3×30 is too large.

$$\begin{array}{r} 22 \text{ R24} \\ 28\,\overline{)\,640}\phantom{\text{ R24}} \\ -56{\downarrow}\phantom{\text{ R24}} \\ \hline 80\phantom{\text{ R24}} \\ -56\phantom{\text{ R24}} \\ \hline 24\phantom{\text{ R24}} \end{array}$$

Think: $24 < 28$

Check by multiplying the quotient by the divisor and adding the remainder.

$$\begin{array}{r} 22 \\ \times 28 \\ \hline 176 \\ +440 \\ \hline 616 \\ +24 \\ \hline 640 \end{array}$$

Practice writing your answer as a multiplication and an addition, followed by an inequality.

$$640 = (28 \times 22) + 24 \qquad 24 < 28$$

Adjusting the Quotient

Sometimes when you round the divisor to the nearest ten, the quotient you try will be too large or too small. Then you need to adjust the quotient. Here's an example:

$$36 \overline{)\,146}$$

You can't divide 14 tens by 36. Divide 146 ones by 36. Round 36 to 40. $40 \times 3 = 120$. Try 3 as a quotient.

$$
\begin{array}{r}
3 \\
32 \overline{)\,146} \\
-\ 96 \\
\hline
50
\end{array}
\qquad 50 > 36
$$

The remainder is greater than the divisor. So the quotient you tried was too small. Make the quotient one number larger. Try 4.

$$
\begin{array}{r}
4 \quad \text{R2} \\
32 \overline{)\,146} \\
-\ 126 \\
\hline
20
\end{array}
$$

$$146 = (36 \times 4) + 20 \qquad 20 < 36$$

Here's a similar problem for you to try: $13 \overline{)\,851}$

Dividing Thousands

You divide numbers in the thousands by two-digit numbers in the same way.

To solve $32 \overline{)\,6{,}659}$, follow these steps:

1. Divide 66 hundreds by 32.

2. Subtract 64 from 66. Bring down the 5 tens. You cannot divide 25 tens by 32. Write a zero in the tens' place of the quotient.

3. Bring down the 9 ones. Divide 259 ones by 32. **Think:** what times 30 is about 259?

4. Check your work by multiplying the quotient by the divisor, and adding the remainder to that product.

$$
\begin{array}{r}
2\,0\,8 \text{ R.3} \\
32\,)\,\overline{6,6\,5\,9} \\
-\,6\,4\,\downarrow\downarrow \\
\hline
2\,5\,9 \\
-\,2\,5\,6 \\
\hline
3
\end{array}
$$

Check.

$$
\begin{array}{r}
208 \\
\times\,32 \\
\hline
416 \\
+\,6\,2\,4 \\
\hline
6{,}656 \\
+\,3 \\
\hline
6{,}659
\end{array}
$$

Practice writing your answer like this:

$$6{,}659 + (32 \times 208) + 3 \qquad 3 < 32$$

Long division is a very good way to practice both multiplication and division. Here are a few long division problems you can use for practice:

$$39\,)\,\overline{4{,}132} \quad 27\,)\,\overline{1{,}007} \quad 45\,)\,\overline{2{,}503}$$

Estimating Quotients

When you estimate a quotient, you can round the dividend or the divisor to a number that makes the division easy, rather than to the greatest place value. Here are two examples:

$$\text{Estimate } 6 \overline{\smash{\big)}\, 383}$$

Round the dividend (383) to 360 because you can divide 360 by 6 easily. You cannot divide 400 by 6 easily.

$$6 \overline{\smash{\big)}\, 360} = 60$$

$383 \div 6$ is about 60.

$$\text{Estimate } 28 \overline{\smash{\big)}\, 1{,}143}$$

Round the divisor to the greatest place value. 28 rounds to 30. 30 does not go into 1,000 easily. 30 does go into 1,200 easily.

$$30 \overline{\smash{\big)}\, 1{,}200} = 40$$

$1143 \div 28$ is about 40.

Letters That Stand for Numbers

Sometimes in math we use a letter to stand for a number. Here's an example:

$$A = 6 + (8 \times 5)$$

In an equation like this, A stands for a mystery number, and your job as a math detective is to figure out what A equals. In this case, you can solve the mystery by multiplying and then adding. $8 \times 5 = 40$, $40 + 6 = 46$. So $A = 46$.

See if you can figure out the mystery number in this equation: $B = (8 \times 3) - 4$

Equality Properties

Equality properties are rules that can help you solve equations like the ones above. One equality property says that *equals added to equals are equal*. This property can help you figure out the mystery number in the following equation.

$$Y - 25 = 15$$

The equality property you just learned says that, if you add an equal quantity to both sides of any equation, it will still be an equation. Look what happens if we add 25 to both sides of this equation.

$$Y - 25 = 15$$
$$(Y - 25) + 25 = 15 + 25$$
$$Y = 40$$

If you subtract 25 from Y and then add 25, the addition and subtraction cancel each other out, and you are left with just Y on the left side of the equation. On the right side of the equation, you add 25 to 15 and get 40. So you know that Y = 40.

Use the same technique to solve $Z - 12 = 17$ and $P - 29 = 17$.

Now let's learn another equality property: *equals multiplied by equals are equal*. This is also very useful for solving equations. Here's an example:

$$Y \div 2 = 37$$

The equality property tells us that we can multiply both sides of an equation by the same number and we will still have an equation. Look what happens when we multiply by 2:

$$Y \div 2 = 37$$
$$(Y \div 2) \times 2 = 37 \times 2$$
$$Y = 74$$

If we divide Y by 2 and then multiply it by 2, the multiplication undoes the division, and we are left with just Y on the left side of the equation. Meanwhile, on the right side of the equation, we multiply 37 times 2 and get 74. So Y = 74.

Try to solve another problem of this sort on your own: $Z \div 6 = 23$

Remembering these equality properties will help you as you begin to study the kind of math called algebra.

Fractions and Decimals

Fractions

Can you read these numbers?

$$\frac{1}{2} \qquad \frac{1}{3} \qquad \frac{1}{4} \qquad \frac{1}{5} \qquad \frac{1}{6} \qquad \frac{1}{7} \qquad \frac{1}{8} \qquad \frac{1}{9} \qquad \frac{1}{10}$$

These numbers are all *fractions*. They are all smaller than one but larger than zero. Each one is made up of two digits, the numerator and the denominator.

$$\frac{1}{3} \begin{array}{l} \leftarrow \text{numerator} \\ \leftarrow \text{denominator} \end{array}$$

These numbers are all fractions, too.

$$\frac{3}{4} \qquad\qquad \frac{3}{5} \qquad\qquad \frac{5}{5} \qquad\qquad \frac{7}{11} \qquad\qquad \frac{11}{12}$$

Can you identify the numerator and denominator for each fraction?

Improper Fractions

When the numerator of a fraction is equal to or greater than the denominator, the fraction is called an improper fraction. Here are some examples of improper fractions:

$$\frac{5}{5}, \frac{7}{4}, \frac{12}{3}, \text{ and } \frac{18}{5}$$

When the number in the numerator equals the number in the denominator, as in $\frac{5}{5}$, the fraction equals the whole number 1. (Remember that the bar in a fraction means the same thing as a division sign, and any number divided by itself equals 1.) The fraction $\frac{5}{5}$ means the same thing as 5 ÷ 5, and 5 ÷ 5 = 1.

$$\frac{2}{2}, \frac{3}{3}, \frac{1}{1}, \frac{100}{100}, \text{ and } \frac{197}{197} \text{ all equal 1.}$$

When the numerator of an improper fraction can be divided evenly by the denominator, with no remainder, the improper fraction equals a whole number.

$$\frac{12}{4} \quad \rightarrow \quad 4\overline{)\begin{array}{r} 3 \\ 12 \\ -12 \\ \hline 0 \end{array}} \quad \text{so,} \quad \frac{12}{4} = 3.$$

Mixed Numbers

When the numerator of an improper fraction cannot be divided evenly by the denominator, the fraction cannot be written as a whole number. Instead, it must be written as a mixed number. Mixed numbers have one part that's a whole number and one part that's a fraction. $2\frac{2}{3}$, $5\frac{1}{4}$, and $1\frac{1}{6}$ are all mixed numbers.

The improper fraction $\frac{18}{5}$ can be written as a mixed number. Remember that $\frac{18}{5}$ means 18 ÷ 5. If you solve this division problem, you will get a whole number and a remainder.

$$5\overline{)\begin{array}{r} 3 \ \text{R}3 \\ 18 \\ -15 \\ \hline 3 \end{array}}$$

$\frac{18}{5}$ is the same as the mixed number $3\frac{3}{5}$. To write the remainder as a fraction instead of "R3," use the remainder (3) as the numerator of the fraction and the divisor (5) as the denominator of the fraction. A remainder always shows that there is a fractional part left over after a division. The answer to every division problem you have solved that had a remainder could be written as a whole number plus a fraction.

Improper fractions can always be written as either whole numbers or mixed numbers. Take a look at the improper fractions below. Which ones can be written as whole numbers? Which ones can only be written as mixed numbers?

$$\frac{9}{9} \qquad \frac{8}{3} \qquad \frac{8}{2} \qquad \frac{16}{5}$$

Equivalent Fractions

Even if two fractions have different numbers in the numerator and denominator, they can name the same amount. Such fractions are called equivalent fractions.

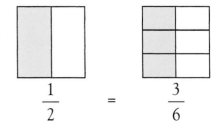

$$\frac{1}{2} \quad = \quad \frac{3}{6}$$

You can make an equivalent fraction by multiplying or dividing both the numerator and the denominator by the same number. Here are two examples:

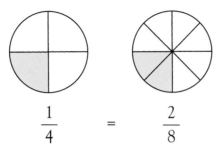

$$\frac{1}{4} \quad = \quad \frac{2}{8}$$

Multiply the numerator and denominator by 2.

$$\frac{1}{4} \quad = \quad \frac{1 \times 2}{4 \times 2} \quad = \quad \frac{2}{8}$$

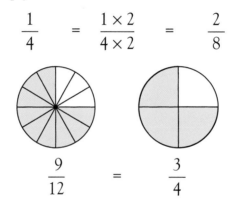

$$\frac{9}{12} \quad = \quad \frac{3}{4}$$

Divide the numerator and denominator by 3.

$$\frac{9}{12} \quad = \quad \frac{9 \div 3}{12 \div 3} \quad = \quad \frac{3}{4}$$

Can you figure out what should go in place of the question mark in the problems below?

$$\frac{2}{3} = \frac{?}{12} \qquad \frac{3}{4} = \frac{?}{100} \qquad \frac{8}{16} = \frac{1}{?}$$

Putting Fractions in Lowest Terms

A fraction is in its lowest terms when its numerator and denominator have no common factor greater than 1—in other words, when no number larger than 1 can divide into both the numerator and denominator. So, to put a fraction in lowest terms, divide the numerator and denominator by common factors, until there is no common factor left greater than one.

Here is an example. Put $\frac{3}{9}$ in lowest terms. You can divide both 3 and 9 by 3. They have 3 as a common factor.

$$\frac{3}{9} \quad = \quad \frac{3 \div 3}{9 \div 3} \quad = \quad \frac{1}{3}$$

1 and 3 have no common factor greater than 1. Therefore, $\frac{1}{3}$ is in lowest terms.

Now try putting $\frac{12}{18}$ in lowest terms. You can divide both 12 and 18 by 2.

$$\frac{12}{18} \quad = \quad \frac{12 \div 2}{18 \div 2} \quad = \quad \frac{6}{9}$$

But you can go further. You can divide both 6 and 9 by 3.

$$\frac{6 \div 3}{9 \div 3} \quad = \quad \frac{2}{3}$$

There are no more common factors greater than 1.

$$\frac{12}{18} \quad = \quad \frac{6}{9} \quad = \quad \frac{2}{3}$$

$\frac{2}{3}$ is the only one of these equivalent fractions that is written in lowest terms.

You could have done this problem in one step by noticing that 12 and 18 have 6 as a common factor. 6 is the greatest common factor of 12 and 18.

$$\frac{12 \div 6}{18 \div 6} \quad = \quad \frac{2}{3}$$

When you divide the numerator and denominator by their greatest common factor, you put a fraction into lowest terms in one step.

Comparing Fractions

You can compare two fractions with the same denominator by comparing their numerators. For example, the fractions $\frac{2}{6}$, $\frac{4}{6}$, $\frac{5}{6}$ have a common denominator.

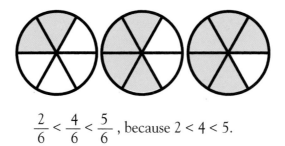

$$\frac{2}{6} < \frac{4}{6} < \frac{5}{6} \text{ , because } 2 < 4 < 5.$$

To compare fractions with different denominators, you must first give them a common denominator. Once their denominators are the same, you can easily compare them. Which fraction is larger, $\frac{2}{3}$ or $\frac{3}{6}$?

First, you need to find the equivalent fraction for $\frac{2}{3}$ with a denominator of 6. You can make an equivalent fraction by multiplying the numerator and the denominator by the same number.

$$\frac{2}{3} = \frac{?}{6}$$

Ask yourself, what do I need to multiply my denominator $\frac{2}{3}$ by to get 6? The answer is 2, because $3 \times 2 = 6$. Now you can find the equivalent fraction by multiplying both the numerator and the denominator by 2.

$$\frac{2}{3} = \frac{2}{3} \times \frac{2}{2} = \frac{4}{6}$$

Therefore, $\frac{2}{3}$ is equivalent to $\frac{4}{6}$. You can now compare $\frac{2}{3}$ and $\frac{3}{6}$ because you have common denominators.

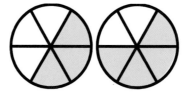

Since 4 is greater than 3, the fraction $\frac{4}{6}$, or $\frac{2}{3}$, is greater than $\frac{3}{6}$.

Can you compare $\frac{2}{3}$ and $\frac{5}{12}$? Which fraction is larger?

Adding Fractions

You can add fractions with the same denominator by adding the numerators. You write each sum in lowest terms.

$$\frac{2}{5} + \frac{1}{5} = \frac{3}{5} \qquad\qquad \frac{4}{9} + \frac{3}{9} = \frac{7}{9}$$

Be sure to add only the numerators. The denominators stay the same. The picture in the example shows why. You are adding the equal parts shown in each numerator. You are not changing the size of the equal parts shown in the denominator.

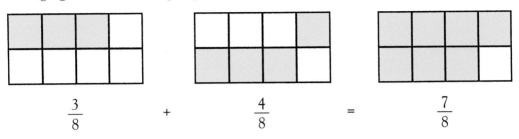

$$\frac{3}{8} \qquad + \qquad \frac{4}{8} \qquad = \qquad \frac{7}{8}$$

Practice adding fractions that have the same denominator. Make sure to write the sum in lowest terms. If the sum is an improper fraction, write it as a whole number or a mixed number in lowest terms. Here are three examples.

$$\frac{5}{9} + \frac{7}{9} = \frac{12}{9} = 1\frac{3}{9} = 1\frac{1}{3} \qquad \frac{5}{12} + \frac{1}{12} = \frac{6}{12} = \frac{1}{2} \qquad \frac{7}{13} + \frac{6}{13} = \frac{13}{13} = 1$$

Subtracting Fractions

You can subtract two fractions that have the same denominator by subtracting the numerators. The denominators remain the same. Here is an example.

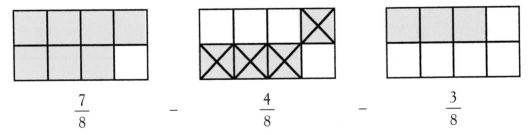

$$\frac{7}{8} \qquad - \qquad \frac{4}{8} \qquad - \qquad \frac{3}{8}$$

When you subtract fractions, make sure to write the difference in lowest terms. here are two examples.

$$\frac{5}{16} - \frac{3}{16} = \frac{2}{16} = \frac{1}{8} \qquad \frac{5}{12} - \frac{5}{12} = \frac{0}{12} = 0$$

Notice that $\frac{0}{12} = 0$. All fractions with a numerator of 0 equal 0.

Expressing Simple Outcomes

Sometimes we use fractions to express simple outcomes. For instance, suppose you took a survey to see how many fans at a football game were rooting for the home team and how many for the visitors. After asking a lot of people, you found that for every 4 fans you asked, 3 supported the home team and only 1 supported the visitors. You could use fractions to explain these outcomes. You might say that $\frac{3}{4}$ of the crowd was rooting for the home team and only $\frac{1}{4}$ for the visitors.

Suppose there are 25 students in your class, 15 girls and 10 boys. That means $\frac{15}{25}$ of the class is girls. Can you put that fraction in lowest terms? What fraction, in lowest terms, would tell what part of the class is boys?

Decimals

You can write the fraction $\frac{1}{10}$ as the decimal 0.1. You read both the same way—one tenth. The period to the left of the 1 is called a decimal point. The decimal point shows that the value of the digits to its right is anywhere between 0 and 1, like a fraction. A decimal is any number that uses places to the right of the decimal point to show a fraction.

The first place to the right of the decimal point is the tenths' place.

ones	.	tenths
1	.	7

You can write the mixed number $1\frac{7}{10}$ as the decimal 1.7. You read both the same way: one and seven tenths.

The second place to the right of the decimal point is the hundredths' place. $\frac{1}{100}$ can also be written 0.01.

ones	.	tenths	hundredths
0	.	0	1

You read both the same way—one hundredth.

$2\frac{47}{100} =$

ones	.	tenths	hundredths
2	.	4	7

You read both as two and forty-seven hundredths.

Notice that when there are both tenths and hundredths in a decimal, you read the tenths and hundredths together in terms of hundredths. Also remember to put an "and" between the whole number part and the fractional part of a decimal, just as in mixed numbers.

The third place to the right of the decimal point is the thousandths' place. You can write $\frac{1}{1000}$ as 0.001.

ones	.	tenths	hundredths	thousanths
0	.	0	0	1

You read both as in the same way—one thousandth.

Notice that as you move from the left to the right, each place value gets 10 times smaller: first tenths, then hundredths, the thousandths. In the decimal system, each place has a value one-tenth as large as one to its left.

$$3\,\frac{857}{1000} = 3.857$$

You read both as three and eight hundred fifty-seven thousandths. Notice that, because there are thousandths in the decimal, you read the tenths and hundredths in terms of thousandths.

Reading and Writing Decimals

Practice writing decimals in words. 0.27 is twenty seven hundredths; 3.8 is three and eight tenths. Also practice writing decimals that are in words with digits. Three hundred fifty-four thousandths is 0.354. Five hundred and fourteen hundredths is 500.14. Can you write seven hundred and one thousandth?

Practice writing decimals in expanded form. 176.04 is 100 + 70 + 6 + 0.04. What is 600 + 40 + 0.7 + 0.08?

Decimals as Fractions

You can write decimals as fractions and fractions as decimals. $\frac{39}{100}$ can be written as 0.39; and 0.02 can be written $\frac{2}{100}$. Rewrite $\frac{25}{100}$ and $\frac{101}{1000}$ as decimals. Rewrite 0.16 and 0.599 as fractions. Ready for something more challenging? Find the decimal equivalents of the fractions that follow. You'll need to convert the fractions to equivalents with a denominator of 100.

$$\frac{1}{2}, \frac{1}{4}, \frac{1}{8}, \frac{1}{10}$$

Convert these decimals to fractions, in lowest terms: .25, .75, .875

Rounding Decimals

You round decimals the same way you round whole numbers. To decide whether to round a decimal up or down, look at the digit to the right of the place to which you are rounding.

Round 6.85 to the nearest tenth. Look at the digit to the right of the 8 in the tenths' place. It's a 5, so round up to 6.9.

Round 7.453 to the nearest hundredth. Look at the digit to the right of the 5 in the hundredths' place. It's a 3, so round down to 7.45.

Rounding a decimal to the nearest *whole* number means rounding it to the ones' place, so that there is no fractional part left. Round 76.47 to the nearest whole number. Look at the digit to the right of the ones' place. 76.4 is closer to 76 than 77. So round down to 76.

Comparing Decimals

Remember that when you compare numbers, you start with their greatest place values.

Compare 7.77 and 7.82. First, compare the ones: 7=7. Next, compare the tenths: 0.7 < 0.8. So 7.77 < 7.82.

Compare 7.77 and 7.7. Remember that you can write 7.7 as 7.70. Then you can compare 7.77 and 7.70. Compare the ones: 7=7. Compare the tenths: 0.7 = 0.7. Compare the hundredths: 0.07 > 0.00, so 7.77 > 7.7.

Practice comparing decimals in problems like these. Remember that you can add zeros to the end of decimals without changing their value.

Comparing Decimals and Fractions

You can also compare decimals and fractions. For example, compare $1\frac{7}{10}$ and 1.15. First rewrite the mixed number $1\frac{7}{10}$ as a decimal: 1.7. Now compare 1.7 and 1.15 Compare the ones: 1 = 1. Compare the tenths: 0.7 > 0.1. So 1.70 > 1.15.

Which is greater, $\frac{1}{4}$ or 0.27? Hint: convert .27 to a fraction and then convert $\frac{1}{4}$ to a fraction with the same denominator.

Reading Decimals on a Number Line

We can show decimals on a number line.

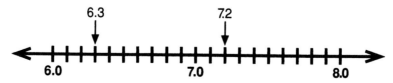

On this number line, each mark shows a tenth. The first arrow is at 6.3, three tenths past 6. The second arrow is at 7.2. You can see from the number line that 7.2 > 6.3.

Adding and Subtracting Decimals

You add and subtract decimals the same way that you add and subtract whole numbers. You must make sure the decimal points and the place values are lined up correctly. Line up the tenths with the tenths, the hundredths with the hundredths, and the thousandths with the thousandths.

Add 0.167 and 2.346.

$$
\begin{array}{r}
0.167 \\
+\ 2.346 \\
\hline
2.513
\end{array}
$$

Make sure to put the decimal point in your answer.

Subtract 1.846 from 5.072.

$$
\begin{array}{r}
{\scriptstyle 4\ 10\ 6\ 12} \\
\cancel{5}.0\cancel{7}\cancel{2} \\
-\ 1.846 \\
\hline
3.226
\end{array}
$$

Make sure to put the decimal point in your answer.

Sometimes it is helpful to put in zeros when you are adding decimals to help you line up the place values correctly. It is not necessary to add zeros, however, as long as you can keep the place values straight.

Add 9.307 + 8 + 0.53 + 6.2

One way is to put in decimal points and zeros.

$$
\begin{array}{r}
9.307 \\
8.000 \\
0.530 \\
+\ 6.200 \\
\hline
24.037
\end{array}
$$

Another way is to leave the numbers as they are.

$$
\begin{array}{r}
9.307 \\
8 \\
0.53 \\
+\ 6.2 \\
\hline
24.037
\end{array}
$$

When you subtract decimals, often you *must* put in zeros. Here is an example. When you subtract 2.63 from 5, you must write 5 with a decimal point and two zeros, to match 2.63. Then subtract.

$$
\begin{array}{r}
{}^{4}\!\!\!\!\!{}^{9}{}^{10} \\
5.00 \\
+\,2.63 \\
\hline
2.37
\end{array}
$$

Making Change

We express dollars and cents using decimals. We write three dollars and forty-five cents like this:

$$\$3.45$$

Suppose you are selling cookies to raise money for your favorite club. Each box of cookies costs $2.75. A man gives you $5.00 for one box. How much change should you give him. Line up the decimal points and do the subtraction:

$$
\begin{array}{r}
\$5.00 \\
-\,2.75 \\
\hline
\$2.25
\end{array}
$$

You should give the customer two one-dollar bills and 25 cents in change. The change might be a quarter, or two dimes and a nickel, or 25 pennies.

Measurement

Measuring Length in U.S. Customary Units

In the United States, we generally measure length using U.S. customary units: inches, feet, yards, and miles. The following chart shows you the U.S. customary units and their abbreviations. It also shows some equivalences among the units. An equivalence shows that two things that appear different are really of equal value.

$$1 \text{ foot (ft.)} \quad = \quad 12 \text{ inches (in.)}$$
$$1 \text{ yard (yd.)} \quad = \quad 3 \text{ feet}$$
$$1 \text{ mile (mi.)} \quad = \quad 5280 \text{ feet}$$
$$1 \text{ mile} \qquad\quad = \quad 1760 \text{ yards}$$

A ruler often measures one foot. To help you measure lengths more quickly, many rulers have lines that mark the inches and fractions of an inch. The longest lines on the ruler below mark the inches. The next longest lines mark half ($\frac{1}{2}$) inch intervals. The lines marking each quarter ($\frac{1}{4}$) of an inch are a bit shorter, and the lines for the eighths ($\frac{1}{8}$) are even shorter. The shortest marks on many rulers mark sixteenths of an inch ($\frac{1}{16}$). Notice that only the inches are labeled. You have to be able to recognize the halves, quarters, and eighths. See if you can measure the nail that sits next to the ruler.

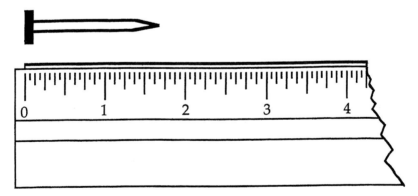

When measuring the length of a real object, we often estimate to the nearest unit. Look at the nail in the picture.

To the nearest inch, the nail is 2 inches.

To the nearest half inch, the nail is $1\frac{1}{2}$ inches.

To the nearest quarter inch, the nail is $1\frac{3}{4}$ inches.

To the nearest eighth inch, the nail is $1\frac{5}{8}$ inches.

The smaller the unit of measure, the more precise your measurement of the length of the screw will be.

Find some small items and measure them to the nearest eighth of an inch using the ruler above or a ruler of your own.

It's also important to practice converting from one unit to another. For instance, you should be able to figure out how many feet there are in half a mile. You know from the table of equivalences that 1 mile equals 5280 feet. To find $\frac{1}{2}$ of any number, you divide it by 2. $5280 \div 2 = 2640$, so a half mile equals 2640 ft.

You should memorize the equivalences listed in this book. That way you can switch from one unit to another without having to look at a table.

Measuring Length in Metric Units

Not everyone uses the U.S. customary units of measurement. In fact, most people in other countries use a different system of measurement, called the metric system.

Some important metric units for measuring length are shown below:

1 centimeter (cm.) = 10 millimeters (mm.)
1 meter (m.)   = 1,000 millimeters (mm.)
1 meter (m.)   = 100 centimeters (cm.)
1 kilometer (km.)   = 1,000 meters (m.)

A meter is a little longer than a yard. A meter stick is typically divided into centimeters and millimeters. Can you measure the paper clip below?

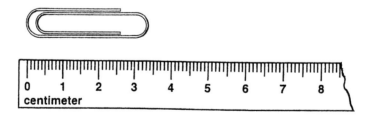

The paper clip is about 3.4 centimeters long, or 34 millimeters long. Take the small objects you gathered when you were measuring inches and measure them to the nearest tenth of a centimeter, or to the nearest millimeter.

Because the metric system is based on the decimal system, it is easy to change from one metric unit to another. It's like working with place value. Here are two examples:

1. How many meters are there in 3 kilometers? Since 1 km = 1000 m, multiply by 1000 to change kilometers to meters. $3 \times 1000 = 3000$. So 3 km = 3000 m.

2. How many meters are there in 400 centimeters? Since 100 cm = 1 m, you divide by 100 to change centimeters to meters. 400 ÷ 100 = 4, so 400 cm = 4 m.

Measuring Weight in U.S. Customary Units

In the United States we measure weight using ounces, pounds, and tons.

$$1 \text{ pound (lb.)} = 16 \text{ ounces (oz.)}$$
$$2{,}000 \text{ lb.} = 1 \text{ ton (t.)}$$

When a baby is born, we usually describe its weight in pounds and ounces, like 8 pounds, 4 ounces. When a child gets older and bigger, we usually express his or her weight in pounds, estimating to the nearest pound. We might use tons if we were measuring the amount of a weight a truck or airplane can transport.

If you have a bathroom scale in your house you can practice weighing household items in pounds. First weigh yourself. Then weigh yourself holding the object. The difference between what you weigh holding the object and what you weigh by yourself is the weight of the object.

Practice converting from pounds to ounces and ounces to pounds. How many ounces are in 8 lb., 3 oz.? To solve this problem, find out how many ounces are in 8 pounds, and then add 3 ounces. From the table of equivalences you know that 1 pound = 16 ounces. So 8 pounds would be 8×16 ounces.

$$8 \text{ lb. } 3 \text{ oz.} = (16 \times 8) \text{ oz} + 3 \text{ oz}$$
$$= 128 \text{ oz} + 3 \text{ oz}$$
$$= 131 \text{ oz}$$

Measuring Weight in Metric Units

The main units for weight in the metric system are the milligram, the gram, and the kilogram. Here are some equivalences:

1 centigram (cg.)	=	10 milligrams (mg.)
1 gram (g.)	=	1,000 milligrams (mg.)
1 gram (g.)	=	100 centigrams (cg.)
1 kilogram (kg.)	=	1,000 grams (g.)

Notice again how the metric system is based on the decimal system, with each unit 10, 100, or 1000 times larger than another unit. There are 1000 grams in a kilogram. You could also say that one gram equals $\frac{1}{1000}$ of a kilogram.

If one egg weighs 84 grams, how much would a dozen eggs weigh? To find the answer, you multiply 84 times a dozen, or 12. $84 \times 12 = 1,008$ grams. How else could you say that? One kilogram, eight grams.

Measuring Capacity in U.S. Customary Units

When cooks prepare food, they use measuring cups, with different sized cups for one cup, $\frac{1}{2}$ cup, $\frac{1}{3}$ cup, and $\frac{1}{4}$ cup. When you buy milk or juice, you often buy a pint, a quart, or a gallon. All of these measurements tell how much liquid is inside.

Here are the equivalences for the U.S. customary measurements of capacity, or volume.

1 cup (c.)	=	8 fluid ounces (oz.)
1 pint (pt.)	=	2 cups
1 quart (qt.).	=	2 pints
1 gallon (gal.)	=	4 quarts

How many cups of milk are in the measuring cup shown? How many ounces?

Measuring Capacity in Metric Units

As with the other measurements, capacity is measured differently in the metric system. Here are the metric units:

1 centiliter (cl.)	=	10 milliliters (ml.)
1 liter	=	1,000 milliliters (ml.)
1 liter	=	100 centiliters (cl.)

If you had a one-liter can of oil and you poured half of it into your car's engine, how many milliliters would be left?

Getting to Know the Metric System

The metric system is used in most foreign countries and in most scientific research. It is being used more and more often in the United States as well. So it's useful to have a good sense of the metric units.

For instance, it's useful to know that a meter is a little longer than a yard, that 100 kilometers is about the same distance as 60 miles, and that a small bag of potato chips weighs about 40 grams.

Adding and Subtracting with Different Units

When you add or subtract lengths that are in different U.S. customary units, you need to regroup in different ways.

Add the inches first.
Regroup 15 in. as 1 ft. 3 in.

$$
\begin{array}{rr}
\mathbf{1} & \\
3 \text{ ft.} & 7 \text{ in.} \\
+ 2 \text{ ft.} & 8 \text{ in.} \\
\hline
& \mathbf{15} \\
6 \text{ ft.} & 3 \text{ in.}
\end{array}
$$

You can't take 9 in. from 4 in.
Regroup 21 ft. 4 in. as 20 ft. 16 in.

$$
\begin{array}{rr}
\mathbf{20} & \mathbf{16} \\
21 \text{ft.} & 4 \text{ in.} \\
- 15 \text{ ft.} & 9 \text{ in.} \\
\hline
5 \text{ ft.} & 7 \text{ in.}
\end{array}
$$

You can also regroup in the same way to add or subtract feet and yards, or yards and miles.

When you add metric measurements, you write the measurements in the same unit first.

To add 2.68 liters and 27 milliliters, you can write both measurements in either liters or milliliters.

$$27 \text{ l} = 0.027 \text{ l}$$

$$2.68 \text{ l} = 2680 \text{ ml}$$

2.68 l	2680 ml
+ 0.027 l	+ 27 ml
2.707 l	2707 ml

Always write metric measurements in a single unit before you add them.

Changing Units of Time

There are 24 hours in a day, 60 minutes in an hour, and 60 seconds in a minute. So how many minutes are there in 5 hours and 11 minutes? To find out the answer to this question, multiply 5 by 60 to find out how many minutes are in 5 hours. Then add 11 minutes. $(5 \times 60) + 11 = 300 + 11$. There are 311 minutes in 5 hours and 11 minutes.

How many minutes and seconds are there in 147 seconds?

Adding and Subtracting Time

When you add and subtract time, you may need to regroup, but in a different way. Instead of regrouping so that 10 ones make 1 ten, when you add hours and minutes, regroup 60 minutes as one hour whenever there are 60 minutes or more. Here is an example of adding two times:

A train journey lasts 7 hours and 45 minutes. If the train leaves at 1:43 P.M., when will it arrive at its destination?

You add: hours minutes

$$
\begin{array}{r}
1 \\
1 \; : \; 43 \\
+7 \; : \; 45 \\
\hline
88 \\
9 \; : \; 28
\end{array}
$$

88 minutes = **1** hour **28** minutes
Add the 1 hour to the other hours.

The train will arrive at 9:28 P.M.

You add or subtract minutes and seconds in the same way. When you subtract minutes and seconds, you may need to regroup 1 minute as 60 seconds.

Emily ran a race in 37 minutes and 22 seconds. Stella ran it in 28 minutes and 47 seconds. How much faster was Stella's time?

Geometry

Planes, Points, and Segments

A plane is a flat surface that keeps going on forever in all directions. It has no thickness. Here's a diagram of a plane.

Plane geometry is the study of points, lines, segments, and figures that can be drawn on a plane. Let's learn about some of these.

Take a pencil and make the tiniest dot you can. In geometry, a tiny dot like that is called a point.

Now draw a second point and connect the two points with a ruler. This is called a line segment, or segment.

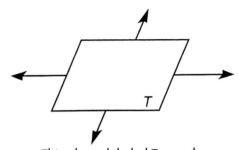

This plane, labeled T, stretches in all four directions.

Points are named with letters, and so are segments. The two points in the illustration are G and H. The segment could be called either $\overline{GH}$ or $\overline{HG}$. The segment over the name tells us this is a segment.

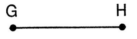

Lines and Rays

What's the difference between a line and a line segment? A segment has a beginning and an ending point. A line goes on forever in both directions.

Since it is not possible to draw a line that goes on forever, we draw an arrow on both ends of a line, to show that it keeps on going in both directions. A line can be named for any two points along the line. This is line BE, or $\overleftrightarrow{BE}$:

Vertical lines run up and down; horizontal lines run side to side (like $\overleftrightarrow{BE}$). You can remember which is which by remembering that horizontal lines run side to side, like the horizon.

A ray is part of a line. It has one end point, and continues forever in only one direction—away from its end point. To name a ray, begin with its end point and add another point along the ray. This is ray EF, or $\overrightarrow{EF}$:

Angles

An angle is formed by two rays that have the same end point. The end point is called the vertex of the angle. Here is angle WXY.

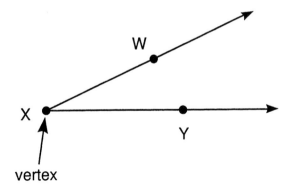

Point X is the vertex of angle WXY. When you name an angle, you always put the vertex in the middle. You can begin by naming either of the other two points, so this angle can also be called angle YXW. The word "angle" is sometimes abbreviated like this: ∠YXW.

Types of Angles

There are three kinds of angles: right angles, acute angles, and obtuse angles. Here's what they look like:

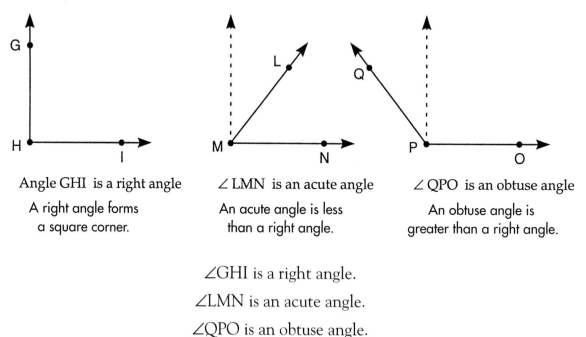

Angle GHI is a right angle

A right angle forms a square corner.

∠ LMN is an acute angle

An acute angle is less than a right angle.

∠ QPO is an obtuse angle

An obtuse angle is greater than a right angle.

∠GHI is a right angle.

∠LMN is an acute angle.

∠QPO is an obtuse angle.

Look around you for angles. What kind of angle does the corner of a windowpane form? How about the corner of a slice of cake?

Intersecting, Perpendicular, and Parallel Lines

When two lines meet, we say they intersect. Here are two intersecting lines.

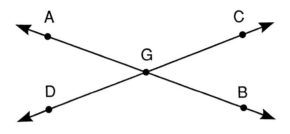

$\overleftrightarrow{DC}$ and $\overleftrightarrow{AB}$ intersect at point G. When two lines intersect to form right angles, we say they are perpendicular.

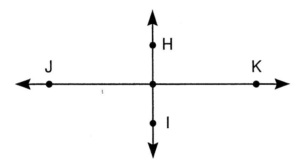

Lines $\overleftrightarrow{HI}$ and $\overleftrightarrow{JK}$ are perpendicular. Where they meet, they form 4 right angles. Lines $\overleftrightarrow{AB}$ and $\overleftrightarrow{DC}$ above are not perpendicular.

Parallel lines are lines that never intersect. Line $\overleftrightarrow{BE}$ and Line $\overleftrightarrow{GH}$ are parallel lines.

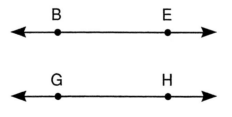

Polygons, Triangles

A polygon is a closed plane figure with three or more line segments as its sides. Polygons also have three or more angles inside them. In fact, the word polygon comes from a Greek word meaning many angles.

Polygons that have three sides are called triangles. The prefix "tri" means three. All triangles have three sides and three angles. They also have three vertices, or points where the sides of a triangle meet.

The vertices of triangle ABC are points A, B, and C. We name polygons by their vertices. Triangles that have three sides of the same length are called equilateral triangles. Because their sides are all of equal length, their angles will be the same measure, too. Triangle ABC is an equilateral triangle.

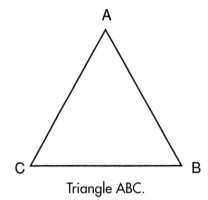

Triangle ABC.

Quadrilaterals and Diagonals

The prefix "quadri-" means four and "lateral" means side. Quadrilaterals are polygons with four sides.

The figures below are quadrilaterals.

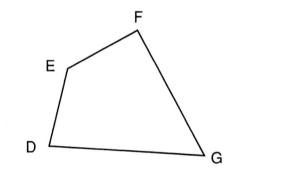

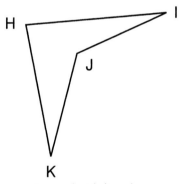

In a quadrilateral, vertices that are not connected by a side are called opposite vertices. A line segment that joins two opposite vertices of a quadrilateral is called a diagonal.

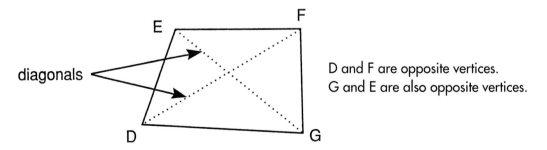

diagonals

D and F are opposite vertices.
G and E are also opposite vertices.

Segments $\overline{DF}$ and $\overline{EG}$ are the diagonals of quadrilateral DEFG.

Kinds of Quadrilaterals

A quadrilateral with only *one* pair of parallel sides is called a trapezoid.

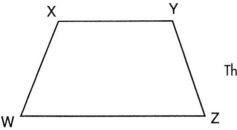

This quadrilateral is a trapezoid.

Quadrilateral WXYZ is a trapezoid. A line that included segment $\overline{XY}$ would be parallel with a line that included segment $\overline{WZ}$, so we say these two sides are parallel.

A quadrilateral with two pairs of parallel sides is a parallelogram.

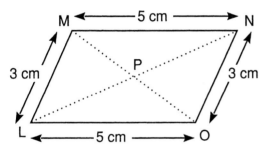

Quadrilateral LMNO is a parallelogram. $\overline{MN}$ is parallel to $\overline{LO}$. $\overline{ML}$ is parallel to $\overline{NO}$.

In a quadrilateral, sides that do not meet at a vertex are called opposite sides. The opposite sides of a parallelogram are parallel: sides $\overline{MN}$ and $\overline{LO}$ are parallel; sides $\overline{ML}$ and $\overline{NO}$ are also parallel. Opposite sides of a parallelogram also have the same length. $\overline{MN}$ and $\overline{LO}$ are both 5 cm. long. $\overline{ML}$ and $\overline{NO}$ are both 3 cm. long.

Rectangles and Squares

Rectangles are special kinds of parallelograms. Rectangles are parallelograms with four right angles.

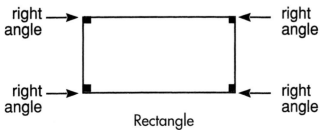

Rectangle

Rectangles can have two sides measuring one length, and two sides measuring a different length. Or, all four sides can be the same length. A rectangle whose four sides are all the same length is called a square.

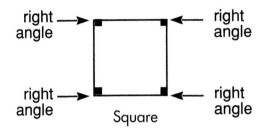

Other Polygons

A polygon with five sides is called a pentagon. A polygon with six sides is called a hexagon. A polygon with eight sides is called an octagon.

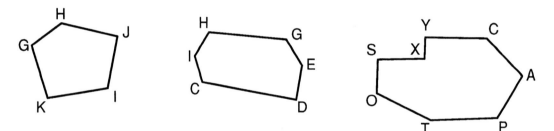

A regular polygon has sides of equal length and angles of equal measure. The hexagon and octagon shown below are regular polygons.

a pentagon   a hexagon   an octagon

Are the three polygons shown above regular or irregular? What well-known, red traffic sign is shaped like a regular octagon?

Circles

A circle is a closed figure, but not a polygon. Polygons have line segments for sides. A circle curves in such a way that every point along the circle is exactly the same distance from the center of the circle.

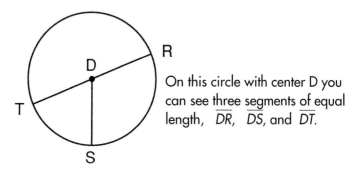

On this circle with center D you can see three segments of equal length, $\overline{DR}$, $\overline{DS}$, and $\overline{DT}$.

A line segment whose end points are the center of a circle and a point on the circle is called a "radius" of the circle. Radius is a Latin word, and the plural is "radii" [RAY-dee-eye]. Segments DR, DS, and DT are radii of the circle above. Since all the radii of a circle have the same length, we also call the length of any radius of a circle its radius.

A line segment whose end points are both on the circle and which passes through the center of a circle is called a "diameter" of the circle. Segment RT is a diameter of the circle above. All the diameters of a circle have the same length. The diameter of a circle is always twice as long as its radius.

With a compass, practice drawing circles with a certain radius or a certain diameter. To do this, make a dot for the center of the circle you want to draw, and open the compass to the length of the radius of the circle. Put one point of the compass on a piece of paper. Keeping the point still, swing the arm of the compass around until it draws a circle.

Similar Figures

Congruent figures have both the same shape and the same size. We say two figures are similar when they have the same shape, but not necessarily the same size. When two figures have the same shape and the same size, they are both similar and congruent. All congruent figures are similar, but not all similar figures are congruent.

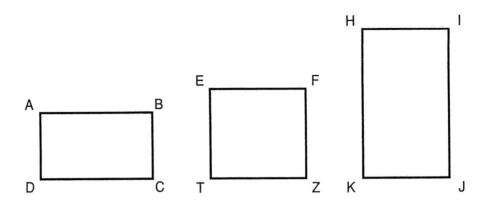

For example, rectangles ABCD and HIJK are similar. Though they have different sizes, they have the same shape.

Rectangles ABCD and EFZT are not similar. They do not have the same shape.

All squares are similar, and all circles are similar.

The Area of a Rectangle

The length and width of a rectangle are called its dimensions. A rectangle has two dimensions. The length of a rectangle is the length of either of its two longer sides. The width of a rectangle is the length of either of its two shorter sides.

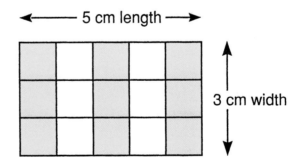

There are 5×3 square centimeters in this rectangle. Its area is 15 cm.[2]. You can find the area of a rectangle by multiplying its length by its width.

Here is the formula for the area of a rectangle. A formula is an equation written with letters that tells you a relationship that is always true. In this formula, A stands for the area of a rectangle, l for its length, and w for its width.

$$A = l \times w \text{ or Area} = \text{length} \times \text{width}$$

You can always find the area of a rectangle by substituting real numbers for l and w and then multiplying the rectangle's length by its width. This is one of many useful formulas in mathematics.

Square Units

You always measure area in square units.

Some U.S. Customary units of area:	Some metric inits of area:
mi.^{2} (*square mile*)	km.^{2} (*square kilometer*)
yd.^{2} (*square yard*)	m.^{2} (*square meter*)
ft.^{2} (*square foot*)	cm.^{2} (*square centimeter*)
in.^{2} (*square inch*)	mm.^{2} (*square millimeter*)

1. What is the area of this rectangle? To find the area of a rectangle, you multiply its length by its width. $27 \times 24 = 648$. The area of this rectangle is 648 square feet.

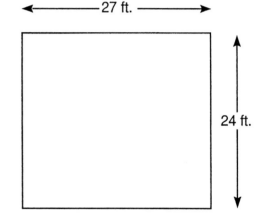

2. How many square inches are there in a square foot? Remember that there are 12 inches in 1 foot.

$$12 \times 12 = 144$$

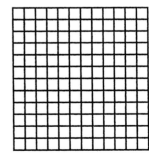

There are 144 in.^{2} (*square inches*) in 1 ft.^{2} (*square foot*). Notice that there are not 12 square inches in a square foot, even though there are 12 inches in a foot! Changing units of area is different from changing units of length. Work out how many mm.^{2} there are in 1 cm.^{2}, how many ft.^{2} there are in 1 yd.^{2}, and how many cm.^{2} there are in 1 m.^{2}.

3. You know the length of this rectangle (12 cm.) and its total area (84 cm.²). Find its width.

You know that 12 cm. × _____ cm. = 84cm.². So you must divide the area by the length to find the width:

$$12 \overline{)84} \atop 7$$

$$\begin{array}{r} 7 \\ 12 \overline{)84} \\ -84 \\ \hline 0 \end{array}$$

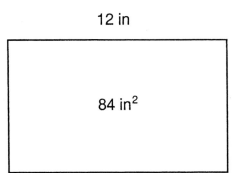

12 in

84 in²

?

The width is 7 cm.

When you know the measurement of one dimension of a rectangle and its total area, you can divide to find the measurement of the other dimension.

Volume

So far we've been looking at figures with two dimensions—figures that can be drawn on a plane. Now let's look at a three-dimensional figure called a rectangular prism. A rectangular prism looks like a box.

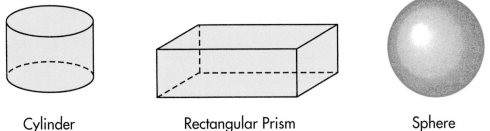

Cylinder
two flat circular faces
no vertexes

Rectangular Prism

Sphere
no flat faces

Notice that all of the faces of this prism are rectangles. There are six faces in all: top and bottom, left and right, and front and back.

The volume of a three-dimensional figure is how much space it occupies. You measure space in cubic units. One example of a cubic unit is a cubic centimeter. The abbreviation for cubic centimeter is cm.³.

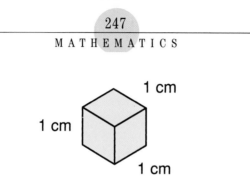

One cubic centimeter (1 cm³)

Notice that a cubic centimeter is a cube. All cubic units are cubes.

By counting cubic units, you can find the volume of a figure—how much space it occupies. Sometimes you have to count cubic units that you know are there but you cannot see.

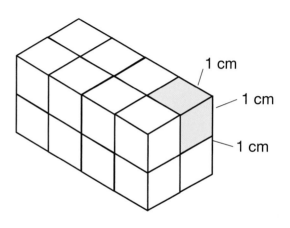

You can count cubic units that are hidden by thinking about the pattern of those that you can see. On one layer of this rectangular prism, there are 8 cubes. There are two layers. 8 × 2 = 16. There are 16 cubic centimeters in the rectangular prism.

See if you can figure out the volume of the next figure. Notice that there are two sections: the top section is a cube 2 cm. on each side. The bottom section is a rectangular prism 4 x 4 x 2. To figure the total volume, you'll have to figure each section separately and then add them together.

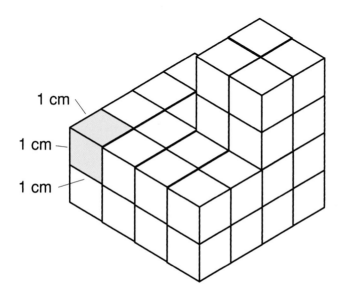

VI.

Science

Introduction

This chapter treats the circulatory and respiratory systems, electricity, atoms, chemistry, geology, and meteorology. It also profiles several eminent scientists.

Parents and teachers can supplement this chapter by taking children to science museums and doing simple science experiments. Many books of fun, safe experiments are now available.

Children should also be encouraged to view the world scientifically: to ask questions about nature and seek answers through observation, to collect, count, and measure, to start a rock collection, or monitor weather conditions, or learn about wind by flying a kite.

Hands-on experience is so important that some educators now reject the very idea of teaching young children about science from books. But book learning should not be neglected altogether. It helps bring system and coherence to a young person's developing knowledge of nature and provides essential building blocks for later study. Book learning also provides knowledge not likely to be gained by simple observations; for instance, books can teach us about things that are not visible to the naked eye, like white blood cells, subatomic particles, and continental drift. And we should not forget that some children enjoy book learning even more than they enjoy experiments and field trips. Both kinds of experience are necessary to ensure that gaps in knowledge will not hinder later understanding.

The Human Body

Circulation and Respiration

Put your hand on your chest and feel your heart beat. Now take a deep breath and feel the air expanding your chest. Every time your heart beats, blood pumps through a network of blood vessels, from the heart to all the parts of your body. Every time you breathe in, air fills your lungs. Oxygen in that air travels from your lungs into your bloodstream, ready to feed the cells in your body.

The heart and the blood vessels are parts of your body's circulatory system. The lungs and windpipe are parts of your respiratory system. These two systems work together to keep you alive. To understand them, though, let's study them separately.

The Heart

The heart is a powerful muscle. It works every second of every day, from the moment you are born until the day you die. Most of the time, you don't even know it is working. But if you sprint up some stairs, you can feel it working harder, thump-thump-thumping as it pumps blood through your body.

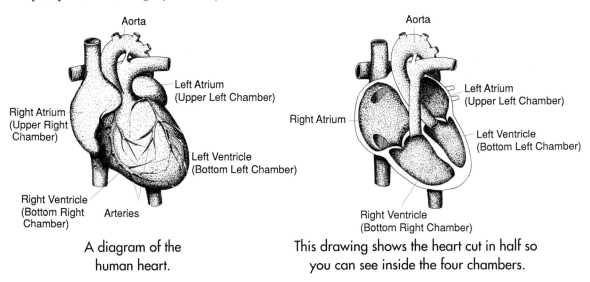

A diagram of the human heart.

This drawing shows the heart cut in half so you can see inside the four chambers.

Your heart is about the size of your fist. It is divided into four chambers. The top two chambers are called the *atriums*; the bottom two, the *ventricles*. Valves in between the ventricles and atriums open and close to allow the blood to flow through the heart.

Blood needing oxygen comes into the heart through the right atrium. It squeezes through a valve and into the right ventricle. From there, it flows out to the lungs for a new supply of oxygen. From the lungs, it flows back into the left atrium of the heart, squeezes through a valve into the left ventricle, and then is pumped out of the heart through the *aorta*, the biggest blood vessel of all. The aorta divides and branches out to take the blood to all the different parts of the body.

The Blood Vessels

The heart pumps blood through your body in hollow, stretchy tubes called *blood vessels*. The blood vessels that carry the oxygen-rich blood away from your heart are called *arteries*. The blood vessels that carry blood back to your heart for more oxygen are called *veins*.

Smaller blood vessels, called *capillaries*, branch off from arteries and veins. The tiny capillaries bring blood in contact with the cells in the body. Capillary walls are so thin that nutrients, oxygen, and waste products pass back and forth through them easily. Capillaries connect arteries and veins. They are the endpoint of arteries, through which oxygen and nutrients are delivered, and the starting point of veins, which pick up and carry waste materials away.

You can see some capillaries by looking in the mirror and *gently* pulling down on your lower eyelid. See those tiny red squiggles on your eyeball? Those are capillaries.

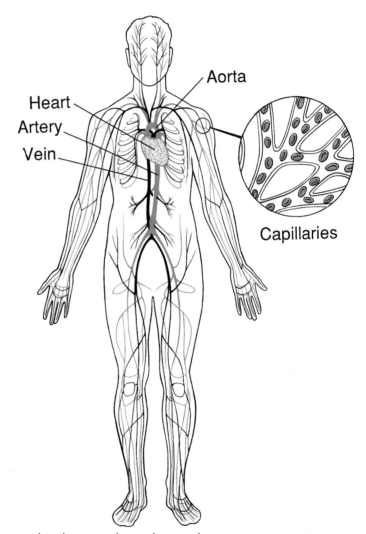

This diagram shows the circulatory system. Arteries are shown in orange and veins are shown in black.

Blood Pressure and Heart Rate

Each time the heart pumps, the stretchy blood vessels swell and shrink as the blood courses through them. The pushing force, caused by the pumping heart, that moves blood through the body is called *blood pressure*. Blood pressure is one of the things that nurses and doctors check to make sure that your circulatory system is working properly.

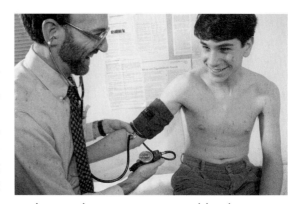

A doctor taking a young man's blood pressure.

Your pulse, or heart rate, indicates how often your heart squeezes to pump blood through your body. To measure your heart rate, press your fingertips on the pulse point in your wrist. Use a watch with a second hand and count the number of pulses in 30 seconds. The average human heart rate is about 90 pulses a minute, so you will probably count about forty-five in half a minute.

But what happens to your heart rate when you exercise? Hop on one leg ten times, then wave your arms over your head ten times. Then measure your heart rate again. When you exercise, your cells use lots of oxygen and soon need more. That's why exercise makes you breathe harder and makes your heart pump faster.

What Is Blood and Why Do We Need It?

Blood never stops moving through your body. It delivers nutrients from food and oxygen to the cells in organs, muscles, bones, and nerves. It picks up waste materials from the cells in your body and carries that waste to organs that can process it. Cells give off a gas called carbon dioxide, which blood carries back to the lungs. When you breathe out, you release carbon dioxide.

If you look at blood under a microscope, you can see tiny objects of several different shapes, all floating in a thin, clear liquid. The liquid part of blood is called the *plasma*. The most common shapes you

This photo of red and white blood cells shows them as they would appear under a microscope—magnified to many times their real size. The red blood cells look like doughnuts with the centers not quite punched out. The round cells with the bumpy surfaces (lymphocytes) are another kind of blood cell.

would see floating in the plasma are the *red blood cells*. There are over 25 trillion—that's 25,000,000,000,000!—red blood cells in one person's body. Red blood cells contain a substance called *hemoglobin*. It's the hemoglobin that does the work of carrying oxygen and carbon dioxide.

Looking through the microscope, you would also see *white blood cells*. White blood cells are like a special forces team that travels in the blood, ready to fight disease on a moment's notice. When an infection develops, white blood cells attack.

If you have ever had a cut, then you've seen *platelets* in action. Platelets are tiny solids in the blood. Their job is to help stop bleeding. Platelets make blood *coagulate*, or get thicker, so a scab develops, protecting the wound while it heals.

Cleaning the Blood

Because your red blood cells work hard, they only last for about four months before they die and are replaced by new ones. Red blood cells die at a rate of 8 million a second! That means a lot of dead red blood cells are floating in your blood right now.

Removing those dead blood cells is one of the jobs of the *liver*, your body's largest organ. The liver breaks down dead cells and reuses what it can as nutrients. The *spleen*, another cleansing organ, helps filter your blood and remove harmful wastes.

Understanding and Preserving Your Heart

For a long time, people did not know that the heart pumps blood in a circuit through the body. One of the men who helped us understand this was an English doctor named William Harvey (1578–1657).

Harvey suggested that the heart was at the center of a blood-circulating system. For a while no one believed him. A few years later, though, the newly invented microscope was used to investigate his claim. Through the microscope, doctors watched blood flowing in the tail of a live fish and realized Harvey had been right.

Today we know much more about the circulatory system and how to keep it healthy. For example, we understand that exercising makes your heart muscle grow stronger, and can help you live longer.

Eating smart is another key to a healthy heart. If you eat more fat than your body can use, it may build up on the inside of blood vessels like crud in an old sink pipe. Then less blood flows through and less oxygen gets to the fingers and toes, brain and heart. When the heart does not receive enough oxygen, heart muscle cells die. The result is called a *heart attack*.

Jogging is a good way to keep your heart healthy.

What's Your Blood Type?

In 1900 a doctor from Austria discovered that not everyone has the same type of blood. For years doctors had been trying to perform *transfusions*—that is, helping badly injured people by giving them blood from another person. It seemed like a good idea, but the patients often died.

The doctor noticed that when he mixed blood from two different people in a lab, the blood cells would often clump together and clot. After many experiments, the doctor concluded that there were four different types of blood. He named them Type A, Type B, Type AB, and Type O. One type of blood just wouldn't flow well in the veins of a person with a different type of blood. From that point on, doctors understood that people donating and receiving blood had to match in blood type.

The Lungs

You breathe in and out more than 20,000 times a day. Each time, you replenish the oxygen in your body's systems and release carbon dioxide that your body cannot use. Your lungs and your respiratory system work together with your heart and circulatory system to keep you healthy and keep your cells alive.

Inside your chest, on either side of your heart, are two inflatable sacs called "lungs." They are like warm, wet sponges inside. They expand and contract as your breathing fills them with air, then pushes the air out again. Take a deep breath and imagine the air, filling those two warm, wet sacs inside your chest.

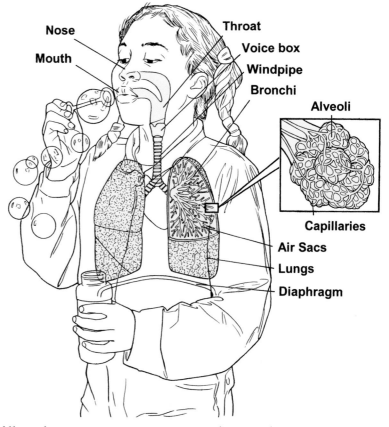

Nose
Mouth
Throat
Voice box
Windpipe
Bronchi
Alveoli
Capillaries
Air Sacs
Lungs
Diaphragm

As you take a breath, air flows through your nose or your mouth and travels down the windpipe, or *trachea* [TRAY-kee-ah]. It moves past the *voice box* and into tubes inside your lungs called *bronchi* [BRON-kye]. Bronchi branch into smaller and smaller tubes. At the very ends of the tiniest bronchi are air sacs called *alveoli* [al-VEE-oh-lye]. These alveoli contain tiny capillaries where the respiratory and the circulatory systems meet. Hemoglobin in red blood cells absorbs the oxygen from the breath you took and carries it to all the cells in your body

The process happens in reverse, too. As blood circulates through your body, it picks up carbon dioxide, which is of no use to your body. When the red blood cells carrying the carbon dioxide reach the capillaries in the alveoli, they unload the waste products into the lungs. Then you breathe out and get rid of the unneeded gas.

Breathing in and out happens because of the diaphragm [DIE-uh-fram], which is a stretchy sheet of muscle underneath your lungs. When the diaphragm arches down, it opens up space in your lungs and air rushes in to fill them. When the diaphragm arches up, it pushes the lungs together and forces air out of them, through the windpipe.

What about Smoking?

Smoking cigarettes is one of the worst things you can do to your lungs and heart. Every pack of cigarettes carries a warning, like this:

> *Surgeon General's Warning:*
> *Smoking causes lung cancer, heart*
> *disease, emphysema, and may*
> *complicate pregnancy.*

When a person inhales cigarette smoke, 4,000 different chemicals invade the lungs. Some of these chemicals are poisons that cause lung cancer. Cigarette smoke also contains sticky, black tar. When the nooks and crannies of a smoker's lungs become clogged with tar, the alveoli can become so stiff with goo that they cannot expand and pass oxygen to the blood. With less of their lungs working, smokers cannot exercise without running out of breath. Their hearts pump harder and harder, but less oxygen reaches their cells.

Healthy (*above*) and unhealthy lungs (*below*).

Chemistry

Cutting a Cube

Have you ever wondered what would happen if you tried to cut something into smaller and smaller pieces? Could you go on doing this forever? Or is there some "smallest" piece, beyond which you cannot go?

Take a look at the big cube below.

Now, imagine using a blade to cut the cube in half along all three directions, so that the big cube becomes eight smaller cubes. Next, you cut each of the small cubes into eight smaller cubes. How many cubes do you have now? If you said sixty-four, you are correct!

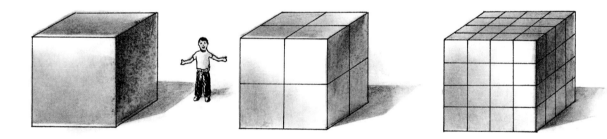

How many rounds of cutting can we do? Eventually, we will have to use a different cutting technique, because our saw will be too thick. But, no matter what we do, and no matter what the cube is made of, we can only perform about 30 rounds of cutting. After that, we will have reached the very smallest piece of the material that still has the properties of that material. This smallest piece is called an *atom*.

Atoms are extremely small: a human hair has a width of about 100,000 atoms! Not all atoms are the same size. For example, an aluminum atom is larger than a helium atom. But even the largest atoms are far too small to see with your eyes.

What Are Atoms Made Of?

As small as atoms are, you might suppose they are the smallest things in the universe. Not really. An atom is simply the smallest part of a material that retains any property of that material. But atoms themselves are composed of even smaller things!

All atoms, whether helium or aluminum or hydrogen or oxygen, are composed of tiny particles called protons, neutrons, and electrons. Protons and neutrons are tightly packed in the center of the atom, called the nucleus. Electrons are found on the outside of the atom. Protons have positive electric charge (shown by the symbol +), electrons have negative electric charge (−), and neutrons have no charge at all. Just as the north pole of one magnet repels the north pole of another magnet, positive electric charges repel each other. Negative electric charges also repel each other. But, just as the north pole of one magnet will attract the south pole of another magnet, positive and negative electric charges attract each other.

Drawing an Atom

Maybe you're wondering what all these parts look like. It would be helpful if we could draw a scientifically accurate picture of atoms. Unfortunately, it is impossible to draw a *completely* accurate picture of an atom. Any picture we try to draw of an atom shows some characteristics correctly but shows other characteristics incorrectly.

This is one possible way to draw a hydrogen atom.

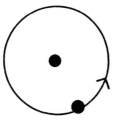

Some things about this drawing are accurate. For example, it shows the proton at the center and the electron on the outside. But scientists now realize that some things about this picture are incorrect. They have learned that the electron is more like a fuzzy cloud of negative charge that surrounds the nucleus. It does not really move around and around the proton, and it does not just exist at one particular distance from the proton. It can simultaneously exist at a lot of different distances—so drawing it like a planet orbiting a sun is misleading.

So maybe we should draw a hydrogen atom more like this.

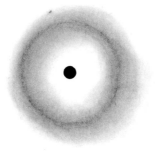

Do you see the trouble we are having? Scientists know that the electron is more like a fuzzy cloud, but they also know that it does not crowd into the nucleus. In fact, the electron cloud sort of spins. But how do we draw that?

Pictures are still very helpful, though. For purposes of this chapter, we will use the simple, not-quite-right picture of electrons in orbit around a nucleus. At least this kind of drawing helps us keep track of the number of particles contained in the atom.

Larger Atoms

Hydrogen is the smallest atom. The second smallest atom is helium. Helium has two electrons, one more than hydrogen has. How many protons do you think a helium atom has? If you said two, you are correct! This is because all atoms are electrically neutral—which is a way of saying that there are equal numbers of positive and negative charges, and they cancel each other out, just as positive two plus negative two equals zero. Since a helium atom has two electrons (negative charges), it must also have two protons (positive charges) to make all the charges exactly cancel out or equal zero.

The next question is: How many neutrons does a helium atom have? It is not possible to guess how many neutrons an atom has, because neutrons have no electrical charge. But through careful experiments, scientists have determined that *most* (but not all) helium atoms have two neutrons. About one out of every million helium atoms has only one neutron. But *all* helium atoms have two electrons and two protons.

There are different types of atoms, such as hydrogen and helium, but there are not different types of electrons, protons, and neutrons. Scientists strongly believe that all electrons are exactly the same. It doesn't matter whether they come from hydrogen, or helium, or any other atom, from atoms on the Earth, or Mars, or a star in a faraway galaxy. All electrons are identical. And the same is true for protons and neutrons.

Because of this, all atoms of a given type are identical. For example, all "regular" helium atoms (the ones with two neutrons) are identical.

Can We Break Open an Electron?

You might be saying to yourself, "I thought atoms were the smallest thing. But it turns out that they can be broken into electrons, protons, and neutrons. Can these particles be broken into pieces, too?"

That's a good question. At present, scientists believe that electrons cannot be broken into anything smaller, but that protons and neutrons can be broken into smaller particles called "quarks."

Can quarks be broken into still smaller particles? Scientists don't know. Science is an ongoing project, and we don't have all the answers yet.

Different Kinds of Atoms

Atoms are also called "elements." Remember our definition of an atom as "the smallest particle of a material that retains the properties of that material?" Each material is called an "element."

This word may be new to you, but the idea isn't. When you see a piece of aluminum foil and ask what it is made of, your answer is "aluminum." Aluminum is an element. Do you know what a soda or juice can is made of? Aluminum. Aluminum foil and aluminum cans are made of the same element.

Atoms are labeled as elements according to the number of electrons they contain, which is also the same number of protons they contain.

The diagram below shows a single atom of each of the first six elements. Notice how each atom has one electron more than the previous atom?

These are only the first six elements. Scientists have discovered more than one hundred elements. After carbon, the next two are nitrogen (N) and oxygen (O). Other elements you may know about are copper, silver, gold, and uranium.

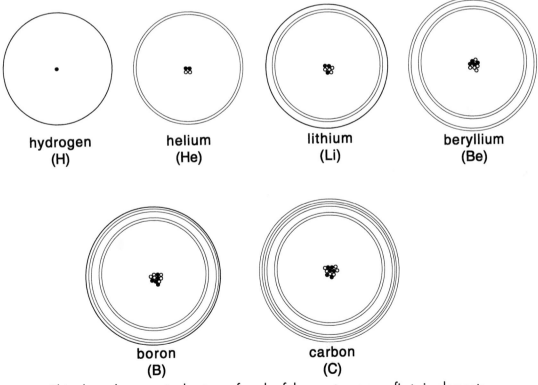

This chart shows a single atom of each of the most common first six elements.
The black circles stand for protons; the hollow circles stand for neutrons.

Few things are made of only one element. Many are a combination of two or more. For example, the smallest particle of water is made of two hydrogen atoms and one oxygen atom. Because it is made of three atoms, two of one element and one of another, we can't call water either an "atom" or an "element." We call this smallest unit of water a "molecule," which means atoms that combine to make up a particle of something new.

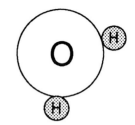

Here's a simple way of drawing a water molecule. This picture shows two small hydrogen atoms, labeled H, attached to a single, larger oxygen atom, labeled O.

There are millions of other substances made of molecules, rather than single elements, such as sugar, salt, alcohol, and gasoline. Even odors consist of molecules. When you smell perfume, some of the molecules of the perfume are traveling through the air and into your nose. That's how you smell things! Many substances, like milk, paint, and concrete, are mixtures of different kinds of molecules. Living things are the most complicated of all. Trees, flowers, fish, dogs, and *human beings* are made up of many different kinds of molecules. And, in living beings, these molecules don't always stay in the same configuration. The molecules in you or in your dog are constantly breaking apart, moving around, and recombining, forming new molecules.

Yet everything we have been talking about here is composed of electrons, protons, and neutrons. Take those three basic units and combine them many, many, many different ways, and you get the huge variety of stuff that makes up the universe.

Measuring That Stuff

To measure the amount of a substance, scientists use the term *mass*. In the metric system, mass is measured in kilograms. For example, a 12-fluid-ounce can of soda has a mass of about 0.38 kilograms. An object's mass is the same everywhere in the universe, as long as it doesn't lose any molecules or pick up any extra ones.

At first, *mass* might sound like weight, the number you get when you stand on the scales to find out how heavy you are. But *weight* depends on how much gravity there is, and mass is the same no matter what the gravity. For example, a can of soda will weigh less on the Moon than on the Earth, because there is much less gravity on the Moon. But the mass of the can of soda is the same at either location.

There is another measurement scientists make to describe the stuff they're studying. They ask how much space an object occupies, and they call their answer *volume*. In the metric system, volume is often measured in liters. Two ways to measure volume are to calculate it with geometry or to determine it through a process called water displacement. With geometry, you can measure the height and the area of the base of a soda can and use those numbers to calculate its volume. Or, using water displacement, you can submerge the

A can of soda weighs about one sixth as much on the moon, even though its mass remains the same.

unopened can in water and see how much it makes the level of the water rise. Both methods will give you, for a standard-sized can, the answer that the volume is about 0.375 liters.

If we know both the mass and the volume of an object, we can calculate another measurement important to scientists: *density*. Density is mass divided by volume. Objects with more density have more mass packed into the same space. For example, pour out the liquid from a soda can and pack it full of rocks. Now the can

You can measure the volume of an object by submerging it in water and comparing the water levels before and after the object was added.

has the same volume, but higher mass, and therefore higher density.

Because water is so common on Earth, it is used as the basis of the metric system. Water has a density of exactly one kilogram per liter.

But which do you think is more dense, water or ice? If you said water, you are correct. When water freezes, the molecules move apart slightly. The mass stays the same, but the volume increases. Since density is mass divided by volume, freezing water makes its density decrease. Ice is a little bit less dense than water. This is why ice cubes float in a glass of water.

Can there be a volume, or space, in which there is no matter at all, not even air? Yes. It is called a *vacuum*. You can imagine a vacuum in your mind, but it is rare to find a perfect vacuum in the real world. Even in outer space, a few atoms float around. When a certain space contains many fewer atoms than normal, we can call it a *partial vacuum*.

Here is an experiment that will show you the effect of a partial vacuum. Ask an adult to help you try it. Empty a small plastic bottle of water. Keeping the cap off, hold it briefly over a hot burner of the stove for a few seconds. You don't want to melt the plastic. As the stove burner heats up the air inside the bottle, some of it will escape. With the bottle still warm, quickly screw the cap back on and put the sealed bottle in a freezer. What do you think will happen?

As the air inside the bottle cools and contracts, a partial vacuum is created. The denser freezer air outside will crush the bottle.

Solutions

You may have noticed that oil and water don't mix very well. Even if you shake a bottle containing oil and water, they separate again when you put the bottle down. One way of explaining this is to say that water molecules stick to each other really well, but they don't stick to oil molecules very well.

But what if you put a spoonful of sugar into a glass of water and stir it up? If you stir long enough, the sugar seems to disappear. Unlike oil, sugar molecules blend well with water molecules. Sugar is one of a certain kind of molecule that attracts water molecules well, pulls them apart, and manages to mingle in between those water molecules.

When this happens, we say the sugar has *dissolved* in water. We call the water the *solvent* and the sugar the *solute*. The sugar is still there, even though you can't see it!

Of course, you can't go on adding sugar to the solution forever. A solvent (in this case water) can only dissolve a certain amount of a solute (in this case sugar). When the maximum amount of a solute is dissolved in a solvent, we say that the solution is *saturated*.

Electricity

Zap!

Someone knocks at the door. You shuffle across the carpet to open it. But when you touch the doorknob, you feel a zap on your fingertip. What's going on?

While unloading the clothes dryer, your sister's socks keep sticking to your pajamas. Why is that?

You're in your bedroom in the dark and when you take off your sweater, you see tiny sparks. Where did they come from?

The answer to each of these questions lies in the movement of tiny electrons.

Static Electricity

Electrons, as you remember, are the subatomic particles that zip around the nucleus of an atom. Electrons have a negative electrical charge, while protons in the nucleus have a positive electrical charge. Attraction between opposite charges keeps electrons from flying free of the atom, but it doesn't hold them very tightly. When objects rub together, electrons can get knocked loose and go off on their own.

For instance, as clothes tumble together in a dryer, electrons from atoms in some pieces of clothing rub off onto other pieces. Your sister's fuzzy socks might lose electrons while your pajamas pick them up. The socks end up with more protons than electrons, and thus more positive electrical charge than negative electrical charge. The pajamas, on the other hand, end up with more electrons than protons: they become negatively charged. That means that the socks and pajamas develop opposite charges—and, as you've learned already, opposite charges attract each other. That's why the socks and the pajamas cling together in the dryer.

When rubbing, or friction, makes an electrical charge build up, that charge is called static electricity. As you take off your sweater, it rubs against your shirt, picks up extra electrons, and builds up a charge. The sparks you see in the darkness are electrons flowing away in a sudden discharge of static electricity.

The zap you felt from the doorknob is discharged static electricity, too. As you rubbed your feet against the carpet, your body picked up extra electrons, which flowed to the doorknob when you reached for it.

Making Light out of Electrons

When you turn on a light, you are starting up a flow of electrons through an electric circuit. It all happens instantaneously, with just the flick of a light switch. Let's see what is really happening at the level of electrons.

Here is an example of a simple circuit, consisting of four parts:

1. a circular copper wire
2. a light bulb
3. a battery
4. a switch.

The battery is the source of energy. It has a positive and a negative pole. When the switch is turned on, electrons travel through the wire, making the full circuit from the negative pole of the battery, through the switch and the light bulb, and back to the positive pole of the battery. This is called a *closed circuit*, because the electrons go in a complete circle.

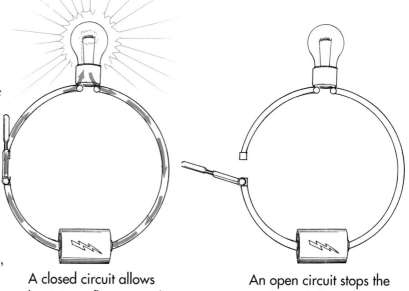

A closed circuit allows electricity to flow around the circuit.

An open circuit stops the flow of electricity.

When the switch is turned off, the circuit is broken and the flow of electrons stops. This is called an *open circuit*, because the electrons do not travel in a complete circle.

Take a look inside an ordinary clear light bulb. Do you see the two wires sticking up? Stretched between them is a very fine wire called a *filament*. When you turn on the switch and create a closed circuit, electrons travel through the circuit and into the light bulb. When the electrons reach the filament, they begin to pile up because the filament is a very narrow passageway for them. It's as if traffic moving in eight lanes had to merge onto a one-lane bridge.

This electric traffic jam is caused by *resistance*—the narrow filament *resists* the large flow of electrons. As the crowd of backed-up electrons presses ahead, they cause the atoms in the filament to vibrate, get hot, and glow. Thanks to resistance, light bulbs turn electrons into light.

Conductors and Insulators

Most household wires that carry electrical current are made of copper, the same metal used to make pennies. Electrons move readily from atom to atom in copper, so electricity flows well through copper. That makes copper a good *conductor* of electrical current. Other metals make good conductors, too.

Some materials do not conduct electrical current at all (in other words, electricity will not flow through them). These materials are called *insulators*.

You see examples of conductors and insulators every day. Anything that you plug into a wall socket for electricity uses a wire made of both a conducting and an insulating material. The wire is probably copper inside, but the part that you see on the outside is made of plastic or rubber. The copper conducts the electricity, but the plastic or rubber insulates it from your hands. Thanks to the insulation, you don't get a shock when you touch the wire.

The last thing you want to do is to become a conductor of electricity! Respecting the power of electrons could save your life. Never fiddle around inside electrical appliances when they are plugged in. Water is a good conductor, so it is especially important not to touch light switches or appliances when your hands are wet or when you are in water. In other words, don't use your hair dryer while you are in the bathtub. The shock could kill you!

Insulation also prevents bare wires from touching each other. When bare wires touch, current can flow between them and take a short cut instead of completing the full circuit. This causes a *short circuit*. Current in a short circuit moves through a smaller loop without doing work. Energy from speeding and bumping electrons builds up. As too

Insulating material (rubber)
Plug
Conducting material (copper)

The electrical cords for televisions, radios, and other electrical appliances contain insulating materials and conducting materials.

The circuit on the right is a closed circuit, working normally. The circuit on the left is a short circuit in which no electricity is reaching the light bulb.

much current flows through the wires, they become hotter and hotter. The situation can get dangerous, because the wires can get hot enough to start a fire. Some good safety measures include replacing worn-out electrical cords, keeping pets from chewing on cords, and keeping cords away from heaters and places where they can be rubbed or pinched.

Overloading a circuit by plugging in too many appliances can cause wires behind the walls to heat up, too. Safety devices such as fuses and circuit-breakers are designed to interrupt the circuit if too much current threatens to heat up the wiring. A fuse is a tiny glass tube surrounding a thin metal strip. If too much current runs through the fuse, the metal strip melts, breaking the circuit and stopping the flow of electricity before the wires get too hot.

Electromagnets

Electric current can be switched on and off by opening and closing a circuit. Some magnets can be turned off and on in the same way. They are called *electromagnets*.

If you were to take an iron nail and wrap an electrical wire around it about ten times, then connect it to a circuit, you would be making a very simple electromagnet. When you close the circuit (or turn the system "on"), the current flows through the wire coiled around the nail. That movement of electricity creates a magnetic field that changes the ordinary nail into a magnet. The more times the wire is coiled around the nail, the stronger a magnet that nail becomes. Switch off the electric current, and the nail loses most of its magnetic force of attraction. It becomes an ordinary nail again.

Magnets that can be turned on and off are useful in many ways. Television receivers, loudspeakers, metal detectors, and motors and brakes in some cars depend on electromagnets to work. Cranes move tons of steel using powerful electromagnets. They can use those magnets to pick up loads and, with a flip of the switch, drop those loads.

Electromagnets are also used in special trains called "maglevs" (for "magnetic levitation"). Instead of wheels that run on a track, maglev trains use electromagnets that run along a guide rail. Electric current flows through the electromagnets. The magnetic pole in the tracks is opposite to the pole of the train's magnets, so magnetic force pushes the train cars off the tracks. They hover above the guide rail and glide smoothly along at high speed.

This Japanese maglev train flies along its magnetic track at speeds up to 300 miles per hour.

Geology

Layers of Planet Earth

Have you ever wondered what it would be like to journey down, down, down to the center of the earth? To get there, you would have to dig a hole 3,872 miles deep, through four different layers of the earth.

The top layer—the layer on which you live—is called the crust. The crust is about 25 miles deep, made of dirt on top of solid rock.

Once you dig through the crust, you reach a very hot second layer called the *mantle*. Here it is so hot that instead of hard rocks, the Earth's material melts and flows like thick syrup, which geologists call magma. The mantle of magma is 1,800 miles deep.

Continuing down toward the center of the earth, you come next to the third layer—the outer core. This layer, made of searing hot liquid metal, is nearly as thick as the mantle.

Deeper still, you reach the inner core at the Earth's center, estimated to be about the size of the Moon. Here at the inner core, the temperature is hotter than at the surface of the Sun! But the pressure from all the layers of Earth around the inner core keeps it from melting.

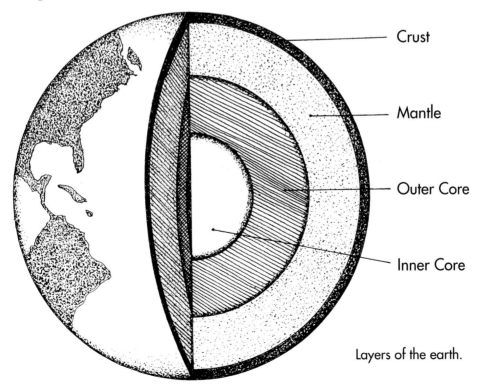

Crust

Mantle

Outer Core

Inner Core

Layers of the earth.

The word "geology" comes from the Greek word *gaia*, which means "earth." Geology is the study of the Earth, its matter, and its history.

Earthquakes

It was early morning on April 18, 1906, in the city of San Francisco, California. Eva Campbell was fast asleep when her bed began to lurch violently across the room. Her whole house was trembling: "It rocked like a ship on a rough sea. . . . Quiver after quiver followed . . . until it seemed as if the very heart of this old earth was broken and was throbbing and dying away slowly and gently."

On that terrible morning, San Francisco was destroyed by one of the most destructive earthquakes ever to take place in the United States. Many people died, crushed by falling buildings or trapped in fires that started when gas lines broke.

An earthquake is a sudden and violent shaking of the earth's crust. Earthquakes can be strong enough to shake buildings

The San Francisco earthquake of 1906 destroyed many buildings.

and bridges off their foundations, to open cracks big enough that cars fall into them, and to cause huge avalanches. On the other hand, some earthquakes can be so mild that people don't even notice them. In fact, an earthquake happens somewhere in the world every thirty seconds.

Geologists record the vibrations from earthquakes with machines called *seismographs*. Seismographs measure tremors underground and plot them like a graph. To compare the *magnitude*, or strength, of different earthquakes, geologists often use a chart called the Richter [RIK-ter] scale.

The Richter scale gives scientists a way to compare earthquakes. An earthquake measuring 2 on the Richter scale is 10 times stronger than an earthquake rated 1. No earthquake has ever measured greater than 9 — thank goodness, because when an earthquake measures 9 on the Richter scale, its magnitude is equal to an explosion of 200 million tons of dynamite!

This man is monitoring a seismograph.

Earth's Moving Plates

The earth's crust is something like a big, messy jigsaw puzzle, made of many pieces called *plates*. Some of the pieces fit together well. Some fit more loosely. Some of them lie on top of each other.

The boundary line where two plates meet is called a *fault*. Deep cracks in the earth's crust sometimes occur at faults. San Francisco sits right on a fault called the San Andreas Fault, which runs the length of California, and that is one reason why California experiences so many earthquakes.

Part of the San Andreas Fault in California, seen from the air. The fault runs up the center of the picture, like a vertical line.

It feels as if the ground we stand on is solid and motionless, but in fact the plates that make up the Earth's crust move. They push, pull, and rub against each other.

What makes the plates move? Like rafts on water, the Earth's plates float on the magma of the mantle. When magma moves, so do the plates. Magma is always circulating. Hotter magma rises to the surface, cools, then sinks. These movements jostle the plates.

The sliding of rock against rock in the Earth's crust can cause pressure to build up over time, until suddenly—CRACK!—rock fractures, stored energy is released, and the ground trembles.

Sometimes an earthquake happens on the ocean floor. Its energy pushes seawater into a giant wave called a *tsunami* [tsoo-NAH-mee]. A tsunami can travel more than 400 miles per hour. As it approaches shore, where the water is shallower, it grows taller and taller, pushed by the energy behind it. A tsunami can grow as tall as a ten-story building before the curling wall of water crashes down on land.

Earthquakes beneath the ocean can send gigantic waves, called tsunamis, tumbling towards land.

TSUNAMI
VERTICAL DROP CAUSED BY EARTHQUAKE

OCEAN FLOOR

Volcanoes

Volcanoes are like safety valves for the planet's furnace. They release built-up pressure from inside the earth. Volcanoes form when hot magma from the mantle squeezes up through weak spots in the earth's crust, usually where plates meet. The volcano erupts when that incredibly hot liquid comes gushing out of the earth. Once it flows out of a volcano, magma is called lava. A volcanic eruption can keep going for hours, days, even months. Ash and hunks of fiery rock spew from the opening in the earth, and over time they pile up and harden into a mountain.

Sometimes volcanoes erupt quietly, without a lot of noise and explosions. Glowing-hot lava oozes out from the opening on top and runs down the sides of the volcano. Other times volcanoes erupt violently, flinging hot lava, gases, and pieces of rock into the air. Volcanoes often erupt many times over the course of centuries, sometimes quietly and sometimes explosively, building up a mountain of layers of hardened lava, cinders, and ash.

World-Famous Volcanoes

Mount Vesuvius, on the western coast of Italy, erupted in A.D. 79 and buried the ancient Roman cities of Pompeii and Herculaneum in ash and cinders. Twenty thousand people were killed. The tons of ash that entombed Pompeii kept it almost perfectly preserved for centuries. Archeologists digging in the area more than 1,500 years later unearthed the entire town, complete with houses, shops, restaurants, temples, signs, and paintings. Even the bodies of people who had lived in Pompeii were well preserved, trapped and hardened by ash.

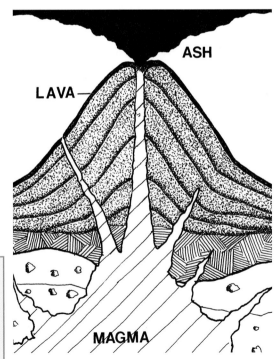

A volcano erupts: hot magma forces its way through cracks in the earth's crust and erupts on the surface as lava.

An "active" volcano is one that is erupting or is expected to erupt sometime in the future. "Dormant" means a volcano has not erupted for a while, and no one knows for sure whether it will ever erupt again. "Extinct" means the volcano has not erupted since humans have been recording history, and probably never will again.

Krakatoa, a volcano on an Indonesian island, erupted in 1883 with an explosion so powerful that it was heard almost three thousand miles away. Volcanic ash shot seventeen miles up into the Earth's atmosphere, darkening the skies for almost twenty hours. The force of the eruption created a 100-foot tsunami that took the lives of 36,000 people on the nearby islands of Java and Sumatra. The ash sent into the atmosphere by Krakatoa changed the color of sunsets around the world for months after the eruption.

When Mount Saint Helens, in Washington, erupted in 1980, 230 square miles of forest were blown down or burned. Temperatures reached 1,100 degrees Fahrenheit near the blast. The winds from the blast were measured at more than 600 miles per hour, and trees were flattened for 15 miles around. Rocks as big as a hilltop tumbled down, filling up a valley 150 feet deep—the largest landslide in recorded history. Hot ash, three feet thick, blanketed the area nearest the volcano.

Mount St. Helens erupted in 1980, sending huge clouds of volcanic ash into the air.

Despite all this devastation, life has returned to Mt. St. Helens in the years following the eruption. Plants have sprouted through the ash. These plants have created a little bit of humus in which more seeds, brought by the wind, have taken root and begun to grow. Scientists predict that by 2200, a forest will cover Mt. St. Helens once again.

Hot Springs and Geysers

In some places in the world, a lot of volcanic activity is going on under the Earth's surface. Magma that is forcing its way up through the crust heats up water that has percolated down through cracks. Sometimes the hot water bubbles up to the surface and forms steamy ponds called *hot springs*. Sometimes the Earth's underground shape makes that hot water shoot up into the air, creating geysers. Geysers form when water collects in underground caves and chambers. The water gets hotter and hotter, until finally it boils and turns to steam. Just like the steam pressure that makes a tea kettle whistle, the force of this underground steam blasts through the cracks in the Earth's crust.

Old Faithful, in Yellowstone National Park, was already a tourist attraction in 1878, when this photo was taken.

Yellowstone National Park, in the state of Wyoming, sits on a hot spot of underground volcanic activity. When you visit Yellowstone, you can see explosions of water and steam from underground. One famous geyser at Yellowstone sends a hissing fountain of water and steam 160 feet into the air. It erupts regularly and so it is called Old Faithful.

Drifting Continents

If you could go back in time 300 million years, before the time of the dinosaurs, and look down from space, the Earth would look very different. Geologists believe that back then, the continents we know today were crowded together in one giant land mass. They have named that land mass "Pangaea" [pan-JEE-uh], a word made up from the Greek for "all the world." Over 100 million years, the super-continent of Pangaea gradually broke into pieces. Oceans flowed in between the newly-formed continents. Even though the continents only drifted a few inches apart each year, a few inches per year for millions of years adds up to a lot of changes. Geologists call those changes continental drift.

Building Mountains Over Time

From space the earth looks like a smooth blue and white marble. But down here on the planet, we know its surface is anything but smooth. The land is wrinkled and bumpy. Mountains poke up from every continent and from the ocean floor. Scientists divide mountains into several categories based on how they were formed.

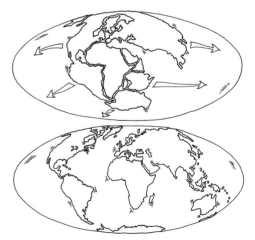

PANGAEA

PRESENT

These two maps show how the plates of Pangaea drifted to the location of our current continents.

Dome-shaped mountains

Volcanoes can build mountains by spitting out piles of lava, cinders, and ash. Volcanic mountains can also form without an eruption. Magma beneath the surface swells and pushes up a mountain-sized bump. Before it finds a vent, the magma cools and hardens into *dome-shaped mountains*. The Black Hills of South Dakota and Wyoming are dome mountains.

Folded mountains

Imagine a dish towel, spread on the table. Now picture what happens when you push the edges toward the center. The more you push, the more the towel wrinkles and crumples into folds. The same kind of thing has happened to the crust of the Earth in different places, making formations called *folded mountains*. The Earth's tallest mountains, the Himalayas, formed 45 million years ago when two crustal plates collided deep beneath an ancient ocean. The tremendous force of the impact made the ocean floor between the plates bend and fold into mountains and valleys. You may have a hard time believing that the Himalayas were once part of an ocean floor, but fossils of ocean creatures can still be found embedded in the rock on the mountains' peaks! The Alps in Europe are folded mountains, too, and the Appalachians in the eastern U.S. are part of a very old chain of folded mountains.

Fault-block mountains

Sometimes, when plates collide on a fault line, the rock is brittle. Then the crust doesn't bend and fold, but instead it cracks into huge blocks. As the two plates keep pushing against each other, the blocks on one side of the fault slowly lift up into a tilted ridge. These are called *fault-block mountains*. The Sierra Nevada Mountains, which run through southern California and western Nevada into Mexico, are examples of fault-block mountains.

The Grand Tetons, in the western U.S., are fault-block mountains.

Making Rocks

Mountains are made of rocks, but what are rocks made of? Rocks are made of chemicals called minerals. There are over 2,000 kinds of minerals on Earth. Some rocks are made of a single mineral, and others are combinations. To classify a given rock, geologists consider how it was formed.

Rocks that were made from cooling magma or lava are called igneous [IG-nee-us] rocks. The name comes from *ignis*, the Latin word for "fire." Heavy, speckled granite; light, powdery pumice; black, glassy obsidian—even though they all look different, these are all igneous rocks. They started as hot magma and cooled into rock.

Rocks that were made when layer upon layer of sand and debris settled down together are called *sedimentary rocks*. Their name comes from the Latin word sedo, which means "settle down." Over millions of years, layers of sediment pressed down in the bottom of ancient oceans and rivers. The pressure cemented tiny grains together into rock. Limestone is a sedimentary rock, made mostly of the compressed bones and shells of millions of tiny sea creatures. Sandstone is another sedimentary rock.

The last family of rocks is called *metamorphic* [met-uh-MORE-fick] rock. This family gets its name from the Greek words *meta*, meaning "change," and *morph*, meaning "form"—because metamorphic rocks are rocks that have changed form.

Some metamorphic rocks have changed

When this lava flow from a volcano in Hawaii cools and hardens, the rocks will be igneous rocks.

Pressure can turn the layers of sediment on the bottom of this river into sedimentary rock.

through heat. When magma collects underground, it heats the surrounding rock to such high temperatures that the minerals get cooked. They change into new minerals, and the rocks containing them change form. Others have changed through pressure. Immense weight, like the weight of a mountain, can press down and change minerals. Marble, for example, used for its beauty in sculpture and buildings since the time of the ancient Greeks, is a metamorphic rock. Heat and pressure underground turn limestone into the rock we know as marble.

From Boulder to Rock to Pebble to Soil

While plate movement is building mountains up, other forces are wearing them down. Wind, water, ice, and plant roots crack and crumble rock over time, taking huge boulders and turning them into fist-sized rocks, then pebbles, then sand, and finally into tiny particles that contribute to the Earth's soil. This process is called "weathering."

Imagine a boulder on a mountainside. After a million years a little crack appears in its surface. When it rains, water trickles into the crack. On chilly nights—and there are many chilly nights on the top of a mountain—the water in the crack freezes and expands. Like a wedge, that ice pushes the sides of the crack in the boulder wider and wider apart. Freezing, thawing, and freezing again works on the crack until it becomes a network of cracks. Particles of dust and dirt carried by wind and water settle into those cracks. Seeds blown by the wind land in the soil collected in the cracks. The seeds sprout, and small plants' roots push against the sides of the cracks and make them wider still. Then one sunny day, a jagged piece of the boulder cracks off and somersaults down the side of the mountain, crashing into other boulders in its path and chipping pieces off them. That's the first step in the boulder's crumbling journey from big rock to future soil.

> How long does it take for an entire mountain to crumble away? Geologists have calculated that a mountain gets approximately 3 inches shorter every 1,000 years.

The ocean weathers rocks as well. Have you ever noticed that most of the pebbles on a beach are round and smooth? Rocks and sand tumble together in the surf, grinding off all the rough edges. Over time, the action of the waves turns rocks into pebbles and then into sand.

Water and wind, plants and ice, all cause *physical weathering*. But rock also gets weathered by chemicals that occur naturally in the Earth. When water mixes with certain gases from the atmosphere, for example, it sometimes results in a weak acid, which can eat away at the surface of rocks. Some plants also produce weak acids, which seep into the Earth and affect the rock around them. These are examples of *chemical weathering*.

Erosion

Weathering is just one way that the surface of the Earth changes. Another way has to do with gravity. Because of gravity, water, soil, and rocks are constantly tumbling down Earth's slopes, hills, and mountains. This process is what we call *erosion*, another important way that the surface of the Earth changes.

Suppose a small pebble slides down a mountain slope, and heavy rains wash it into a stream. The pebble is carried by rushing water over a waterfall and down the mountain, where the stream dumps into a river. The pebble falls to the river bottom and is pushed along by the current. It tumbles among other pebbles, rocks, sand, and soil. Gradually it becomes a rounder, smoother, and smaller pebble than it was when it began its journey, its sharp edges worn away by the constant rubbing against other pebbles and sand on the riverbed.

As the pebble approaches the sea, it may be deposited on one of the islands at the river's delta, or swept out to sea.

Every day, this process of erosion is happening on Earth. Streams and rivers carry millions of tons of sediment—rocks, pebbles, sand, and soil—from land to ocean daily. Why don't the oceans fill up with sediment? The answer is: because nature recycles.

Over millions of years, layers of sediment are squeezed into sedimentary rock on the ocean floor, which has as many

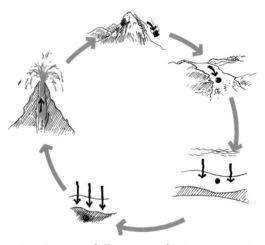

This diagram follows a rock's journey as it tumbles off a mountain, drifts down a river, lands on the ocean floor, sinks into the undersea sediment, and melts into magma, which then bursts out of an erupting volcano. The whole process could take millions of years.

mountains and valleys as the surface of the Earth above water. The deepest undersea valleys are places where the Earth's plates meet. There, sedimentary rock is pressed down into the mantle, where it melts into magma. The magma circulates under the Earth's crust, and when it finds weak spots, it shoots up lava, which builds up new mountains—and the cycle begins again.

Wind can also change rock and soil on the surface of the Earth. Windblown sand, especially in desert areas, works like a sand-blaster over time, smoothing sharp rock edges or carving away softer rock on cliffs and mountainsides. Wind can carve unusual rock formations, creating caves, mesas, towers, and arches.

Ice is a rock carver, too. Huge masses of ice and snow called *glaciers* [GLAY-shurs] form on high mountains and in very cold regions. Glaciers are like rivers of ice. Even though they seem frozen solid and motionless, glaciers creep slowly downhill. Stones trapped by glaciers scrape the ground beneath them and carve grooves in the rock. Large glaciers carve out the landscape.

The Saskatchewan Glacier in Canada is part of a series of connected glaciers called the Columbia Icefield, which formed many years ago, during the Ice Age.

About 10,000 years ago, the Earth emerged from an *Ice Age*, a period of more than a million and a half years when colossal glaciers, nearly two miles thick, moved over much of what is now North America, northern Europe, and northern Asia. The glaciers gouged out huge areas as they advanced and grew. At the end of the Ice Age, when the glaciers melted, the holes gouged out by the glaciers filled up with water. Today we call some of those water-filled, glacier-made holes the Great Lakes!

Layer upon Layer

If you were to dig a hole in the ground, going down many feet, you would see several layers of different colors of soil.

The top layer, probably darker than the rest, is the *topsoil*. Topsoil contains tiny pieces of weathered rock mixed with *humus* [HYOO-mus], or decaying matter from plants and animals. Air and water move through the tiny spaces between grains of topsoil. Plants spread broad networks of roots in the topsoil, and their roots help hold the soil down and prevent erosion. As plants die, they decay and add to the humus, which will feed future plants—another one of nature's many recycling projects.

Beneath the topsoil, the next layer down is called the *subsoil*. It is made mostly of weathered rock and clay, with very little

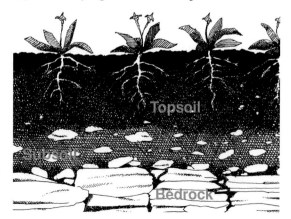

humus. While topsoil replenishes itself every year, it takes hundreds of thousands of years for the subsoil to form. Some tree roots grow long enough to reach the subsoil.

Under the subsoil is a layer made of solid rock, called the *bedrock*. Bedrock is far enough underground to be well protected from wind, water, and freezing, and so it has not weathered into soil.

Meteorology

The Fascinating World of Weather

The sky darkens with threatening storm clouds. Suddenly, there's a brilliant flash — crackle — ka-BOOM! Thunder rumbles around and rattles the windows. "It must be the angels' bowling night," someone says, or "That's Thor, the Viking god, in his big boots clomping across the sky." All around the world, all through history, human beings have made up stories to explain the powerful forces that we witness as weather.

Human beings have also spent centuries making a scientific study of the weather. The study of weather is called *meteorology*, coming from a Greek word *meteoros*, meaning "high in the air" and the suffix *-ology*, meaning "study of." The people who study weather are called *meteorologists*.

Layers of Air

Weather happens because our planet is wrapped in layers of air, called the Earth's *atmosphere*, and because the Sun is constantly bombarding the Earth with energy. Without an atmosphere, Earth would look like the Moon, a waterless, lifeless hunk of rock. Our atmosphere is constantly absorbing energy from the Sun, and that energy moves around from place to place, creating weather.

Earth's atmosphere is made of four layers of air: the outermost

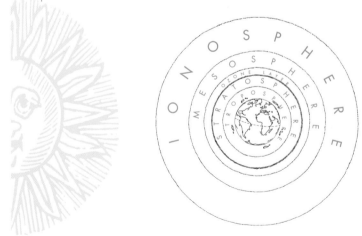

The earth's atmospheric layers. Part of the stratosphere is the ozone layer, which filters out dangerous radiation before it reaches our atmosphere.

layer, the *ionosphere* [eye-AHN-oh-sfeer]; the *mesosphere* [MEZ-oh-sfeer]; the *stratosphere* [STRAT-oh-sfeer]; and the lowest layer, which touches the surface of the Earth, the *troposphere* [TROH-poh-sfeer].

When you breathe, you are inhaling air from the troposphere. But clouds are also in the troposphere. Most of Earth's weather happens in the troposphere.

The stratosphere, from seven to thirty miles above the Earth, contains a tiny amount of a gas called ozone, which protects us from ultraviolet radiation, part of the energy that comes from the Sun.

The Ozone Layer

Ozone in the stratosphere absorbs ultraviolet radiation from the Sun, which in high quantities can be very harmful, even deadly, to many creatures on Earth. Recently, scientists discovered that a hole has developed in the ozone layer over the Earth's Southern Hemisphere. This may allow unhealthy amounts of ultraviolet radiation to reach Earth. Scientists are trying to figure out what's causing the hole. They are watching it carefully and hoping that the ozone layer can mend itself.

The mesosphere, from thirty to fifty miles above the Earth, acts as a protective shield in another way. Perhaps you have seen shooting stars streaking across the night sky. These are meteors, hunks of rock streaking through space at incredible speeds. Sometimes they come so close to Earth that they enter the atmosphere. But when they rub against air in the mesosphere, all but the largest meteors heat up so intensely that they burn to cinders before reaching Earth.

The ionosphere, fifty miles above the Earth and higher, is constantly showered by X-rays, ultraviolet radiation, and electrons thrown off by the Sun. So much energy from the sun reaches the high levels of the ionosphere that temperatures climb as high as 2,200 degrees Fahrenheit!

Have you ever climbed into a car that has been all closed up on a hot, sunny day? Then you know what it's like when the Sun's energy shines into a place and gets trapped inside. It gets hot!

In much the same way, the Sun's energy shines into the Earth's atmosphere. Sunlight passes through the layers of the atmosphere and warms up the land and the oceans. Some of the sunlight bounces back into the atmosphere and heats up gases in the air. The gases absorb the heat energy, holding it in the Earth's atmosphere rather than allowing it to return to space. Thanks to that process, the Earth is a comfortable place for life instead of a freezing cold planet.

Uneven Heating

When you look at the weather maps in the newspaper or watch the weather report on TV, you can see that weather isn't the same everywhere on Earth —it isn't even the same in different towns in the same state! From warm breezes and gentle rains to hurricanes, blizzards, and ice storms, weather is always changing. It changes because the Earth is heated unevenly, and because heat energy moves around in the Earth's atmosphere.

The Sun doesn't shine with the same intensity on every region of Earth. It shines on the area near the equator the most directly of all, so the air around the equator heats up the most. It shines the least directly at the North and South Poles, so the air at the poles stays the coldest. These differences in temperature make the air in the atmosphere move around.

Television weather reporters watch high and low pressure areas to predict tomorrow's weather.

Have you ever noticed that when you open an oven, hot air rises up on your face, but when you open a refrigerator, cold air spills down on your feet? Hot air rises and cold air sinks. As air is heated, its molecules spread out. It becomes less dense. It is lighter and puts less pressure on the Earth. When we talk about a mass of warmer, less dense air in the atmosphere, we call it a *low-pressure* air system. Cooler air contains molecules that are denser, or closer together. It puts more pressure on the Earth, and we call it a *high-pressure* air system.

Near the equator, low-pressure air systems rise, spread apart, and move toward the earth's poles. At the same time, high-pressure air systems sink and move toward the equator, filling the spaces left vacant as low-pressure air moves away. Before long, the intensity of the Sun at the equator heats up the high-pressure systems, transforming them into low-pressure systems, and the cycle continues. This continual exchange of warm and cool air creates wind.

Winds

A famous poem asks, who has seen the wind? No one, of course. But we certainly see what wind can do. Meteorologists have developed ways to describe wind by measuring its speed and direction. For instance, a north wind at 20 miles per hour is a wind coming from the north and moving as fast as a car travels when it drives 20 miles per hour.

A wind that blows 10 or 20 miles per hour is called a breeze. If the wind gusts up to 40 or 50 miles per hour, it is called a *gale*. If it travels 75 miles per hour or faster, it qualifies as a *hurricane*.

To measure wind speed, meteorologists use an instrument called an *anemometer* that looks like a pinwheel, with three arms and a cup at the end of each arm. Wind blows into the cups and makes the pinwheel spin. By counting its spins during a certain time period, meteorologists can measure the speed of the wind.

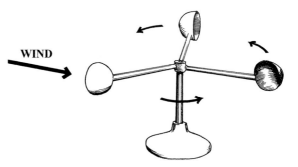

An anemometer measures wind speed. The faster it spins, the faster the wind.

Weather Patterns

Some wind patterns continue their movements almost all the time and in the same general direction. These winds are called the Earth's *prevailing winds*. They are our strongest, most persistent winds, and they shape big weather patterns. Different parts of the globe experience different prevailing winds. During the Age of Exploration Christopher Columbus and other explorers and traders used the prevailing winds, also known as trade winds, to carry them back and forth across the Atlantic Ocean.

There are many other weather patterns that remain generally constant in certain areas of the world. Average temperatures, the amount of rainfall or snowfall, and the average amount of moisture in the air (that is, the *humidity*), all determine the *climate* of every region in the world. Climate is the average weather pattern for a region. Climate is influenced not only by weather patterns but also by geological patterns, such as whether the region is a large land mass or a group of islands, whether it is flat or mountainous, and whether it is near a body of water. The world has many different climates. Each climate supports a different group of plants and animals and a particular kind of human community.

Tropical climates occur in places near the equator. Temperatures stay hot and day length changes little throughout the year. Polar climates occur in places near the North and South Pole. Temperatures stay cold, even below freezing, and there is extreme variation in day length between seasons. Imagine how different the animals, plants, and human habitations must be in these two climates.

Cloud Families

Clouds can look like fat gingerbread men or two-headed fire-breathing dragons or your Aunt Louise. No two clouds look just the same, but scientists sort clouds into categories, according to their shape. Identifying clouds can help you understand—and even predict—the weather.

Cumulus [KYOOM-yuh-luss] clouds form on sunny days when updrafts of warm, wet air rise to a cooler level. Cumulus clouds in the sky usually mean fair weather.

Stratus clouds look like flat sheets that can stretch out to the horizons, blocking out sunshine. They are often a signal that rain is on the way.

Cirrus [SIHR-us] clouds ride highest in the troposphere, where the air is coldest. Made of ice crystals, they look like wispy curlicues. Cirrus clouds often come to fair skies before a rain.

When Push Comes to Shove

Air masses with different levels of humidity and different temperatures are moving constantly above the surface of the Earth. They don't always mix. Often they collide. As you can imagine, a lot of things can happen when wet, low-pressure air meets dry, high-pressure air. The boundary where one air mass meets another is called a *front*.

This picture shows three different kinds of clouds. At the top are wispy, feathery cirrus clouds. In the middle are big, puffy cumulus clouds. At the bottom are low-lying, sheetlike stratus clouds.

Sometimes a cold air mass wedges in under a warm air mass. The boundary between them is called a *cold front*. The cold air below forces the warm air to rise swiftly. The warm air cools rapidly and its water vapor forms heavy clouds, full of precipitation. These conditions result in thunder, lightning, and rainstorms, followed by bright, clear weather.

Sometimes a warm air mass overtakes a cold air mass. The boundary between them is called a warm front. The low-pressure mass of warm air rides up on top of the cold air and slowly pushes it out of the way. These conditions result in stratus clouds and a long, steady rain.

Lightning and Thunder

Dark, massive clouds signal the approach of one of nature's loudest and most dazzling sound and light shows: a thunderstorm. As a cold front moves through an area, especially during spring and summer, it plows up warm, humid air. The moist air piles up higher and higher into towering, miles-high, flat-topped clouds called *thunderheads*.

At the top of thunderheads, condensed droplets quickly cool into ice crystals. Strong air currents jiggle the ice crystals up and down inside the cloud. As the ice crystals crash, bump, and rub against each other, electrons loosen and zing around as static electricity, just as they do when your socks and pajamas tumble against each other in the clothes dryer.

Electrons that have been bumped loose collect in the bottom of the cloud, giving it a negative charge. That negative charge interacts with the positive charge of the earth itself. Electrons zing down toward the positively charged ground. When the two charges meet— crackle! zap!—energy is released in a giant electrical discharge. The brilliant white flash of lightning that we see is a powerful electrical current, flowing through the air.

A lightning bolt heats up the air around it five times hotter than the surface of the sun. That air expands FAST —and vibrates the air all around it violently. Those vibrations reach our ears when we hear the thunder that so often accompanies lightning.

Light travels much faster than sound. The flash of a bolt of lightning travels to our eyes at 186,000 miles per second. Sound from the same event—the clap of thunder accompanying the lightning bolt —travels only one-fifth of a mile per second.

You can use this information to make a rough estimate of how far away lightning has struck. As soon as you see a flash of lightning, count the seconds until you hear the thunder. Divide the number you reached by five, and you have the distance in miles between you and the bolt of lightning.

Lightning strikes over the U.S. Capitol building, in Washington, D.C.

Tornadoes

The most dangerous thunderstorms are the ones that create tornadoes—whirling, funnel-shaped clouds that reach down to the surface of the earth and suck things up. Tornadoes can be so powerful that they pick up freight trains and toss them around.

Meteorologists think that tornadoes are caused by the interaction of warm, humid updrafts (or swift winds moving from the Earth upwards) and cool downdrafts (swift winds moving from the sky down to Earth). They do not know exactly why the air begins to spin around and forms the funnel cloud. To find out, scientists track tornadoes and post measuring instruments in their paths. They hope the data they collect will help them understand more about tornadoes.

A tornado tears across the Great Plains.

Hurricanes

Hurricanes form over tropical oceans in areas of low pressure. Warm, moist air rises rapidly from the warm water and forms clouds. More warm, moist air rushes in to replace it. Air gets sucked up faster and faster, creating storm clouds and a tall, spiraling column of wind. The column of wind pulls more and more moisture from the ocean, growing larger and picking up speed. The *eye* of the hurricane is a hole in the storm at the center of the spiral. In the eye, the air pressure is very low and the winds are calm.

Huge waves pound a Florida beachfront hotel during a 1964 hurricane.

To track hurricanes and learn more about them, meteorologists fly airborne laboratories directly into the storm. They fly in jets equipped with instruments designed to photograph and measure the storm from high above.

Forecasting the Weather

When you wake up in the morning, do you sometimes wonder what you ought to wear —long pants or shorts, a rain jacket or a sun hat? How do you decide? Chances are, you listen to the weather report. It tells you how hot the day is predicted to be, whether it may rain or snow, and how low the temperature will drop after the sun goes down in the evening.

How do people forecast the weather? To predict the weather, people need both a general knowledge of weather patterns and specific information about what's happening at the present moment. A complicated network of instruments, placed all over the world—and above the world—create pictures of air masses as they move in the earth's atmosphere. Weather balloons carry instruments high into the atmosphere. Radar equipment sends out signals that bounce off rain and ice crystals inside clouds to create pictures of clouds and measure how fast they are moving. Every three hours at 600 weather stations around the United States, weather watchers record temperature, humidity, air pressure, wind speed, and wind direction. Each station sends that data to the National Weather Service in Asheville, North Carolina, where all this information is combined into a big picture of current weather conditions.

Even with all this information, meteorologists cannot always be certain what the weather will bring tomorrow.

Air moves from areas of high pressure into areas of low pressure, and as it moves, the weather changes. The gauge on a *barometer* (seen here) tells whether the air where you are has high or low pressure. When the barometer is falling, it means that air pressure is getting lower. Clouds will probably move in and rain or snow may fall. When the barometer is rising, it means that air pressure is getting higher, and you can expect clear skies and less humidity.

Science Biographies

Elizabeth Blackwell

Sometimes a person's whole life can change in an instant. Elizabeth Blackwell's life changed one afternoon in 1844, when she was twenty-three. Blackwell went to visit a friend who was dying. The dying woman asked her why she did not think of studying medicine. When Blackwell reminded her friend that there *were* no women doctors, the woman sighed and said if she had been treated by a "lady doctor," she might not be dying.

At that time, it was not considered proper for women to talk about or know anything about their bodies. Elizabeth Blackwell's sick friend had been so ashamed to mention her internal problems to a man that she hid her pain for too long. When she finally sought treatment, it was too late to save her life.

Blackwell couldn't get the dying woman's suggestion out of her mind. She

Elizabeth Blackwell.

decided to try to become a doctor. She wrote to twenty-nine medical schools asking for admission. Most didn't even reply, and several of the ones that did were very rude. Friends suggested that she dress up as a man to attend medical school, but Blackwell wanted to be accepted for what she was. Finally, a small medical college in upstate New York said "yes." Blackwell graduated in 1849 at the head of her class, the first woman in the United States to receive a medical degree.

No American hospital would hire Doctor Blackwell, so she went to work in European hospitals. When she returned to the U.S. she opened her own clinic, the New York Infirmary for Indigent Women and Children. The clinic's patients were very poor; few had ever seen a doctor before.

Elizabeth Blackwell worked at her clinic, wrote articles, and made speeches teaching women about nutrition for babies, the need for exercise and clean air, and the importance of cleanliness. Her clinic grew into an institution that included a medical college for women. Over the next ninety years, more than a million patients were treated at the clinic she helped start.

Elizabeth Blackwell made many sacrifices. She even lost an eye from infection after caring for a sick baby. Nevertheless, she remained determined to teach women to care for their bodies and those of their children. She was also determined to open new career opportunities for other women. Today, almost 200,000 women doctors follow in her footsteps.

Charles Drew

Charles Drew was born in Washington, D.C., in 1904. When Drew was fifteen, his sister died of tuberculosis. As he watched her condition deteriorate, Drew wished he could do something to help. It was then that he first thought about the possibility of becoming a doctor.

There was only one problem with this idea: Drew was an African-American. In those days, much of American society was segregated, or separated, on racial lines: black people and white people went to different schools and could not sit together in restaurants or on buses. Only a handful of colleges would accept African-American students—and medical school would be another hurdle beyond college. But Charles Drew managed to succeed against the odds.

In high school, Drew was a strong student and an outstanding athlete. Eventually he was offered a scholarship to

Charles Drew.

Amherst College. At Amherst, Drew was a star quarterback, the most valuable player on the baseball team, the captain of the track team, and the national high hurdles champion. He could probably have become a professional athlete, but he remained interested in science and medicine. In 1928, he entered a medical school in Canada and began his lifelong study of blood.

Earlier in this section you learned a little about blood and the various substances it contains. But much of what we know today was not known in the 1930s and 40s, when

Charles Drew was studying blood. Doctors did know that people who lost a lot of blood could be given new blood in a procedure called a blood transfusion, but it wasn't easy to get a blood transfusion in 1940. There was no way to keep blood fresh or take it where people might need it. Charles Drew discovered that if he removed the solid cells (like red blood cells) in blood, and kept only the liquid part, called plasma, the blood could be stored for a long time. It could then be used in transfusions whenever and wherever it was needed. After making this discovery, Drew set up the first blood bank in New York City.

When World War II broke out overseas, many people were wounded and needed blood transfusions. Charles Drew suggested sending plasma instead of whole blood. He started collecting blood, separating the plasma, and shipping it safely to injured people. His work saved thousands of lives.

After America entered World War II, Charles Drew became the first director of the blood bank of the American Red Cross. He led efforts to collect blood for our country's soldiers and sailors. But the Army told the Red Cross to keep blood donated by black people separate from blood donated by whites. Some white people disliked blacks so much that they did not want to get any "black" blood, even if it might save their lives. Charles Drew explained that this was not right: there is no such thing as "black" and "white" blood. Blood is blood. But no one listened. This made Drew very angry. To make his point, Drew resigned from the Red Cross in protest. The Red Cross continued to segregate blood on racial grounds throughout World War II, but civil rights reformers eventually persuaded the organization to stop this racist practice.

After resigning from the Red Cross, Drew returned to Washington, D.C., where he taught medicine at Howard University and became famous as a surgeon. In 1943, he received a special award from the National Association for the Advancement of Colored People (NAACP). He died in 1950, after a tragic car accident.

By using his talents to help other people, Charles Drew set an example for people of all races. He proved that it is what you achieve in life, not the color of your skin, that shows your true worth as a person.

Michael Faraday

Many scientists start out by asking questions that begin, "what would happen if. . ." One of the greatest "what if" question-askers of all time was Michael Faraday (1791–1867). This man's curiosity led him to discoveries about the nature of electricity that changed the world.

Faraday was the son of a poor English blacksmith. He had very little schooling and at age thirteen was sent off to work as an apprentice to a bookbinder. For years Faraday made the most of his job by reading all the books that came into the shop to be bound. Faraday also attended public lectures and kept a journal of his thoughts.

Michael Faraday.

At one series of lectures by the famous scientist Sir Humphry Davy, Faraday wrote down everything the speaker said and bound it up into a beautiful book for Davy. Not long after, Davy was temporarily blinded by an explosion in his laboratory. He sent for Faraday and asked if he would be his right-hand man and help with experiments. In return, Faraday would be allowed to use the laboratory and equipment for his own experiments. Faraday made the most of this opportunity. This would be his lab for the next 50 years.

Faraday's most famous experiments had to do with electricity and magnetism. Another scientist had noted that a magnet would move when an electric current was sent through a nearby wire. This gave Faraday an idea. If the current could move the magnet, then maybe the magnet could

move the current. He wondered, "What if electricity and magnetism are really two examples of the same force and can be converted back and forth?"

To test this idea, Faraday set up an experiment to see if the movement of a magnet could produce an electric current. He made a coil of wire and attached it to a current detector. When he moved a magnet in and out of the coil, a current was produced. Next he attached a copper disc to wires and spun the disc between the two

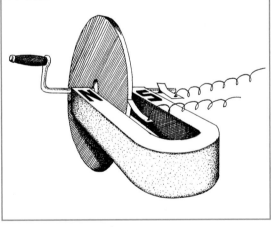

Faraday's generator.

poles of a horseshoe magnet. This made a steady current through the wires. Faraday had built the first electrical generator!

Faraday is remembered as one of the greatest scientists of all time. His discoveries gave other scientists and inventors the knowledge they needed to invent electric motors, generators, the telegraph, the telephone, and just about every other electrical device we use today.

Faraday was also one of the first scientists to think that it is important to share scientific experiments with everyone, not just other scientists. He held events especially for children to show them his experiments. Sometimes his experiments did not go as he had expected. Then he would say, "The failures are just as important as the successes." Michael Faraday was always learning, even from his failures.

Illustration and Photo Credits

The Metropolitan Museum of Art, Rogers Fund, 1955. (55.4): 158
The Metropolitan Museum of Art, Rogers Fund, 1907. (07.160) Photograph by Schecter Lee: 163 (b)
Monticello / Thomas Jefferson Memorial Foundation, Inc.: 165
Museum of Fine Arts, Boston: 163 (a)
Susan Nees: 7
Photo Researchers, Inc. © David M Phillips: 254 (a)
Photo Researchers, Inc. © Laurence Pringle: 76 (a)
Photographs and Prints Division, Schomburg Center for Research in Black Culture, The New York Public Library, Astor, Lenox and Tilden Foundations: 105
Scurlock Studio Collection Archives Center, National Museum of American History, Smithsonian Institution: 289
Gayle Sherwood: 170, 171 (a), 172, 173
Joel Smith: 125 (a)
South Tyrol Museum of Archaeology, Italy, www.iceman.it, author: Sara Welponer: 78 (b)
Guiseppe Trogu: 274 (b), 280 (a)
US Geological Survey: 270 (b), 271 (a), 273, 275, 276 (a), 279 (a)

Text Credits and Sources

POEMS

"George Washington" from *A Book of Americans,* by Rosemary and Stephen Vincent Benét, Holt, Rinehart and Winston. Copyright © 1933 by Rosemary and Stephen Vincent Benét, copyright renewed © 1961 by Rosemary Carr Benét, reprinted with permission of Brandt & Hochman Literary Agents, Ltd.

"The Rhinoceros" from *Verses from 1929 On* by Ogden Nash. Copyright © 1933 by Ogden Nash, renewed. Reprinted by permission of Curtis Brown, Ltd.

"Life Doesn't Frighten Me" from *And Still I Rise* by Maya Angelou. Copyright © 1978 by Maya Angelou. Reprinted by permission of Random House, Inc.

"Humanity" from *The Collected Poems of Elma Stuckey* by Elma Stuckey. Copyright © 1988; all rights reserved. Reprinted by permission of Sterling Stuckey.

"Dreams" from *Collected Poems by Langston Hughes.* Copyright © 1994 by the Estate of Langston Hughes. Reprinted by permission of Alfred A. Knopf, a Division of Random House, Inc.

"Things" from *Honey, I Love,* by Eloise Greenfield. Copyright © 1978 by Eloise Greenfield. Used by permission of HarperCollins Publishers.

"Fog" from *Chicago Poems* by Carl Sandburg. Copyright © 1916 by Holt, Rinehart and Winston, renewed 1944 by Carl Sandburg. Reprinted by permission of Harcourt, Inc.

"the drum" from *Spin a Soft Black Song* by Nikki Giovanni. Copyright ©1971,1985 by Nikki Giovanni. Reprinted by permission of Hill and Wang, a division of Farrar, Straus and Giroux, LLC.

"Clarence" from *A Light in the Attic,* by Shel Silverstein. Copyright © 1981 by Evil Eye Music, Inc. Selection reprinted by permission of HarperCollins Publishers.

STORIES

"The Fire on the Mountain" from *The Fire on the Mountain and Other Ethiopian Stories,* by Harold Courlander and Wolf Lelau. Copyright © 1978 by Harold Courlander. Reprinted by permission of the Emma Courlander Trust.

"The Wonderful Chuang Brocade" from *The Magic Boat and Other Chinese Folk Stories,* by M. A. Jagendorf and Virginia Weng. Copyright © 1980 by M. A. Jagendorf and Virginia Weng. Reprinted by permission of Vanguard Press, a division of Random House, Inc.

Index

References to illustrations appear in italics.